Conduct Unbecoming

Conduct Unbecoming

The Ethics Crisis at the Supreme Court and How Legitimacy Can Be Restored

Richard W. Painter

OXFORD
UNIVERSITY PRESS

OXFORD
UNIVERSITY PRESS

Oxford University Press is a department of the University of Oxford.

It furthers the University's objective of excellence in research, scholarship, and education by publishing worldwide. Oxford is a registered trade mark of Oxford University Press in the UK and in certain other countries.

Published in the United States of America by Oxford University Press
198 Madison Avenue, New York, NY 10016, United States of America.

Library of Congress Cataloging-in-Publication Data
Names: Painter, Richard W., 1952- author
Title: Conduct unbecoming : the ethics crisis at the supreme court and how legitimacy can be restored / Richard W. Painter.
Description: New York : Oxford University Press, 2026. | Includes bibliographical references and index.
Identifiers: LCCN 2025053837 (print) | LCCN 2025053838 (ebook) |
ISBN 9780197832271 hardback | ISBN 9780197832288 epub | ISBN 9780197832301
Subjects: LCSH: United States. Supreme Court | Judges—Professional ethics—United States | Judicial ethics—United States | Conflict of interests—United States | Separation of powers—United States | Judicial independence—United States
Classification: LCC KF8742 .P325 2026 (print) | LCC KF8742 (ebook)
LC record available at https://lccn.loc.gov/2025053837
LC ebook record available at https://lccn.loc.gov/2025053838

DOI: 10.1093/9780197832301.001.0001

Printed by Sheridan Books, Inc., United States of America

The manufacturer's authorized representative in the EU for product safety is Oxford University Press España S.A. of Parque Empresarial San Fernando de Henares, Avenida de Castilla, 2 – 28830 Madrid (www.oup.es/en or product.safety@oup.com). OUP España S.A. also acts as importer into Spain of products made by the manufacturer.

FSC
www.fsc.org
MIX
Paper | Supporting responsible forestry
FSC® C008955

Contents

Acknowledgments

The author thanks the many scholars and lawyers who have shared with him valuable insights on ethics at the Supreme Court with comments on the manuscript for this book, and on the author's 2024 article in the *Georgetown Journal of Legal Ethics* discussing ethics problems at the Court and potential solutions, such as an inspector general for the Court. Norman Eisen, Virginia Canter, and Amanda Frost shared uniquely valuable insights on judicial ethics and ways to hold the justices accountable. E. Thomas Sullivan shared helpful insights on the Court's separation of powers jurisprudence in connection with a separate co-authored book on use and abuse of presidential power.

The author also thanks the late Judge John T. Noonan, Jr. of the Ninth Circuit Court of Appeals for introducing him to the subject of judicial ethics as a law clerk (1987–88) and later as a coauthor of three editions of a casebook on legal ethics.

The University of Minnesota provided invaluable research and administrative assistance for work on this book, and for the author's other publications addressing ethics in all three branches of government.

Introduction

The nine United States Supreme Court justices are among the most powerful people in the US government. The presidency is powerful but changes hands every four to eight years. Supreme Court justices retain power until they retire. The justices occasionally have a hand in choosing the president.[1] The justices often tell presidents what they may and may not do,[2] but presidents cannot tell Supreme Court justices what to do. The justices have bestowed on past, present, and future presidents immunity from criminal prosecution for official acts,[3] a use of judicial power that exceeds the president's power to grant pardons after the fact. Acts of Congress may be stricken down by the justices as unconstitutional,[4] but Congress cannot change the constitutional rulings of the court.

The author of this book, as head of the White House ethics office, advised President George W. Bush in nominating two of the current justices—Chief Justice John Roberts and Justice Samuel Alito. Filling a Supreme Court vacancy is an important job, often undertaken with considerable care to maximize the impact a new justice will have on the jurisprudential trajectory of the court and to minimize the chances of the nomination failing in the Senate. And one would hope that the new justice would also be ethical.

The White House ethics office did not focus on judicial philosophy or whether a prospective nominee was a liberal or a conservative. Other political appointees in the White House, and political appointees in the Justice Department, addressed those issues. The White House ethics office vetted nominees' compliance with judicial ethics rules and any other matter that might be used to attack a nominee's character and fitness in a Senate confirmation hearing. Some potential Supreme Court nominees didn't make the short list for this reason—they had participated in cases involving companies they owned stock in, they had received gifts they shouldn't have, or their annual financial disclosure forms had omissions.

[1] *See Bush v Gore*, 531 U.S. 98 (2000).
[2] *See e.g. Youngstown Sheet & Tube Co. v. Sawyer*, 343 U.S. 579 (1952).
[3] *Trump v. United States*, 603 U.S. __ (2024).
[4] *See e.g. Citizens United v. Federal Election Commission*, 558 U.S. 310 (2009) (striking down campaign finance reform legislation).

Conduct Unbecoming. Richard W. Painter, Oxford University Press. © Oxford University Press (2026).
DOI: 10.1093/9780197832301.003.0001

Chief Justice Roberts and Justice Alito, however, passed the ethics vetting. They also passed the "political" vetting by senior officials in the White House and Justice Department. At least this author had done his job—there were virtually no serious ethics issues in either confirmation hearing. Both nominees were confirmed (Roberts by a vote of 78–22 and Alito by a vote of 58–42).

But did we—all of us involved in the confirmation process in the White House and in the Senate—really do our job?

What was done by the White House or the Senate to obtain a credible commitment from either nominee that they would adhere to specific norms of judicial ethics once they were on the court? What was done to obtain a credible commitment from the Chief Justice that he would enforce specific ethics norms on the court for all the justices? Not much. In that respect, the process failed. The White House and Senate similarly failed in the nomination and confirmation of every other justice on the court.

A credible and enforceable commitment to adhere to ethics rules has never been obtained by any president from any nominee to the court. Once a justice is on the court with lifetime tenure, the justice, save for impeachment, is beyond the reach of Congress and is beyond the reach of the executive branch except for the extremely unlikely event that the justice is prosecuted for a crime. Even then, the Supreme Court justices could in the future bestow upon themselves the same immunity from criminal prosecution for official acts that they bestowed on the president in 2024.[5] The justices may very well be beyond the reach of the law.

A Supreme Court nominee's answers given in confirmation hearings are almost always very general—for example, the nominee recites an unenforceable promise to adhere to generally accepted standards of judicial ethics. Occasionally, questions will be asked about whether the nominee will recuse from a very few specific cases known at the time, and the nominee's answers will vary from a firm commitment to recuse when there is an obvious conflict to a noncommittal or evasive answer when the nominee, and the White House, probably intend for the nominee to participate in the case.[6]

Nothing can be done when a justice later chooses to interpret ethics rules differently from other judges or to ignore ethics rules and then say that a clear violation was a "mistake." Once they are on the court, the justices have the

[5] *Trump v. United States*, *supra*.

[6] Compare, for example, Justice Jackson's firm commitment at her confirmation hearing that she would recuse from the Harvard affirmative action case, discussed in Chapter 1, with the evasive answer by Justice Kagan at her confirmation hearing about her participation in cases involving the constitutionality of the Affordable Care Act, discussed in Chapter 3.

power to interpret the law, and they interpret the ethics rules that apply to themselves the way they see fit.

That is the subject of this book. The problem addressed here is that there is no effective way of requiring Supreme Court justices to adhere to ethics rules that bind other judges as well as public officials in the legislative and executive branches of government. Rules restricting gifts, outside income, and conflicts of interest all too often are ignored, as are rules requiring financial disclosure and recusal from cases in which a justice's impartiality might reasonably be questioned.

The justices collectively decide what the law is for other Americans and decide what the law is for themselves. But they don't make their ethics decisions collectively by issuing rulings on Supreme Court ethics and the conduct of their colleagues; rather, they decide individually. Each justice is allowed to decide what the law is for themselves, with nobody telling them "no" if they get it wrong, even egregiously wrong. Their decisions about their own ethics almost always are never written down.

The court is a law unto itself.

Why is this important? As a general matter, it is offensive to democracy to have a branch of government that is unaccountable to the other branches and ultimately to the people. The people are supposed to choose their government rather than have it imposed upon them, and this requires accountability in all three branches government.

Public confidence in the court is undermined when ethics rules are ignored. This feeds distrust in the legitimacy of the court's rulings and the legal system. Ultimately, such distrust could make it hard to enforce some of the court's rulings. Not since the desegregation era of the 1950s and 1960s has the Supreme Court needed the backing of the president against elected officials who otherwise would ignore the court's rulings. But if such a moment were to arise today, what would happen? A president, a member of Congress, or a governor could take advantage of public disrespect of the court to disobey the court's orders. Lower federal courts and state courts might do the same. Would the court have sufficient credibility in the public eye so that defiance of its orders would be viewed across the political spectrum as unacceptable?

Furthermore, in several broad categories of law, unethical conduct of the justices can have a harmful effect on the substance of the court's jurisprudence.

First, many cases before the court involve the economy and commerce. The side that wins makes money, and the other side loses money. It's not just the parties to a case who are affected but similarly situated companies and individuals as well. A ruling favoring one coal company likely helps all coal companies; a ruling favoring one big bank often helps all big banks. On the losing side may be smaller competitors, public safety, public health, the environment, and other interests. There could be millions of losers in some cases, but they will never get their day in court.

Consider a recent example. In 2024, the court in *Loper Bright Enterprises v. Raimondo*[7] overturned decades of precedent and decided that federal courts shall no longer defer to executive branch agencies in interpreting statutes that Congress has placed under their purview.[8] This is a huge win for industry in healthcare, energy, finance, and just about every other area of the economy regulated by the federal government. Hundreds of statutes may have to be amended by Congress to prohibit conduct that heretofore courts have assumed is prohibited because administrative agencies said so. Perhaps the court's decision in this case is the right one—that the federal courts should interpret acts of Congress deferring only to Congress and not to executive branch agencies—but one would hope that justices who make such monumental decisions conduct themselves in their personal and professional lives so as not to appear to be captives of industries that benefit from those decisions. Americans should not have to worry that the jurisprudential framework of the majority opinion in *Raimondo* was formulated by one or more Supreme Court justices on some billionaire's yacht.

Supreme Court justices should free themselves of personal and financial relationships with the wealthiest people who have the most to gain in some cases before the court while other people potentially have the most to lose. But the justices won't do that. As discussed in Chapter 2 of this book, just about any relationship with a wealthy individual or organization other than an outright bribe is tolerated. And it might not even be disclosed.

For the justices, "freedom of association"—the idea that regardless of one's official position one can associate with anyone one chooses to associate with—takes priority over impartiality. Freedom of association ordinarily does not come with freedom to accept special favors—free jet travel, cruises on yachts, or a personal loan for an expensive recreational vehicle—but for some members of this court it does. Even those justices who do not indulge in such generosity are apparently unwilling to stop their colleagues from accepting it.

When billionaires fly justices on jets to the Caribbean or fishing trips to Alaska, perhaps they do so with no intended purpose besides friendship. It is possible that a billionaire may want to enjoy downtime with a justice talking about the weather, fishing, sports, or anything except the work of the

[7] *Loper Bright Enterprises v. Raimondo*, 603 U.S. ___ (2024).
[8] *Ibid.*

court. It is possible that the justice might prefer the company of the billionaire even if the justice were to pay his own way. Possible, but not likely. Chapter 2 of this book discusses this exchange of lavish gifts for proximity to a justice after Chapter 1 discusses how many of these same wealthy people and organizations are active in deciding who gets appointed to the court to begin with.

Next is the large body of cases that pertain to elections discussed in Chapter 3. The Supreme Court is the referee in the electoral process by which the other two branches of government are chosen, and the court often makes the rules for choosing all three branches of state government as well. The court by a 5–4 majority, perhaps prematurely, chose the president in 2000 in *Bush v. Gore.*[9] In 2024, the court in *Trump v. United States*[10] ruled that Donald Trump had immunity from prosecution for his official acts as president trying to overturn the 2020 election.

Perhaps even more important are the many election law cases the court has decided on topics as far ranging as campaign finance, gerrymandering, voter ID requirements, and other rules that can determine the outcome of elections, as discussed in Chapter 3. One of the court's most notorious and unpopular rulings, *Citizens United v. Federal Election Commission*, struck down campaign finance reform legislation and opened the floodgates for unlimited expenditures from corporate treasuries on electioneering communications, making candidates increasingly dependent on wealthy supporters.[11] That is yet another case Americans should not have to worry about being decided on the yacht or private jet of a billionaire.

Federal law provides that "[a]ny justice, judge, or magistrate judge of the United States shall disqualify himself in any proceeding in which his impartiality might reasonably be questioned."[12] It's one thing for a justice to be appointed to the court because of party loyalty, which often includes relationships with the financial backers of a political party. But a justice continuing to maintain these relationships and showing partisanship after joining the court reinforces the appearance of bias and perhaps actual bias as well. Election related cases should not be decided by justices who cannot distance themselves from the political process in which they are the referees.

Yet some justices pontificate at social gatherings about the battle between left and right in American politics, with a clear preference for one over the other. Sometimes they are caught on tape, which makes one wonder how

[9] *Bush v. Gore, supra.*
[10] *Trump v. United States, supra.*
[11] *Citizens United v. FEC, supra*, 558 U.S. 310 (2010).
[12] 28 U.S.C. § 455(a).

often this occurs when the public doesn't learn about it. Many of the court's conservative justices regularly speak at and attend functions of the Federalist Society, a group of conservative lawyers, while liberal justices do the same at gatherings at universities and other predominantly liberal organizations. Like elected officials, they have their political "base" and go back to it frequently for approval from their admirers.

Watching this court is all too often like watching a football game in which referees come on the field wearing the teams' jerseys, acting as referees and cheerleaders at the same time. Sometimes at critical junctures the referees themselves delay the game—for example, the court's dilatory resolution of the immunity question in *Trump v. United States*[13] weeks before the major party nominating conventions in 2024. But nobody calls them on it, because they are the referees.

And what if their team loses? One justice's spouse flew the American flag upside down outside their house after President Trump lost the 2020 election and some of his supporters in a violent riot failed to stop the counting of the electoral ballots at the Capitol. Justice Alito said that this was about his wife's dispute with a neighbor, but it seemed like the Alitos' dispute was with the results of the election. Virginia Thomas, the spouse of Justice Thomas, was active in the effort to overturn the 2020 election that Joe Biden won by about eight million votes and a wide margin in the Electoral College.

Shortly after that upside-down flag came down, the court heard the cases that came in the aftermath of the insurrection of January 6, 2021. That event, the first violent upheaval over a presidential election since the Civil War, generated cases over congressional subpoenas from the January 6 Committee of the US House, and then criminal cases against the perpetrators, including ultimately a criminal case against the losing candidate, President Trump. Should Justices Alito and Thomas have participated in cases involving these efforts to overturn the 2020 election? Should they have done more to avoid the appearance of partisanship that potentially created a need to recuse?

The recusal statute is clear that justices must disqualify themselves from a case "in which his [their] impartiality might reasonably be questioned,"[14] but who decides this? Justices Thomas and Alito decided for themselves. They did not recuse from any of the cases involving the attempt to overturn the 2020 election. This includes the court's decision in 2024 in *Trump v. United States* bestowing on Trump immunity from criminal prosecution for official acts he took as president to reverse the result of the election. Because Justice

[13] *Trump v. United States*, 603 U.S. ____ (2024).
[14] 28 U.S.C. 455.

Amy Coney Barrett's concurring opinion interpreted the scope of presidential immunity more narrowly than the majority,[15] each of their votes was a deciding factor in the court's presidential immunity ruling being as broad as it was. As discussed in Chapter 3, the court's decision in that case was tainted by partisanship that the court should have done more to avoid.

Chapter 3 also tells how the court narrowly avoided a crisis that would have blown up if Donald Trump had won the 2016 election by a narrower margin in the Electoral College and the court had again decided a case like the court's very controversial decision on the 2000 election in *Bush v. Gore*. In several interviews in 2016, Justice Ginsburg made public comments attacking Trump as a candidate, for which she rightly apologized. These comments would have made it extremely contentious for her to vote in a case determining the outcome of the election, and even more so if she had been the deciding vote on the court handing the election to Hillary Clinton. That did not happen, but it could have, and Justice Ginsburg surely knew this when she made her remarks about Trump.

Finally, there are the social issues that so deeply divide our country. Here, the court has made a lot of new law, even though many of the justices ostensibly are opposed to judicial activism. The court has struck down key provisions of campaign finance laws,[16] struck down state gun laws,[17] reversed abortion rights that had been guaranteed for close to fifty years under *Roe v. Wade*,[18] and prohibited affirmative action in college admissions.[19]

Some of these decisions involve the federal government's relationship with the states. The court expands the power of the states when the majority of the justices agree with state laws (abortion)[20] and restricts the power of the states when a majority of the justices disagree (gun control[21] and affirmative action[22]). This court is extraordinarily powerful, and its decisions can override those of state and local governments on issues that impact Americans' daily lives. But should these cases be decided by justices who have previously been wined and dined, and enjoyed lavish all-expenses-paid vacations, arranged by operatives of nonprofit organizations focused on the outcome of these very same cases? Perhaps not.

***

[15] *Trump v. United States*, *supra* (opinion of Justice Barrett concurring in part).
[16] *Citizens United v. Fed. Election Comm'n*, 558 U.S. 310 (2010).
[17] *New York State Rifle & Pistol Ass'n v. Bruen*, 597 U.S. 1 (2022).
[18] *Dobbs v. Jackson Women's Health Ctr.*, 597 U.S. 215 (2022).
[19] *Students for Fair Admissions v. President and Fellows of Harvard College*, 600 U.S. 181 (2023).
[20] *See Dobbs*, 597 U.S. at 231.
[21] *See Bruen*, 597 U.S. at 11.
[22] *See Students for Fair Admissions*, 600 U.S. 181 (2023).

Mark Lemley in the *Harvard Law Review* made the credible accusation that the only consistent logic of the court's opinions is the justices' intent to consolidate their power by weakening Congress, the presidency, and the states whenever they like.[23] Unfortunately, the court is consolidating its own power while at the same time asserting its independence from external controls over the ethics of the justices. The court is striving to be a law unto itself.

This book is not about suggesting ways to constrain the court's power. Others have addressed that topic, and it is an important one. This book assumes that the court will continue to have such extraordinary power for decades to come. The point here is that it is essential to have accountability—including enforceable ethics rules—to accompany power, and that for the court there is no meaningful accountability.

Broader structural changes to the court have floundered. There is little support in Congress or the White House to expand the size of the court or implement other major changes.[24] As discussed in Chapter 8, impeachment and removal of a justice is close to impossible. This book will assume a neutral stance on structural changes to the court, although Chapter 7 does suggest structural changes to the confirmation process for new justices.

This book also is not about liberal or conservative jurisprudence or political ideology that has shifted over the years. At present, the court is far more conservative than the population of the country. The United States has not experienced such an alignment in the judicial branch since the 1930s when President Franklin Roosevelt confronted an ultra-conservative court and responded with an attempt to pack the court with additional justices.

The court, by contrast, was relatively liberal from the 1940s through the 1970s.

Another thing that has changed is how the court approaches ethics. As discussed in Chapter 4, the court faced an ethics crisis in 1969 when it was discovered that Justice Abraham Fortas had accepted undisclosed outside income from the family foundation of a wealthy businessman. As also discussed in Chapter 4, that controversy was confronted in 1969 by a consensus among other justices, including Chief Justice Earl Warren, and members of Congress that ethics norms on the court had to be enforced. Some liberals, including Senator Walter Mondale (D-MN) called for Fortas's resignation from the court, even though this meant the loss of one of the court's most liberal justices, who would be replaced by President Richard Nixon.

[23] Mark A. Lemley, *The Imperial Supreme Court*, 136 Harv. L. Rev. 97 (2022).

[24] *See generally* Presidential Commission on the Supreme Court of the United States, Final Report (2021) (avoiding endorsement of major changes to the court, including its expansion, but proposing an "advisory code of conduct" for the court).

Fortas resigned. The nagging question today, fifty-seven years later, is what changed? Why is Supreme Court ethics today such a partisan issue, whereas in 1969, also a time of political polarization, people on different ends of the political spectrum could at least agree that ethics norms on the court had to be enforced? Chapter 4 explores answers to that question.

This book does not endeavor to connect the ideology of the justices to their ethics problems, although in some areas, such as gifts from billionaires to justices who consistently rule in favor of big business, the connection between ethics and judicial philosophy is inescapable.

The conservative justices have added to the scoreboard more actual and apparent ethics violations than their dwindling number of liberal counterparts, but the tally is not a shutout. And none of the justices—liberal or conservative—appears willing to be forceful in holding other justices accountable. In 2023, in the midst of the latest ethics crisis, all nine justices signed a public statement insisting that the court was adhering to the highest standards of ethics. As discussed in Chapter 4, colleagues cover for colleagues.

This book also does not address procedural issues such as the court's "shadow docket," in which the justices decide important constitutional and statutory questions in cases that have not reached final judgment—for example, stays and other injunctions—without full briefing and oral argument on the merits.[25] These orders of the court, sometimes not signed by the individual justices and unexplained, raise serious concerns about transparency and bias. Such procedures are "ethics" issues broadly speaking and have been addressed by Stephen Vladeck[26] and other authors.

This book's focus is ethics rules for the court. The justices don't acknowledge that there is a problem. Some members of Congress also deny there is an ethics problem on the court. At a Senate hearing in 2023, this author had a testy exchange on that topic with Senator John Kennedy (R-LA), who distorted a social media post and asked, "Which justices do you think are bought?"[27] As explained in Chapter 8, the answer to that question may

[25] William Baude, *Foreword: The Supreme Court's Shadow Docket*, 9 NYU J. of L. & Liberty 1 (2015).

[26] *See generally* Stephen Vladeck, *The Shadow Docket: How the Supreme Court Uses Stealth Rulings to Amass Power and Undermine the Republic* (2023). The "shadow docket" can also conceal ethics violations. Justice Thomas participated in a 2022 shadow docket case involving enforcement of a House January 6 Committee subpoena in circumstances where he clearly should have recused. This and other cases are discussed in Chapter 3.

[27] On June 21, 2023, the author of this book testified before the US Senate Budget Committee at a hearing on fossil fuel industry dark money and climate change. Senator John Kennedy used his questioning time to attack this author's prior statements about ethics scandals at the Supreme Court and the appearance that justices on the court can be "bought." *See* United States Senate Committee on the Budget, Hearing, June 21, 2023, *Dollars and Degrees: Investigating Fossil Fuel Dark Money's Systemic Threats to Climate and the Federal Budget*, https://www.budget.senate.gov/hearings/dollars-and-degrees-investigating-fossil-fuel-dark-moneys-systemic-threats-to-climate-and-the-federal-budget [https://perma.cc/5G9Z-HD23]; *see also*

turn on what one means by "bought"—the narrow definition in the federal bribery statute or the understanding of corruption the founders had when they adopted the Impeachment Clause of the Constitution.

Unfortunately, political debate over Supreme Court ethics is all too often partisan; Republicans today defend the court or are silent about Supreme Court ethics, but only a decade ago they were castigating the court when it handed down liberal rulings during the Obama administration. As discussed in Chapter 6, Senator Chuck Grassley (R-IA) in 2015 introduced a bill that would install an inspector general (IG) at the Supreme Court.[28] He is silent on that topic today.

Meanwhile, public opinion of the court is at an all-time low.[29] Whether or not corruption impacts the court's adjudication of a particular case, appearance of corruption is enough to undermine the credibility of the court as an institution and ultimately public confidence in our entire system of government.

This book will not attempt to demonstrate a connection between ethics violations and justices' votes in specific cases. It would be very hard to prove "but for" causation or even "proximate cause" linking ethics violations to a particular decision of the court. One can argue that the justices' prior judicial philosophy determines outcomes, that the justices would have ruled the same way anyway (for example, conservative justices would have ruled in favor of businesses controlled by billionaires, even without a free trip on a billionaire's yacht). This might be correct or it might not be. This book will not speculate on that.

In the end, though, the public still believes the court is corrupt, and that itself is worrisome.

In November 2023, the Supreme Court finally gave in to public pressure and promulgated a new code of conduct.[30] It accomplished little.

Richard W. Painter, *How the Supreme Court Can Get Its House in Order*, MSNBC Opinion (May 2, 2023), https://www.msnbc.com/opinion/msnbc-opinion/supreme-court-can-finally-get-house-order-rcna82293 [https://perma.cc/823B-4JBE] (proposing installation of an ethics lawyer and an inspector general at the Supreme Court).

[28] *See* Judicial Transparency and Ethics Enhancement Act, S. 1418, 114th Cong. (2015) (bill introduced by Senator Grassley that would have established an IG's office for the judiciary, including the Supreme Court), 114 Cong. Rec. S3240 (daily ed. May 21, 2015) (floor speech by Sen. Grassley explaining the need for an inspector general for the Supreme Court).

[29] *See* Jeffrey Jones, *Confidence in U.S. Supreme Court Sinks to Historic Low*, Gallup (June 23, 2022), https://news.gallup.com/poll/394103/confidence-supreme-court-sinks-historic-low.aspx [https://perma.cc/2DP6-VXCT] (reporting that only "[t]wenty-five percent of U.S. adults say they have 'a great deal' or 'quite a lot' of confidence in the U.S. Supreme Court"); Devan Cole, *Supreme Court Approval Rating Declines Amid Controversy over Ethics and Transparency: Marquette Poll*, CNN (May 24, 2023), https://www.cnn.com/2023/05/24/politics/supreme-court-approval-rating-poll-ethics-marquette/index.html [https://perma.cc/D57D-W8PW].

[30] Supreme Court of the United States, Statement of the Court Regarding the Code of Conduct (November 13, 2023), https://www.supremecourt.gov/about/Code-of-Conduct-for-Justices_November_13_2023.pdf [https://perma.cc/KS7H-UK39].

The court's new ethics code, for the most part, replicates the ethics code for other federal judges. There are two gaping holes, however. First, unlike the ethics code for other federal judges, the ethics code has no enforcement mechanism. The justices presumably will enforce it themselves. Second, when releasing the ethics code, the justices said that the code of conduct "largely represents a codification of principles that we have long regarded as governing our conduct."[31] In other words, little has changed.[32] That, coupled with the court's April 2023 statement reassuring the public that they are complying with ethics rules,[33] reveals a lot about how the justices interpret the new ethics code to validate what they have already been doing. This book will describe only some examples of violations of existing law on financial disclosure, gifts, and recusal. If what's been going on at the court for the past two decades is compliance with the new ethics code, the code is not going to change anything.

Congress has considered steps to oversee Supreme Court ethics. H.R. 7647, the Supreme Court Ethics, Recusal, and Transparency (SCERT) Act of 2022,[34] would have required Supreme Court justices to adopt and follow a code of ethics, establish advisory review of ethics issues by appellate court judges, require disclosure of gifts and travel, codify recusal standards, and require the court to disclose lobbying and dark money interests appearing before it. On February 9, 2023, Congressman Hank Johnson (D-GA) reintroduced the bill, and Senator Sheldon Whitehouse (D-RI) introduced a companion bill in the Senate.[35] This book, in Chapter 7, will evaluate the advantages and disadvantages of the proposals in this and similar legislation.

This book also proposes a solution not included in the most recent proposals before Congress: an ethics lawyer and an IG for the court. In 2015, Senator Chuck Grassley introduced a bill providing for an IG for the entire

[31] *Ibid.*

[32] The code itself reiterates that the justices have been complying with financial disclosure laws binding on other federal judges. "For some time, all Justices have agreed to comply with the statute governing financial disclosure, and the undersigned Members of the court each individually reaffirm that commitment." *Ibid* at 8. As discussed later in this book, there have been multiple instances in which some of the justices' financial disclosure filings have been inaccurate.

[33] *See* Statement on Ethics Principles and Practices (2023), https://www.judiciary.senate.gov/imo/media/doc/Letter%20to%20Chairman%20Durbin%2004.25.2023.pdf ("The undersigned Justices today reaffirm and restate foundational ethics principles and practices to which they subscribe in carrying out their responsibilities as Members of the Supreme Court of the United States. . . . In 1991, Members of the Court voluntarily adopted a resolution to follow the substance of the Judicial Conference Regulations. Since then, Justices have followed the financial disclosure requirements and limitations on gifts, outside earned income, outside employment, and honoraria. . . . In regard to recusal, the Justices follow the same general principles and statutory standards as other federal judges, but the application of those principles can differ due to the unique institutional setting of the Court.").

[34] Supreme Court Ethics, Recusal, and Transparency Act, H.R. 7647, 117th Congress (2021–22).

[35] Supreme Court Ethics, Recusal, and Transparency (SCERT) Act, S. 359, 118th Cong. (2023–24).

judicial branch, including the Supreme Court,[36] but that bill never advanced out of committee. The time has come to revive that idea and have one or more IGs in the judicial branch, with particular attention to investigating alleged violations at the Supreme Court.

These reforms are necessary but not sufficient. Other reforms, such as mandatory disclosures of funding of amicus briefs, are needed.[37] There also needs to be disclosures of funding of confirmation battles before the court, a topic addressed in Chapter 1 of this book.

Furthermore, the ethics lapses on the court are part of a broader problem of people and organizations with massive amounts of money influencing all three branches of our government. Expenditures that the court protects as free speech in cases such as *Citizens United v. Federal Election Commission*[38] come from some of the same people and organizations that seek to influence the court itself with everything from amicus briefs to fishing trips and yacht excursions for justices. A Supreme Court ethics lawyer and IG can do a lot to fix the court, but we should not overestimate the prospect of reforming judicial ethics without a broader reform of ethics in government in general, and in the political system we use to choose our government. The much-needed broader objective of getting money out of politics, which this author[39] and others[40] have addressed elsewhere, is beyond the scope of this book.

Chapter 1 of this book starts with the nomination and confirmation process and the well-funded outside organizations that are involved in the process, often before there is even an open seat on the Supreme Court. It is at this stage that the successful nominee is aware that without the support of these organizations the nomination never would have made it out of the Oval Office, not to mention confirmation by the Senate. The new justice owes these people and knows it. Chapter 2 addresses financial conflicts of interest of the justices and discusses ethics rules that are supposed to insulate the justices from improper influence on account of gifts, free travel, book royalties, spousal income and stock holdings. These rules are, on their face, insufficient, and, in the case of the court, enforcement is nonexistent. Chapter 3 addresses political conflicts of interest, as some of the justices have increasingly involved themselves in partisan politics, as have their spouses. As pointed out in Chapter 1, partisan politics is what got them on the court to begin with, but presumably

[36] Judicial Transparency and Ethics Enhancement Act, S. 1418, 114th Cong. (2015–16).

[37] *See Ibid.*

[38] *See Citizens United v. Fed. Election Comm'n*, 558 U.S. 310 (2010).

[39] *See generally* Richard W. Painter, *Taxation Only with Representation: The Conservative Conscience and Campaign Finance Reform (Take Back Our Republic)* (2016).

[40] *See, e.g.*, Lawrence Lessig, *Republic, Lost: How Money Corrupts Congress and a Plan to Fix It* (2015).

they would leave politics at the courthouse door upon joining the court. They don't. This undermines the court's credibility in the wide array of cases in which its holdings shape the outcome of elections.

Chapter 4 explains multiple factors that make the Supreme Court justices prone to ethics lapses, perhaps more so than the other two branches of government. Lifetime tenure in a position with incredibly high status, the phenomenon of "colleagues covering for colleagues" that is all too common in other workplaces, the justices' power to interpret the law generally, including their own ethics rules, confidentiality, and the lack of external oversight all contribute to the accountability problem. Chapter 5 addresses the separation of powers problem, the argument that the Constitution prevents the other two branches of government from interfering with the independence of the Supreme Court. Like presidents who argue that Congress and the federal courts cannot check presidential power, some of the justices argue that Congress cannot pass laws imposing ethics rules on the court and mechanisms to enforce those rules. Chapter 6 proposes one such mechanism: an IG who would enforce ethics rules and other laws at the Supreme Court. Chapter 7 evaluates other ethics reforms for the court, some already proposed in pending legislation, as well as changes to the confirmation process for judges and justices. Most structural reforms of the court—for example, increasing the number of justices—will not be addressed in this book.

Chapter 8 addresses impeachment, investigations, and other things Congress can do about the ethics crisis at the court. This involves a complex balancing of separation of powers concerns, and judicial independence, with the need to utilize legitimate oversight and checks and balances contemplated by our Constitution. Chapter 9 addresses proposals for term limits for the justices, a proposal that may be attractive for other reasons but would have an uncertain impact on the court's ethics. Chapter 10 discusses the possibility, and the advantages and disadvantages, of amending the Constitution to address Supreme Court ethics.

Public confidence in the court ultimately depends upon the justices being perceived to be ethical, and the public's willingness to overlook ethics lapses is not boundless, even when some people agree with the court's rulings. Without ethics reform, other political actors, including presidents, members of Congress, and governors, will increasingly attack the court not only for its rulings but also for the character of its justices. We could reach a point where "separation of powers"—a doctrine now embraced with vigor by the court in its jurisprudence—is interpreted by state of federal actors to mean that they can simply ignore the court's rulings.

This book's proposals are not a comprehensive remedy for the weakening of checks and balances in our system of government, whether it be an unconstrained Supreme Court or an unconstrained presidency, but this book will discuss ways to subject the justices to the basic standards of conduct expected of people who hold power in a representative democracy. The court itself should care about this problem, as should we all.

1
Choosing Judges and Justices

This chapter discusses the nomination and confirmation of Supreme Court justices, a process that the author witnessed firsthand as a White House Counsel's Office lawyer screening prospective nominees for two seats on the court, now held by Chief Justice Roberts and Justice Alito.

It is at this stage that ethics problems for justices begin. Most nominees to the court for years have been nurturing close personal relationships with people involved in the political process, which in today's political climate involves the economic and political interest groups trying to influence the direction of the federal judiciary. Justices are nominated and confirmed to the court because powerful people and organizations, not just the president and a majority of the Senate, want them to be there. Substantial sums of money are spent on the nomination and confirmation process to support nominees that advance a particular ideological viewpoint. As described in later chapters of this book, these relationships last with the justices once they are on the court and become the source of many of the ethics problems that have plagued the court.

The argument presented in this chapter is that people and organizations investing so much in the nomination and confirmation process for federal judges and justices are motivated to protect their investment by maintaining close ties once judges and justices are on the bench. Judicial ethics rules push in the opposite direction. Judges' and justices' personal and professional relationships potentially put them on a collision course with judicial ethics rules, but there are some meaningful constraints on the lower federal courts where there is a process for enforcing ethics rules and establishing boundaries between judges and external sources of influence. Not so much at the Supreme Court. Latter chapters of this book explore how these individuals and organizations that influence the nomination and confirmation process also circumvent judicial ethics rules to continue to influence the direction of the Supreme Court.

In sum, the ethics crisis the court faces today is intrinsically linked to the well-oiled and well-financed political machine that puts judges and justices on the federal courts to begin with.

Conduct Unbecoming. Richard W. Painter, Oxford University Press. © Oxford University Press (2026).
DOI: 10.1093/9780197832301.003.0002

There is a parallel process for state courts, which almost always involve elections, whether partisan elections, nonpartisan elections, or retention elections. This book is not about the contentious, and well-funded, process for electing state judges; other authors have written extensively on that topic.[1] Nonetheless, federal and state processes for judicial selection have one thing in common: the enormous amounts of money spent by special interest groups trying to influence who gets on the courts. It would be naïve to assume that these groups will stop trying to influence federal or state judges and justices once they take the bench. The difference is that voters have some say in whether state judges remain in office, and these judges have at least some incentive to comply with ethics rules and norms. Voters have no say in who is on the federal bench once a judge or justice is appointed to lifetime tenure.

The Politically Ambitious Young Lawyer

A seat on the federal judiciary does not come by chance. Lawyers who become federal judges often first set their sights on gaining political connections needed get another important government job, perhaps in the White House, in the Justice Department, or with Congress.

This usually means supporting one of the two major political parties and affiliating also with nonprofit groups ideologically aligned with one of the two parties. Most new federal judges belong to the party of the nominating president, although a few district judges are appointed as part of a "package deal" with senators of the opposing party who agree to vote to confirm the president's other nominees. Either way, political connections are critical. Law firm partners gain entry with political contributions, but younger lawyers, and even law students, can begin their networking within organizations aligned with the judicial philosophy of one party or the other.

For many ambitious lawyers, a judicial clerkship is the first step. Of the nine justices on the Supreme Court, six served as law clerks on the court. Chief Justice John Roberts clerked for Justice William Rehnquist; Justice Elena Kagan clerked for Justice Thurgood Marshall; Justice Neil Gorsuch clerked for Justices Byron White and Anthony Kennedy; Justice Brett Kavanaugh clerked for Justice Anthony Kennedy; Justice Amy Coney Barrett clerked for Justice Antonin Scalia; and Justice Ketanji Brown Jackson clerked for Justice Stephen Breyer. Three of these justices, Roberts, Kavanaugh and Jackson, replaced the justices they had clerked for on the court.

[1] *See* Herbert H. Kritzker, *Judicial Selection in the States* (2020); *see also* Michael S. Kang & Joanna M. Sheperd, *Free to Judge: The Power of Campaign Money in Judicial Elections* (2023).

Judges hire law clerks with strong academic records, but there also is a philosophical alignment between a judge and many of the judge's law clerks, particularly on the Supreme Court.[2] The widening gulf between the predominantly liberal pool of qualified law students applying for clerkships and the increasingly conservative federal judiciary has led conservative judges to hire some liberal clerks, although less so on the Supreme Court[3] (notable exceptions include Dana Remus, a former clerk for Justice Alito, who later became a lawyer in President Obama's White House Counsel's Office and the White House counsel for President Biden).

Connections in political circles are important. Consider, for example, the Federalist Society, a well-funded organization of conservative and libertarian lawyers, law professors, and judges. The Federalist Society, founded by law students at Yale, the University of Chicago, and other law schools in the 1980s, was originally intended to bring conservative and libertarian perspectives into a legal academy where most professors and students were to the left of the political mainstream. Federalist Society speakers in the 1980s and 1990s included judges and justices appointed by President Reagan and President George H. W. Bush. The Federalist Society has made an important contribution to debate in law schools, and the author of this book served as a faculty advisor for Federalist Society chapters at several law schools. The Federalist Society is also a critically important social network for conservative lawyers.

The Supreme Court's more conservative justices often attend the Federalist Society's annual dinner in Washington.[4] Court of appeals judges are there as well, increasing their visibility, recruiting law clerks, and enjoying discussion of legal issues. In the 1990s and early 2000s, Judge Alex Kozinski of the Ninth Circuit, routinely played poker with law students, clerks, former clerks, and

[2] *See* Adam Bonica et al., *The Political Ideologies of Law Clerks and Their Judges* (Coase-Sandor Working Paper Series in Law and Economics No. 754, 2016), https://chicagounbound.uchicago.edu/cgi/viewcontent.cgi?article=2432&context=law_and_economics. This paper found ideological consistency among clerks hired by a federal judge increases with the level of the court and is highest at the Supreme Court, *Id.* at 23, 29, and that the data "shows a clear relationship: the more conservative a judge, the more conservative his or her clerks tend to be." *Id.* at 27.

[3] In courts other than the Supreme Court, "The clerks of Democratic appointees more closely resemble the ideologies of their judges than do the clerks of Republican appointees—a result that is not surprising given the greater prevalence of liberal versus conservative clerks." *Id.* at 29. The overall applicant pool for qualified clerks leans heavily toward the political left, *Id.* at 12, Figure 1. This may limit conservative judges' hiring options on the lower federal courts, but less so on the Supreme Court. With federal courts becoming increasingly conservative since this study was conducted in 2016, some of these observations may be even more pronounced today.

[4] *See* Mark Sherman, *Justices Cheered at Conservative Group's Anniversary Dinner*, Assoc. Press (Nov. 11, 2022), https://apnews.com/article/abortion-voting-rights-us-supreme-court-samuel-alito-donald-trump-f0926d7b4a8bbaf7b698ada1a791ab25 [https://perma.cc/BDP3-EYQE] ("Four of the five Supreme Court justices who overturned the constitutional right to abortion showed up at the conservative Federalist Society's black-tie dinner marking its 40th anniversary.").

prospective clerks[5] at Federalist Society meetings.[6] Judges may also consider the fact that hiring politically connected clerks can improve their chances of a Supreme Court appointment if their clerks later work in the White House Counsel's Office, the Justice Department, or for powerful US Senators.

With more limited success, Democrats and liberals have founded a rival group called the American Constitution Society (ACS). ACS chapters in law schools invite liberal judges and justices to speak. ACS also has a national convention, and ACS members populate the Justice Department during Democratic administrations. Some become judges. But ACS does not have as much money or as broad a reach as the Federalist Society. In 2023, the Federalist Society's total revenues were approximately $21.5 million, while the ACS had revenue of approximately $8.66 million.[7]

Liberals, however, have broader networks within law schools, given the liberal leanings of law professors.[8] Of law professors who made campaign contributions in the 2024 election, 95 percent gave only to Democrats.[9] Professors' recommendation letters are critical to obtaining judicial clerkships, although there is no evidence that these letters are stronger for liberal students than for conservative students. For liberals, the pathway from the professoriate to the court has worked for justices as well as clerks, with Harvard being a clear favorite. President Clinton appointed Justice Breyer, who had been a law professor at Harvard Law School before he joined the court of appeals, and President Obama appointed Harvard Law School Dean Elena Kagan to the court. As dean, Kagan strategically made herself popular with conservatives by appointing a handful of conservative professors to the Harvard faculty.[10]

[5] *See* Alex Kozinski, *Confessions of a Bad Apple*, 100 Yale L. J. 1707 1715 (1991) (acknowledging that he hired desirable clerks "by beating them at poker, losing to them at chess, calling them during ski vacations, introducing [them] to current clerks, wining and dining, bageling and loxing."). As discussed later in this book, Judge Kozinski many years later resigned from the Ninth Circuit in a sexual harassment scandal.

[6] The author of this book also recalls seeing Judge Kozinski playing poker with clerks and prospective clerks at Federalist Society meetings in the late 1980s and 1990s.

[7] *See* Pro Publica Nonprofit Explorer, showing ACS 2023 revenue of $8.66 million, https://projects.propublica.org/nonprofits/organizations/522313694, and Federalist Society 2023 revenue of $21.5 million, https://projects.propublica.org/nonprofits/organizations/363235550. In previous years, Federalist Society revenues were even higher before its co-chairman, Leonard Leo, founded other organizations to fund a lot of his work on judicial nominations and confirmations.

[8] *See, e.g.*, Adam Bonica et al., *The Legal Academy's Ideological Uniformity*, 47 J. Legal Studies 1 (2018) (finding that 15 percent of law professors, compared with 35 percent of lawyers, are conservative).

[9] *See* Derek T. Muller, Law School Faculty Monetary Contributions to Political Candidates, 2017 to early 2023, post to Excess of Democracy blog, March 11, 2024 ("I identified 3148 law faculty who contributed only to Democrats in this 5+ year span—95.9% of the data set of those identified as contributing to either Democrats or Republicans in this period. Another 88 (2.7%) contributed only to Republicans. And 48 others contributed to both Democrats and Republicans"), https://excessofdemocracy.com/blog/2024/3/law-school-faculty-monetary-contributions-to-political-candidates-2017-to-early-2023.

[10] Laura Meckler, *Kagan's Harvard Stint Could Be Selling Point Record as Conciliator in Law-School Post May Help Win Republican Support for Potential Supreme Court Nomination*, Wall St J. (Apr. 27, 2010) (discussing Elena Kagan's hiring of some conservative law faculty while dean of Harvard).

Other justices had close ties with academia while pursuing careers elsewhere. Justice Ketanji Brown Jackson was on the board of overseers of Harvard University before she joined the court and, as discussed in Chapter 2, has recused from some cases involving Harvard.

And it is no surprise that conservatives continue to think that the law schools are aligned against them. Such is a longstanding grievance against academia on the political right going back to William F. Buckley's call for intervention by conservative trustees and alumni in his 1951 book *God and Man at Yale*.[11] Such grievances have intensified in recent years. Some federal judges have joined the chorus by condemning law schools for their political activism—for example, Judge James Ho's announcement in 2022 that he would not hire clerks from Yale.[12] Then, in 2025, came the aggressive, and arguably unconstitutional, executive orders targeting academic institutions by President Trump.[13]

A liberal-dominated legal academy, however, will hardly doom conservative law students' chances of obtaining judicial clerkships. With only three liberal justices on the Supreme Court, liberal law students who think political affinity with a justice will land them a clerkship are at a 1:2 disadvantage. Courts of appeals and federal district courts are more evenly balanced between appointees by presidents of the two political parties, but given the liberal political disposition of most law students, more of them compete for clerkships with judges with whom they are politically aligned than do their conservative classmates. This gap between the left-leaning political ideology of most law students applying for clerkships and the ideology of the federal judiciary is widening as more conservatives are appointed to the bench.[14]

Law professors with ties to the court's six conservative justices also feed the clerkship pipeline. These include Professor Amy Chua of Yale, who made headlines in 2018 by reportedly advising law students on how prepare for an

[11] William F. Buckley Jr., *God and Man at Yale: The Superstitions of "Academic Freedom"* (1951).

[12] Debra Cassens Weiss, *Why This Conservative Federal Appeals Judge Will No Longer Hire Clerks from Yale Law School*, ABA J. (Oct. 3, 2022).

[13] *See President and Fellows of Harvard College v. United States Department of Homeland Security et. al.*, Civil Action No. 25-cv-11472-ADB (D MA) (June 23, 2025), Memorandum and Order, enjoining presidential proclamation suspending "the entry of any alien into the United States as a nonimmigrant to pursue a course of study at Harvard University . . . or to participate in an exchange visitor program hosted by Harvard University" as an unconstitutional retaliation directed at Harvard in response to its exercise of its First Amendment rights. https://www.harvard.edu/federal-lawsuits/wp-content/uploads/sites/17/2025/06/show_temp-234.pdf.

[14] *See* Bonica et al., note 2, *supra* (discussing political leanings of the pool of law clerks compared with judges).

interview with Justice Kavanaugh.[15] Notre Dame Law School, an excellent law school once overlooked for judicial clerkships and for decades looked down upon by an anti-Catholic legal establishment,[16] has now moved toward the top of Supreme Court clerkship rankings with the appointment to the court of former Notre Dame law professor Amy Coney Barrett.[17]

In sum, while legal education provides career opportunities for conservatives and liberals, conservatives are a much smaller group among law students and law faculty. Some feel isolated in their own institutions, but safety in numbers is found in national gatherings—for example, the annual student convention and lawyers convention of the Federalist Society. For conservative lawyers, this may lead to a stronger group cohesion than for the larger group of liberals who predominate on campus but go in different directions when they graduate from law school (a not insignificant number go into corporate law, where they may become less liberal). The relatively small and cohesive networks for conservative lawyers, in turn, may influence the way conservative lawyers respond, or don't respond, to ethics problems involving conservatives in the White House, Congress, or the Supreme Court. This book revisits the groupthink problem in Chapter 4, but here it is important to note that political movements defend their own and the relatively small group of conservative law students and lawyers may be particularly sensitive to criticism of any one of their number, including a Supreme Court justice.

Law firms also are a powerful interest group, shaping young lawyers' careers and preparing some for a career on the bench. Here conservatives have also claimed that a "woke" legal establishment is aligned against them.[18] Large law firms, however, represent mostly corporate clients[19] and have provided conservative lawyers, including John Roberts (a former partner of Hogan & Hartson (now Hogan Lovells) and Brett Kavanaugh (a former partner or Kirkland & Ellis), with an upward career trajectory and pathway for

[15] David W. Chen, *Yale Law School Boasted About Kavanaugh; Now Comes "a Moment of Reckoning,"* N.Y. Times (Sept. 26, 2018) ("Last week, the Guardian reported that Amy Chua, one of the school's star professors, had told female students they needed to have a "certain look" in order to clerk for Judge Kavanaugh, a charge she has denied."). At Yale, Professor Chua was also a mentor to Vice President J. D. Vance.

[16] *See* John T. Noonan, Jr. & Richard W. Painter, *Professional and Personal Responsibilities of the Lawyer* (1997), 550 discussing *Lucido v. Cravath*, 425 F. Supp. 123 (S.D.N.Y. 1977) (employment discrimination suit brought by an Italian American associate denied partnership at Cravath, Swaine & Moore after being the only associate hired by the firm out of Notre Dame).

[17] *Notre Dame Is a Pipeline for Supreme Court Clerks, Magnet for Justices*, Wash. Post (Dec. 3, 2024).

[18] John McGinnis, *The Dangers of Woke Law ("Wokeism in the Legal Profession May Be Even Worse Than on Campus")*, Law & Liberty (Nov. 10, 2022), *reviewing* David Enrich, *Servants of the Damned: Giant Law Firms, Donald Trump, and the Corruption of Justice* (2022), https://lawliberty.org/book-review/the-dangers-of-woke-law/.

[19] *See* Enrich, *Servants of the Damned*, *supra* (discussing law firms' representation of gun manufactures, big tobacco, fossil fuel companies, and other wealthy clients).

appointment to the bench. Law firms also pay very large hiring bonuses to hire law clerks, over $400,000 for Supreme Court clerks.[20] Many of these former clerks argue cases before the court as members of the Supreme Court bar, are an important part of the circle of supporters of the justices and may be reluctant to call out ethics breaches on the court, a phenomenon discussed further in Chapter 4.

Yet, in 2025, the political right turned harshly against elite law firms, with President Trump's executive orders targeting firms that had represented his political opponents or were involved in investigations of his conduct. President Trump's executive orders targeting law firms were probably unconstitutional and so far have not fared well in the courts.[21] Nonetheless, many law firms are unenthusiastic about clashing with the executive branch, and some quickly caved in to President Trump's demands.[22] The broader point is that the legal profession, particularly large corporate law firms, thrives on close relationships with all three branches of government and has been a weak counterweight even when there are egregious abuses of power. As discussed further in Chapter 4, expecting elite lawyers and their firms to call out ethics breaches on the Supreme Court is a bridge too far.

The Court of Appeals

The court of appeals is the path most justices pursue to get on the Supreme Court. On the current court, all the justices but Justice Kagan were federal court of appeals judges. Kagan too held a powerful Senate-confirmed position, solicitor general of the United States, in the Obama administration. Many federal judges were involved in partisan politics and politically important interest groups early in their career. At the time of their nomination, many also had close relationships with home-state senators.

The president's political appointees in the Department of Justice, either in the Office of Legal Policy or the Office of Legal Counsel, do the initial screening of candidates for the federal bench, with further review by lawyers in the

[20] Adam Liptak, *Law Firms Pay Supreme Court Clerks $400,000 Bonuses. What Are They Buying? Inside Information and Influence with the Clerks' Former Bosses May Figure in the Transactions, a New Study Suggests*, N.Y. Times (Apr. 21, 2020).

[21] *See* executive order of the president, addressing risks from Perkins Coie LLP, March 6, 2025 (revoking security clearances of lawyers associated with a law firm that had previously represented the Democratic Party); and *Perkins Coie LLP v. United States Department of Justice et. Al.* (D. D.C. 2025), Civil Action No. 25-716 (BAH), order dated May 2, 2025, enjoining this executive order on constitutional grounds ("[i]t is simply not the case that all security-clearance decisions are immune from judicial review.").

[22] *See* Benjamin Weiser, *What to Know About Paul Weiss, the Law Firm Bowing to Trump's Demands* ("The 150-year-old firm has employed many Democrats, including Manhattan's former U.S. attorney. Its revenue was more than $2.6 billion last year."). N.Y. Times (Mar. 21, 2025).

White House Counsel's Office. Final decisions are made by the president and his political advisors.

But not all people involved in the selection process are federal employees. In Democratic administrations, labor unions and civil rights organizations play a critical role, telling the Justice Department, the White House, and influential senators who should, and should not, be appointed to the federal bench. In Republican administrations, conservative political commentators and organizations perform this role.

The Federalist Society, for example, has transformed from a student organization to one of the most powerful public policy groups in Washington, playing an ad hoc role in advising on judicial nominations in Republican administrations.[23] Giving such advice is a complex balancing act, as installing a "conservative" judge is not a monolithic endeavor. The Federalist Society and other similar groups are divided between social conservatives and libertarians. Some conservatives and libertarians also are skeptical of judicial deference to presidential power even if a Republican is in the White House. Yet conservative opposition to judicial "activism" has waned in recent years as federal courts have overturned statutes conservatives don't like in areas ranging from firearms to affirmative action and campaign finance. Despite these crosscurrents in the conservative movement, however, leaders of conservative groups are usually able to agree on which judicial nominees meet the criteria needed to satisfy most activists in their movement.

Screening of judicial nominees was less ideologically polarized up through the early 2000s when the Justice Department, the White House, and the Senate gave serious weight to a nonpartisan American Bar Association (ABA) committee's rating of nominees to the federal bench. The ABA process was so formalized, and deference to it so ingrained, that the Supreme Court considered whether the ABA committee on judicial selection was a "federal advisory committee" like other outside committees appointed by the executive branch and subject to the transparency provisions of the Federal Advisory Committee Act of 1972 (FACA).[24] The court, however, in *Public Citizen v. Department of Justice*,[25] held in 1989 that the ABA committee that advised the Justice Department on appointment of judges was not a federal advisory committee and did not have to meet the requirements of FACA.

[23] *See* Jeffrey Toobin, *The Conservative Pipeline to the Supreme Court*, New Yorker (Apr. 10, 2017), https://www.newyorker.com/magazine/2017/04/17/the-conservative-pipeline-to-the-supreme-court [https://perma.cc/PZB8-2VDP].

[24] The Federal Advisory Committee Act (FACA) is Pub. L. No. 92-463, 86 Stat. 770 (1972).

[25] *Public Citizen v. Department of Justice*, 491 U.S. 440 (1989).

Republicans, however, believe that the ABA is too liberal. The ABA has been sidelined in Republican administrations as ideologically right-leaning organizations, such as the Federalist Society, have assumed this role in screening judicial nominees, albeit with a much more secretive process than that used by the ABA. And as before, neither the courts nor Congress have been willing to impose the transparency requirements of FACA, which would require that at least some of this outsourcing of judicial selection be conducted in public view.

Federalist Society members were very much involved with judicial selection under President George W. Bush and the first term of Donald Trump.

The Federalist Society point man for judicial appointments from the 1990s through the first Trump administration was Leonard Leo, a conservative lawyer who was co-chair of the Federalist Society as well as the founder of several other conservative organizations. Leo is a master fundraiser. Leo raised over $400 million for judicial confirmation activities from 2014 to 2018.[26] Then, in 2021, he raised $1.6 billion from one man alone, electronics billionaire Barre Seid.[27] Leo also controls a group of for-profit corporations that allegedly received millions of dollars of contracts from his nonprofits.[28]

The extent of Leo's influence over the judicial selection process burst into the open in 2025 when President Trump broke with Leo, unhappy with decisions of conservative judges he had appointed in his first term. Trump accused Leo of giving him bad advice, and as usual ratcheted up the rhetoric in anger:

> I was new to Washington, and it was suggested that I use The Federalist Society as a recommending source on Judges. I did so, openly and freely, but then realized that they were under the thumb of a real "sleazebag" named Leonard Leo, a bad person who, in his own way, probably hates America, and obviously has his own separate ambitions.[29]

[26] Testimony of Lisa Graves, president, Center for Media and Democracy, before the US Senate Comm. on the Jud. Subcomm. on Fed. Courts, Oversight, Agency Action & Fed. Rights, titled What's Wrong with the Supreme Court: The Big-Money Assault on Our Judiciary (Mar. 10, 2021).

[27] "[A] reclusive, far-right billionaire [Barre Seid] supercharged Leo's dark money operation with a $1.6 billion donation. . . . Seid and Leo devised a plan to transfer all the shares in an electronics company to Leo's front group, on the way to selling that company. So when that company sold for $1.6 billion, it all went straight to Leo's group and, by the way, helped Seid avoid what would have been roughly $400 million in taxes." Statement of Senator Sheldon Whitehouse (D-RI), Sept. 13, 2022, https://www.whitehouse.senate.gov/news/speeches/scheme-18_leonard-leos-16-billion-payday/.

[28] Robert Maguire, Leonard Leo–Tied Nonprofits Have Paid His Businesses $90 Million in Just Six Years, Citizens for Responsibility and Ethics in Washington (CREW) (Nov. 2, 2024), https://www.citizensforethics.org/reports-investigations/crew-investigations/leonard-leo-tied-nonprofits-businesses-88-million/.

[29] *See* Charlie Savage, *Trump, Bashing the Federalist Society, Asserts Autonomy on Judge Picks* ("The president has grown increasingly angry at court rulings blocking parts of his agenda, including by judges he appointed.") N.Y. Times (May 30, 2025).

The substance of this dispute exposes tensions between the Trump administration and the conservative legal movement that have been brewing since 2016, when many conservative lawyers refused to support Trump's candidacy, and that appear to have worsened in his second term. Trump was angry that "conservative" judges on the court of international trade did not defer to his tariffs.[30] It was perhaps predictable that originalist judges might oppose Trump on tariffs. A tariff is a tax. Taxation only with consent of the legislature is a principle embedded in the Constitution and goes back to Magna Carta. But for Trump, political disputes are more about power than conservative principles, and he sought to test his power to imposes tariffs unilaterally. It's perhaps predictable that he would lash out at judges and even the conservative legal movement when he lost.

Putting aside the possibility that the Federalist Society's influence over judicial appointments may wane in the second Trump administration, the president has openly acknowledged what journalists covering judicial appointments have said for years: The Federalist Society, and Leonard Leo in particular, have had an extraordinary amount of influence on judicial appointments in Republican administrations.

Leo's power over the judicial selection process comes from his ability to raise money. Even if he is pushed aside by the Trump administration, other similar fundraisers will emerge to take this place. We will revisit Leo in the next chapter of this book, discussing how he facilitated vacation travel for justices with conservative donors who support the Federalist Society and other conservative groups that help judges and justices get appointed.

The focus of this book, however, is not the merits or demerits of any of these organizations. The focus here is on how important "social networking" with these organizations is for prospective court of appeals nominees, particularly those who also aspire to be elevated to the Supreme Court.

After appointment to the bench, the influence game continues. A court of appeals judge has many invitations to choose from—speaking engagements at bar associations and law schools, trade associations, and more. Unlike Supreme Court justices, however, court of appeals judges are bound by an enforceable ethics code, and violating ethics rules can be a deal killer for nomination to the Supreme Court. Most court of appeals judges are careful to stay on the right side of the line.

But there are also many loopholes for judges and their influencers to take advantage of. For example, moneyed special interest groups, often through

[30] *See V.O.S. Selections, Inc., et. al. v. United States, et. al.* (U.S. Ct. Int. Tr. 2025), No. 25-00066. Slip Op. 25-66. The Supreme Court affirmed in *Trump v. V.O.S. Selections, Inc.*, 607 U.S. ___ (2026).

an academic conduit such as George Mason University's Law and Economics Center, invite judges to lavish weekend or even week-long conferences on "law and economics" and similar topics. Free five-star resort lodging, fine food and wine, and golf are interspersed with lectures from supposed experts who present judges with grand theories about the law, never expressly telling judges how to decide cases but drilling into conference participants over and over again the theory that minimizing government regulation in just about any area of the law—antitrust, financial markets, consumer protection, labor and employment, the environment, and so on—is almost always the preferred "efficient" outcome maximizing social wealth for everyone. Judges go away from these conferences having gained a few pounds and, the corporate sponsors hope, enlightenment about how free markets work when courts leave big corporations and billionaires alone.

Attendance at these conferences can help validate a federal judge with corporate interests that participate in the nomination and confirmation process for higher courts, including the Supreme Court. The flip side is that acceptance of free lodging, food, and drink from corporate interests is an ethics problem. But for the "professional" nature of the conference, accepting free attendance would be impermissible under judicial ethics rules. The late Abner Mikva, a court of appeals judge and former White House counsel, was very critical of these conferences and called for judges to be banned from attending without paying.[31] In interviewing Supreme Court nominees at the White House, the author of this book asked about such conferences because a nominee's attendance likely would become an issue in Senate confirmation hearings. (Chief Justice Roberts and Justice Alito apparently did not attend such conferences while on the courts of appeals.)

Nomination

Long in advance of a Supreme Court opening, the White House Counsel's Office usually begins preparing lists of candidates with help from Department of Justice political appointees. Outside interest groups often help build the list. Although a president may nominate someone not on the list at the last moment (Harriet Miers's unsuccessful nomination for the court in 2006 transpired that way), getting on the list for the next Supreme Court opening is a big advantage.

[31] Abner Mikva, *The Wooing of Our Judges*, N.Y. Times (Aug. 28, 2000), https://www.nytimes.com/2000/08/28/opinion/the-wooing-of-our-judges.html ("... so much is built into our judicial system—from the black robe and 'all rise' custom to lifetime tenure for federal judges—to help foster the notion of judicial integrity. It all becomes meaningless, however, when private interests are allowed to wine and dine judges at fancy resorts under the pretext of 'educating" them.').

Because most Supreme Court nominees are court of appeals judges, establishing a politically appealing jurisprudential track record in prior decisions is important. In her first written opinion as a court of appeals judge in 2022, Judge Ketanji Brown Jackson struck down a policy begun under President Trump that restricted the bargaining power of labor unions for federal workers.[32] This, of course, earned her the support of dozens of unions when she was nominated for the court only a few weeks later.[33]

Occasionally, opinions from Supreme Court hopefuls go beyond demonstrating a jurisprudential philosophy and specifically take sides in political disputes. Consider, for example, the 2025 opinion by Judge James Ho of the Fifth Circuit reluctantly following the directives of the Supreme Court in an immigration case but explicitly stating that he agreed with the dissenters, Justices Thomas and Alito, who sided with President Trump, and suggesting that Trump had been disrespected by the courts.[34]

Factors not directly related to judicial philosophy also influence Supreme Court nominations. Geographic representation on the court used to be a major factor, at the beginning of the Republic when creation of new circuits led to the appointments of new justices,[35] and later because geography (North vs. South vs. West) was a proxy for political ideology,[36] but geography is no longer so important. Race, gender, and religion are. Some presidents are transparent about it—for example, Biden announcing in 2021 that he was going to nominate a Black woman to the court, instead of simply just doing it. Republicans go to the other extreme, saying that they refuse to consider race, gender, and religion but often doing so anyway. Roman Catholics, a group historically discriminated against in the United States and rarely represented on the court prior to 1950, have made up for lost ground; all five Republican appointees to the court since 2000 were born Roman Catholic. In 1991, Justice Thomas, Catholic and African American, replaced Justice Thurgood Marshall, also African American but having a very different judicial philosophy. Justice Sandra Day O'Connor was the first woman on the court in 1981; there are now three. The court has had up to three Jewish justices at the same time

[32] Daniel Wiessner, *U.S. Supreme Court Contender Jackson Backs Unions in First Ruling*, Reuters (Feb. 1, 2022), https://www.reuters.com/legal/government/us-supreme-court-contender-jackson-backs-unions-first-ruling-2022-02-01/.

[33] Working People Support the Nomination of Ketanji Brown Jackson to the Supreme Court, AFL-CIO (Feb. 28, 2022), https://aflcio.org/2022/2/28/working-people-support-nomination-ketanji-brown-jackson-supreme-court

[34] *A.A.R.P., W.M.M., and F.G.M., v. Trump* (5th Cir. 2025), https://www.ca5.uscourts.gov/opinions/pub/25/25-10534-CV0.pdf.

[35] Joshua Glick, *On the Road: The Supreme Court and the History of Circuit Riding*, 24 Cardozo L. Rev. 1753 (2003).

[36] William J. Daniels, *The Geographic Factor in Appointments to the United States Supreme Court: 1789–1976*, 31 W. Pol, Q. 226 (1978); Lee Epstein et al, *The Increasing Importance of Ideology in the Nomination and Confirmation of Supreme Court Justices*, 56 Drake L. Rev. 609 (2008).

(Ginsburg, Breyer, and Kagan), all appointed by Democrats, but now there is only one (Kagan). The days of the Supreme Court justice born into a white Anglo-Saxon Protestant family, almost the entire court from the founding up through the 1970s, are over (today there are none). The court, in this way, is more diverse than ever before, except for the fact that every justice but one (Barrett) went to law school at Harvard or Yale, and the court is more conservative than it has been since the 1930s.

Today, political ideology and jurisprudential philosophy are by far the most important factors in selecting Supreme Court nominees. Presumably, the lure of a potential Supreme Court appointment is enough to keep many courts of appeals judges faithful to the judicial philosophy that earns support of outside groups, usually the same groups that helped them get on the court of appeals. But the jurisprudence of a justice on the Supreme Court is more difficult to predict. Appointment to the Supreme Court is the last round of any "tit for tat" political game the court of appeals judge may play with interest groups for elevation to the court. When the game is over, new justices presumably can do as they please.

Until recently, many did. Conservatives have been especially disappointed. President Nixon, after failing to persuade the Senate to confirm two conservatives to the court (Clement Haynsworth and G. Harrold Carswell in 1969 and 1970, respectively), appointed four justices: Chief Justice Warren E. Burger and Justices Harry Blackmun, Lewis F. Powell Jr., and William Rehnquist. Only Rehnquist was a reliable conservative vote on the court. President Ford appointed Justice John Paul Stevens, who, particularly in his later years on the court, aligned with the liberals. President Reagan appointed Justices Antonin Scalia, Sandra Day O'Connor, and Anthony Kennedy, and only Scalia was a reliable conservative. President George H. W, Bush appointed Justices Souter and Thomas, but only Thomas voted with the conservatives. Out of ten Republican-appointed justices from 1969 to 1991, there were only three reliable conservatives, a 30 percent batting average.

Then, beginning with President George W. Bush, more effort was put into assessing the sincerity of the professed conservative judicial philosophy of candidates for the court. Both Bush appointees, Justice Alito (almost always) and Chief Justice Roberts (usually), have been reliable conservatives. President Trump got three appointments, Justices Gorsuch, Kavanaugh, and Barrett, all three of whom have stayed conservative, although Barrett has ruled against Trump in several cases involving presidential power, and these justices may not support Trump's more extreme measures in his second term.

Democrats have had fewer appointments to the court, but generally more luck choosing liberals who stayed liberal: Over the past sixty years, these were Justices Thurgood Marshall, Ruth Bader Ginsburg, Stephen Breyer, Elena

Kagan, Sonia Sotomayor, and Ketanji Brown Jackson. (On average since 1965, there has been one Democratic appointment to the court and one reliable liberal justice every ten years.) In sum, getting an opportunity to appoint any justices at all has been the biggest challenge for Democrats, whereas for Republicans the biggest challenge has been appointing Republican justices who will stay Republican, or at least decide cases the way Republicans would like them to.

Making sure that a Supreme Court justice does not stray from the "desired" jurisprudential outcome is difficult. Republican special interest groups are desperate to avoid appointing another Justice Stevens, Souter, O'Conner, or Kennedy, and see appointments such as Justices Scalia, Thomas, and Alito as the epitome of success. Carefully screening nominees for true ideological commitment is increasingly part of the process. The sought-for objective—which this author witnessed in the Bush White House—is to identify true believers in jurisprudential principles the president has promised interest groups he will advance on the court, and to separate those true believers from nominees who could "defect" after the last round of play with their political patrons.

A lot of this has to do with the genuine philosophical disposition of the justice, which may be discernable at the time of nomination, and getting this right is considered crucial.

Interest groups also choose favorites. Their communications with the White House are covert and perhaps predictably do not involve the White House ethics lawyer (at least that was this author's experience). In the GOP, there are two big groups: business friendly groups and social conservatives. In the Democratic Party, there are several factions; those that want more government regulation of business and those that don't are often at odds. Labor unions scrutinize court of appeals judges' decisions in labor cases. Civil rights groups do the same.

As with court of appeals nominations, the Federalist Society is a major player in Republican administrations. Another important conservative group is the Heritage Foundation, sponsor of the Project 2025 agenda, which was adopted in large part at the beginning of President Trump's second term. Heritage has long been involved in judicial selection as well. In 2016, then President-Elect Donald Trump's list of eleven candidates for the court included five attributed to the Heritage Foundation's John Malcolm, director of the Edwin Meese III Center for Legal and Judicial Studies.[37]

[37] See, "Heritage Expert Helps Shape Supreme Court Nominee List, Heritage Foundation," Sep 14, 2016 ("From the moment Justice Antonin Scalia died unexpectedly in February, Heritage Foundation scholars have been at the forefront of the debate over the Supreme Court vacancy. That now

Finally, prospective nominees, while staying close to the interest groups that support them, also need to be aware of the ethics traps. They can perhaps do anything they please once they are on the court, but not so beforehand. Court of appeals judges who do not follow ethics rules can be disciplined, or overruled, and violations can be used against them in Senate confirmation hearings if they are ever nominated for the Supreme Court. Ethics checks are initially conducted along with other background checks in the White House Counsel's Office. The author of this book, in clearing both Chief Justice Roberts and Justice Alito for nomination, drew up a list of stock holdings and other financial interests of the nominee and his spouse, along with all subsidiaries of these companies, and then conducted several computer checks against the docket of appellate cases in which the nominee had participated to discern whether the nominee had ever violated recusal rules. Neither Roberts nor Alito had, but several other contenders were not so fortunate. Because a closely divided Senate can look for any excuse to reject a nominee, the White House usually will not nominate a judge who appears to have violated judicial conduct rules.

Confirmation

Supreme Court confirmations are increasingly contentious even though none has failed in a vote on the Senate floor since President Reagan's nomination of Robert Bork was rejected in 1988. Special interest groups aligned with the two political parties have opposing interests, and they will spend large sums supporting, or opposing, a nominee.[38]

The Senate confirms a justice by majority vote; the filibuster, still used to block legislation, has disappeared from judicial nominations and has not been used for the Supreme Court. This means that a bare majority of senators, potentially representing less than a majority of the US population can confirm a justice, including one nominated by a president who did not win the popular vote.[39]

includes influencing the list of potential replacements being considered by Donald Trump, the Republican Party's presidential nominee.") https://www.heritage.org/crime-and-justice/impact/heritage-expert-helps-shape-supreme-court-nominee-list

[38] *See* Ilya Shapiro, *Supreme Disorder: Judicial Nominations and the Politics of America's Highest Court* (2020) (describing extreme politicization of the nomination and confirmation process with the two parties representing polar opposite judicial philosophies); Ilya Shapiro, The Politics of Supreme Court Confirmations and Recommendations for Reform, CATO Institute (July 20, 2021), https://www.cato.org/testimony/perspectives-supreme-court-practitioners-views-confirmation-process.

[39] *See* Xiao Wang, *Increasingly Antidemocratic? An Empirical Examination of the Supreme Court Nomination and Confirmation Process*, 11 Calif. L. Rev. Online 242 (2020), https://ssrn.com/abstract=3634951 ("Justices Kavanaugh and Gorsuch are the only members of the court to have been (1) nominated by a

"Murder boards" of lawyers, lobbyists, and politicians prepare the nominee for confirmation hearings and often include persons outside the government who work for outside organizations.[40] This means that up until the Senate confirmation vote and swearing in of a justice, the nominee likely will be in close contact not only with administration officials but also private individuals and organizations that support the nomination.

Throughout this process, there is no workable way for the Senate or the White House to get a meaningful commitment on ethics going forward, even if such an ethics commitment were desired—and it may not be desired if White House staffers and senators are also in alliance with the same interest groups that seek to influence the new justice. The nominee's past record on ethics can be closely scrutinized, but motivation to comply with ethics rules is reduced on the Supreme Court, as discussed in Chapter 4. Supreme Court nominees won't reveal to the Senate how they will decide future cases,[41] and commitments in Senate testimony on ethics are just as elusive. In any event, such commitments cannot be enforced.

A crisis in the confirmation process can make a nominee even more dependent upon supporters and financial backers, so exposure of a past scandal may in the long run solidify personal relationships that give rise to future scandal after the nominee joins the court. For example, Leonard Leo, the Federalist Society co-chair and master fundraiser, worked closely with Senate staff dealing with sexual assault allegations against Brett Kavanaugh during the confirmation process.[42] Clarence Thomas faced an even greater nomination

President receiving less than a majority of the vote and (2) confirmed by Senators representing less than a majority of the U.S. population."). In 2020, weeks before the presidential election, Justice Barrett was added to this list.

[40] According to the records of the Senate Judiciary Committee, the "murder board" preparing Judge Alito for his confirmation hearing consisted of over a dozen lawyers from the Justice Department and the White House Counsel's Office, including the author of this book, US Senator, Dan Coats, (R-IN), and influential lawyers and lobbyists from outside the government: Ed Gillespie, Republican lobbyist and former chairman of the Republican National Committee; Theodore B. Olson, partner of Gibson, Dunn & Crutcher and former solicitor general; Adam Ciongoli, senior vice president and general counsel, Time Warner Inc. and former Alito law clerk; Michael A. Carvin, partner of Jones Day and former deputy assistant attorney general Office of Legal Counsel; Charles J. Cooper, partner of Cooper & Kirk, and a former assistant attorney general Office of Legal Counsel; Timothy Flanigan, general counsel for corporate and international law, Tyco, and a former deputy counsel to the president; Leonard Leo, executive vice president of the Federalist Society; and John Manning, a professor (later dean and provost) from Harvard Law School. *See Alito's "Murder Board" a Mix of the Legal Elite*, Nat'l L. J. (Jan. 26, 2006). https://www.law.com/article/almID/900005446271/; Tricia Bishop, "Advisers Helped Navigate Alito Nomination." *The National Law Journal*, January 30, 2006 (URL link no longer available).

[41] Ray McKoski, *The Refusal of Supreme Court Nominees to Discuss Legal, Political, and Social Issues at Senate Confirmation Hearings: Ethical Obligation or Survival Strategy*? 73 S.C. L. Rev. 1 (2021), https://ssrn.com/abstract=3696086 or http://dx.doi.org/10.2139/ssrn.3696086.

[42] *See* Email from Mike Davis, chief counsel for nominations, US Senate Committee on the Judiciary, Sen. Chuck Grassley (R-IA), chairman, to "Nominations Strategy" [recipient field redacted] (Sept. 16, 2018, 10:20 p.m.) ("Just spoke to Leonard Leo for 30 mins. He is pushing BK [Brett Kavanaugh] to call on us to reopen the hearing, so BK can address these allegations. I made it clear that this is a recipe for

crisis with sexual harassment allegations in 1991, and he and his wife, Virginia Thomas, remained close to his defenders through his next three and a half decades on the court. (Mrs. Thomas's employment with the Heritage Foundation and involvement in conservative political organizations is discussed in the next two chapters of this book.)

Enormous amounts of money are spent by both liberal and conservative interest groups on advertising to support or oppose nominees to the court. A 2006 study by the Brennan Center for Justice in the aftermath of the Roberts and Alito nominations, as well as the failed Harriet Miers nomination, found that a staggering $7,597,675 was spent on ads, liberal groups spending $4,297,190 and conservative groups $3,300,485.[43]

The conservative Judicial Crisis Network is one of the biggest spenders on confirmation battles, including in support of Justices Gorsuch ($10 million),[44] Kavanaugh ($5 million),[45] and Barrett ($10 million).[46] In total, conservative groups may have spent close to $30 million on advertising supporting the Barrett nomination alone.[47] The liberal group Demand Justice spent millions in opposition to each of these nominations.[48] These amounts are perhaps modest in comparison to the hundreds of millions and even billions spent on campaigns for Congress and the presidency, and life tenure ensures that justices, unlike politicians, will not have to rely on this kind of support ever again.

This process brings to the nomination and confirmation of federal judges a component of the, in many ways corrupt, system of campaign finance for elected office that this author has criticized elsewhere.[49] But the Supreme Court has blessed this system in *Citizens United v. FEC* and other decisions holding such expenditures to be constitutionally protected speech. Money in

disaster. I also asked Abegg to call Leonard, to relay the same message. I called Travis Lenkner, BK's point man, and relayed the same."). Travis Lenkner is a former law clerk to Judge Kavanaugh and apparently was very much involved in the confirmation process for his nomination to the Supreme Court.

[43] The Brennan Center for Justice, Three Nominations Reveal Contrasting Influence of Interest Groups in High Court Nomination Process (Jan. 31, 2006). https://www.brennancenter.org/our-work/analysis-opinion/three-nominations-reveal-contrasting-influence-interest-groups-high-court.

[44] Brennan Center for Justice, Conservative Group Behind Kavanaugh Confirmation Has Spent Years Reshaping State and Federal Benches (Sept. 12, 2018), https://www.brennancenter.org/our-work/analysis-opinion/conservative-group-behind-kavanaugh-confirmation-has-spent-years.

[45] *Ibid.*

[46] Judicial Crisis Network, *Judge Amy Coney Barrett Confirmed: Judicial Crisis Network Spent $10 Million on Effort to Confirm Judge Amy Coney Barrett* (Oct. 27, 2020), https://judicialnetwork.com/in-the-news/judge-amy-coney-barrett-confirmed/

[47] Marianne Levine, *Demand Justice Launches Seven-Figure Ad Buy for SCOTUS Fight*, Politico (Sept. 29, 2020), https://www.politico.com/news/2020/09/29/demand-justice-seven-figure-ad-buy-scotus-fight-422886.

[48] *Ibid.*

[49] *See* Richard W. Painter, *Taxation Only with Representation; The Conservative Conscience and Campaign Finance Reform* (2016).

politics, protected from federal regulation by the justices, has an enormous impact on the way the justices themselves are chosen. And this interest group spending on electioneering communications and other advertising, while it does not come with implicit strings attached, comes with expectations as to what the justice will do on the court.

Every justice knows that they probably would not be where they are but for the spending of vast sums of someone else's money. This is the biggest gift a justice will ever receive. While justices do not have to reciprocate, and a nominee agreeing in advance to reciprocate would in fact be a bribe,[50] justices know what is expected in return. If what psychologists say about the predisposition to reciprocate gift giving[51] is true, even absent any promise of further exchange, groups that spend this kind of money giving someone a lifetime appointment on the Supreme Court anticipate that they will probably get some of what they want in return. And if what these groups want is what a justice was philosophically committed to anyway, the relationship is that much easier to rationalize.

This is before any additional gift giving described in the next chapter of this book. Free travel and other gifts to justices, particularly when connected with people and organizations that helped put them on the court, probably cement further a justice's feeling of gratitude. Whether or not such relationships change case outcomes at the court, one reason justices are there at all is because these people and organizations wanted them there.

Lifetime Tenure: End Game or Continued Tit for Tat?

As discussed above, Supreme Court justices are there because somebody—not just the president and the Senate—wanted them there. But as also discussed earlier, what justices do on the court is not always easy to predict. Choosing a nominee who is easier to predict because of an established judicial track record is now a political priority, and with the help of outside organizations such as the Federalist Society and the Heritage Foundation, White House and Justice Department lawyers since the George W. Bush administration have gotten a lot better at doing just that. (Democrats have had far

[50] *See* 18 U.S. Code § 201—Bribery of public officials and witnesses, imposing criminal penalties on "(b)Whoever—(1)directly or indirectly, corruptly gives, offers or promises anything of value to any public official or person who has been selected to be a public official, or offers or promises any public official or any person who has been selected to be a public official to give anything of value to any other person or entity, with intent—(A) to influence any official act."

[51] *See* Robert B. Cialdini, *Influence: The Psychology of Persuasion* (2006) (discussing reciprocation or "the internal pull to repay what another person has provided us").

fewer appointments to the court, but generally have had far fewer justices who "defect" from a liberal jurisprudential philosophy.)

But there's another way of keeping tabs on Supreme Court justices to keep them loyal to the people and organizations that helped put them on the court. Political patrons can continue their relationships with justices after confirmation. This is where the shockingly loose ethics regime at the Supreme Court is useful. Free yachting excursions, plane rides, interest-free (and even sometimes principal-free) loans, real estate deals, and other benefits that probably would have been off limits for court of appeals judges are all available for Supreme Court justices responsible to nobody but themselves.

Old friends also do not go away. The Federalist Society's Leonard Leo, who participated in the judicial selection process informally in the Bush and Trump administrations while never working for the government, was also involved in some of the controversial Supreme Court "gifts" discussed in the next chapter of this book. For example, Leo allegedly arranged the 2008 fishing trip that Justice Alito took with billionaire Paul Singer two years after he joined the court.[52] (Both Singer and Robin Arkley II, the owner of the lodge where the fishing expedition was hosted, were major donors to Leo's political groups.[53]) Book deals, spousal income opportunities, and other benefits of high office also come into play.

In sum, there are two ways to keep a justice loyal to the interest groups that got him on the court. The predominant strategy, implemented in earnest beginning in the George W. Bush administration, is to be careful in nominating justices to begin with, paying close attention to candidates' ideological beliefs and even to the political allegiances of family and friends that could influence them once they are on the court. To the extent this strategy works, there is little that will change justices' rulings. The conflicts of interest, gifts, and other ethics problems discussed later in this book undermine the credibility of the court but will not change its decisions. The secondary strategy is to keep justices loyal to preferred jurisprudential principles, and to the political patrons who helped put them on the court, by encouraging continued interaction between justices and these patrons via many of the same channels they used before. It is to those possibilities for influencing the justices, and the ways in which ethics rules are often ignored to do so, to which this book now turns.

[52] *See* Jake Johnson, *Alito's WSJ Op-Ed Didn't Mention SCOTUS Takeover Architect Leonard Leo's Key Role in Ethics Scandal*, Salon (June 21, 2023), https://www.salon.com/2023/06/21/alitos-wsj-op-ed-didnt-mention-scotus-takeover-architect-leonard-leos-key-role-in-ethics-scandal_partner/ [https://perma.cc/8VVP-8WT3] ("According to ProPublica, Leo 'invited Singer to join' and asked the hedge fund tycoon 'if he and Alito could fly on the billionaire's jet.'").

[53] *Ibid.*

2
Financial Conflicts of Interest

As Chapter 1 discussed, powerful special interest groups propel the nomination and confirmation of a Supreme Court justice. There's a lot of money involved as well. People with money want a particular justice on the court for a reason.

These people aren't about to step back and just hope their expectations are fulfilled after confirmation of a justice if there's an opportunity to continue to influence the court. The Supreme Court's dysfunctional ethics regime provides that opportunity. Gifts, free vacation travel, financial support for relatives, real estate transactions, loans that are interest-free (and principal-free), book royalties, and spousal income present abundant opportunities to keep justices connected with benefactors and tethered to the jurisprudential agenda that put them on the court to begin with. Amicus briefs funded directly or indirectly by some of these same persons follow. Failure to enforce the financial disclosure rules for justices and lack of transparency about funding of amicus briefs prevent parties appearing before the court and the public from knowing what's going on.

The work of the court has a substantial economic impact. The court today is overturning or narrowing more economic regulation than at any time since the 1930s when President Franklin D. Roosevelt had his famous battle with the court over its repudiation of the New Deal. The 2024 holding in *Loper Bright Enterprises v. Raimondo*,[1] overturning the four-decades-old *Chevron* doctrine means that courts will no longer defer to federal agencies in interpreting statutes they administer, substantially weakening agencies' ability to promulgate and enforce regulation of finance, the environment, energy, and healthcare. The court in 2020 held that the president has the right to fire the head of the Consumer Financial Protection Bureau,[2] and may soon overturn eighty-year-old precedent[3] and allow the president to fire members of independent commissions such as the Federal Trade Commission, the Federal

[1] *Loper Bright Enterprises v. Raimondo*, 603 U.S. ___ (2024).

[2] *Seila Law v. CFPB*, 591 U.S. 197 (2020) (holding that the president may remove the director of the Consumer Financial Protection Bureau despite a statute providing for a five-year term).

[3] *Humphrey's Executor v. FTC*, 295 U.S. 602 (1935) (holding that the president may not remove a member of the Federal Trade Commission until expiration of the member's statutory term). The court seems

Conduct Unbecoming. Richard W. Painter, Oxford University Press.
DOI: 10.1093/9780197832301.003.0003

Communications Commission, the Securities Exchange Commission, and the National Labor Relations Board. Regardless of the merits of justices' viewpoints on the underlying legal issues, it is problematic if they decide such cases after discussing these issues, or more general issues such as the impact of law on free markets, during free vacations on a billionaire's private jet or yacht, or with someone who is paying their spouses substantial income, or with someone who has just loaned them a great deal of money with no expectation of being paid back.

For interested persons and organizations, however, a lot of money is at stake. The money spent maintaining a good relationship with a justice will probably be a small fraction of the millions spent on nomination campaigns and confirmation battles. People and organizations will spend money trying to influence the justices to the extent they can get away with it. An objective of judicial ethics rules, combined with good judgment on the part of each justice, is to prevent these outside influencers from getting away with it. Another objective is to reassure the public that these influencers are not getting away with it, and that the court is ethically fit to interpret the laws that impact our daily lives.

It is not certain that external influence changed a justice's vote in a particular case, and in many instances, external influence may merely reaffirm a position the justice would have taken anyway. It is perhaps unlikely that a justice would change a vote to get a free luxury vacation from a billionaire, and it is perhaps likely that the billionaire would invite the justice on a free vacation because the billionaire likes the justice, and part of that may be that the billionaire likes the way the judge votes on cases. The ordinary citizen, however, is not particularly interested in a chicken-and-egg game, and figuring out which came first, if either way it's time to clean out a chicken coop that reeks to high heaven.

And it's also possible that in some instances such gifts may reinforce the justice's views, cementing personal relationships with people whose ideology was important to getting the justice on the court to begin with. Judges are not immune from confirmation bias—the tendency of decision makers to favor information that confirms their prior beliefs.[4] Confirmation bias exists already but is probably magnified by repeated interactions in social settings with people who share the same views. Confirmation bias may be

inclined to overturn *Humphrey's Executor* and allow the president to fire a member of the Commission. See transcript of oral arguments in Trump v. Slaughter, December 8, 2025. 25-332_7lhn.pdf

[4] Peter Wason, *On the Failure to Eliminate Hypotheses in a Conceptual Task*, 12 Q. J. Experimental Psych., 129–140 (1960); Peter Wason, *Reasoning About a Rule*, 20 Q. J. Experimental Psych. 273–281 (1968).

reinvigorated on a free yacht excursion in the Caribbean, an outing at a resort in the Adirondacks, or an all-expenses paid fishing trip.

At least as important as the risk of influence on the court's rulings is damage to public confidence in the court, which, as pointed out in the introduction to this book, is at a low point. Even if not a single case is decided differently because of the court's loose ethics rules, the public will be suspicious and disgusted with the stench of corruption. The potentially devastating impact on democracy of loss of public confidence in the judiciary is a theme to which this book will return later.

Meanwhile, the court interprets and enforces financial conflict of interest rules for itself. Nobody can tell the justices what to do. This theme also will come up repeatedly in this book—*Supreme Court exceptionalism.* The Supreme Court is different because there is no higher court in the land. "It is emphatically the province and duty of the judicial department to say what the law is," according to the ruling in *Marbury v. Madison* (1803).[5] But does this mean that the Supreme Court justices alone interpret the law, including the ethics rules for themselves? So much for the ancient Roman law maxim "*Nemo judex in causa sua,*" meaning "no one should be a judge in his own cause."[6] The Supreme Court is an exception.

Details follow below.

Luxury Travel and Other Gifts

Federal judges may not receive gifts, including free travel, from persons whose interests are substantially affected by their official duties, with very few exceptions. The statute governing all three branches of the federal government is clear on this point, and there is no exemption for Supreme Court justices:

> (a) Except as permitted by subsection (b), no Member of Congress or officer or employee of the executive, legislative, or judicial branch shall solicit or accept anything of value from a person—
>
> (1) seeking official action from, doing business with, or (in the case of executive branch officers and employees) conducting activities regulated by, the individual's employing entity; or

[5] *Marbury v. Madison*, 5 U.S. 137 (1803).

[6] See Justinian *Codex*, 3.5.1. Emperors Valens, Gratian, and Valentinian to Grachus, City Prefect. "We direct by this general law that no one shall be his own judge or decide his own case. For to give anyone power to render a decision in his own case would be iniquitous."

(2) whose interests may be substantially affected by the performance or nonperformance of the individual's official duties.[7]

Subsection (2) covers, among other things, gifts from any person or organization whose interests are affected by cases before the Supreme Court. The statute allows "reasonable exceptions as may be appropriate" promulgated by the "supervising ethics office," which for the federal courts is defined as "the Judicial Conference of the United States for judges and judicial branch officers and employees."[8]

The Judicial Conference regulates the conduct of the federal courts, but that's not true for the Supreme Court. The authorizing statute for the Judicial Conference does not give the conference power over the Supreme Court.[9] Supreme Court exceptionalism is not only embraced by the justices, but in this instance deferred to by Congress.

This implicitly allows the Supreme Court justices to promulgate their own "reasonable exceptions as may be appropriate." The justices do not explicitly make exceptions to the gift statute but instead resort to a more round about method: The justices purport to adhere to the gift statute and the Judicial Conference exceptions but in subtle ways interpret those exceptions differently for themselves.

Furthermore, as discussed in Chapter 5 of this book, several of the justices apparently believe that Congress cannot constitutionally set ethics rules for the court because of separation of powers concerns. Under this approach, the federal gifts statute would not be binding on the court to begin with because imposing such a statute on the court could be unconstitutional.

Chief Justice Roberts's 2011 Year End Report explained that the justices "observe the same limitations on gifts and outside income as apply to other federal judges," and twenty years earlier, in 1991, the justices adopted "an internal resolution in which they agreed to follow the Judicial Conference regulations as a matter of internal practice."[10] The Supreme Court's 2023 ethics code reiterates that point by replicating most of the rules that apply to other federal judges (minus the enforcement procedures that apply to other federal judges).[11]

[7] *See* 5 U.S.C. § 7353 (gifts to federal employees).

[8] 5 U.S.C. § 7353 (b), (d).

[9] *See* 28 U.S.C. § 331 ("The Judicial Conference shall review rules prescribed under section 2071 of this title by the courts, other than the Supreme Court.").

[10] *See* Chief Justice Roberts, 2011 Year-End Report on the Federal Judiciary, 5–7 (Dec. 31, 2011).

[11] Supreme Court of the United States, Code of Conduct for Justices of the Supreme Court of the United States, and accompanying statement of the Court (Nov. 13, 2023) ("We are issuing this Code, which largely represents a codification of principles that we have long regarded as governing our conduct."). The author of this book in 2024 criticized the court's ethics code for lack of an enforcement mechanism and the

The justices, thus, at least say that they are observing the gift statute with the same exceptions promulgated by the Judicial Conference for other federal judges.[12]

The exceptions to the gift rules promulgated by the Judicial Conference include the following:

1. Social hospitality based on personal relationships; [and]
2. Modest items, such as food and refreshments, offered as a matter of social hospitality.[13]

Another exception applies if the "gift consists of an invitation and travel expenses . . . to attend a bar-related function."[14] But traveling on a free vacation with a fabulously wealthy "friend" is not a "bar-related function." There is yet another exception if a "gift is from a relative or friend, if the relative's or friend's appearance or interest in a matter would in any event require that the [judge] to take no official action with respect to the matter."[15] This means that the gift from a relative or friend is permissible because the judge already needs to recuse from any case that could affect the financial interests of the donor. But as pointed out later in this chapter, the justices who receive such gifts often don't recuse.

Finally, under a separate federal statute in the Ethics in Government Act of 1978, all gifts, whether permissible or impermissible, need to be disclosed, with very few exceptions.[16] The act[17] requires annual disclosure forms filed by senior officers in all three branches of government—Congress, the executive branch, and the federal courts—including a brief description of the source and value of all gifts that exceed the reporting threshold. (This is reset every three years by the General Services Administration and currently is $525.) Required disclosure for free travel includes a "brief description (including a travel itinerary, dates and nature of any expenses provided) of travel or reimbursements received from any source."[18]

court's unwillingness to address ethics violations, including some also discussed in this chapter. Richard W. Painter, "SCOTUS House: Can a Supreme Court Ethics Lawyer and Inspector General Help Get This Fraternity Under Control?," *Georgetown Journal of Legal Ethics* 37, no. 1 (2024): 347

[12] *See* U.S. Courts, Guide to Judiciary Policy, Vol. 2C: Codes of Conduct, Ch. 6: Ethics and Professional Guidance, § 620.10 (regulations promulgated by the Judicial Conference of the United States under the authorities of 5 U.S.C. §§ 7351(c), 7353(b)(1), and 7353(d)(1)(C)); *See* Ethics Reform Act of 1989, Pub. L. No. 101-194 (1989).

[13] *Ibid.* at § 620.25.

[14] *Ibid.* at § 620.35.

[15] *Ibid.*

[16] *See* Ethics in Government Act, 5a U.S.C. § 102(a)(2)(A) (disclosure requirements for gifts).

[17] 5 U.S.C. §§ 13103(f)(11), 13101(10).

[18] *Ibid.* at 13104(a)(2)(A)-(B).

The Supreme Court justices have mostly been complying with the gift rules and disclosure rules in practice, but there have been some glaring exceptions.

A 2024 analysis by an independent group, Fix the Court, concluded that the justices have accepted 344 gifts totaling $2.9 million since 2004; gifts valued at $2.4 million were attributed to a one justice alone: Justice Thomas.[19] Some of his gifts were not disclosed until very recently.[20] These are the gifts we know about. The fact that the other justices are silent in the face of Justice Thomas's noncompliance suggests that they too may have liberally interpreted the gift rules and accompanying disclosure rules. Alternatively, the other justices could be complying (mostly), but they are not willing to criticize another justice, a phenomenon explored in Chapter 4, where this book discusses "colleagues covering for colleagues."

Here are some of the specifics.

For more than twenty years, Justice Thomas accepted regular gifts of private jet travel, yacht excursions, and other luxury vacations from billionaire and Republican megadonor Harlan Crow, without disclosing them as gifts on his annual financial disclosure reports filed under the Ethics in Government Act of 1978.[21] Pro Publica estimated that one of these trips alone, a luxury trip to Indonesia, could have cost $500,000 if Justice Thomas had chartered the plane and yacht himself.[22]

At Topridge, Crow's luxury resort in the Adirondacks, hangs a painting of Justice Thomas seated next to Mr. Crow, and sitting nearby is Leonard Leo, the co-chairman and former executive vice president of the Federalist Society.[23] We remember Leonard Leo from Chapter 1 of this book—he has been one of the most influential outsiders in the nomination and confirmation of Supreme Court justices by Republican presidents for the past twenty-five years. (Leo, however, may not be in such good graces with President

[19] Fix the Court, *A Staggering Tally: Supreme Court Justices Accepted Hundreds of Gifts Worth Millions of Dollars* (June 6, 2024) (reporting that the justices received 445 gifts valued at $4,780,720, and a total of $2.4 million in gifts to a single justice, Justice Thomas), https://fixthecourt.com/2024/06/a-staggering-tally-supreme-court-justices-accepted-hundreds-of-gifts-worth-millions-of-dollars/

Fix the Court's (FTC) reporting is unusual because Justice Thomas accepted gifts without reporting them, making it more complicated to produce a clean calculation. FTC's initial account identified 344 gifts to the entire court, totaling $2,993,036. Of this total, Justice Thomas accounted for 103 gifts valued at $2,402,310. However, FTC shared another count that includes Justice Thomas's *likely gifts* raising the total to 445 gifts valued at $4,780,720 for the whole Court. Of that total, Justice Thomas apparently received 204 likely gifts, valued at $4,189,994. Fix the Court's spreadsheet goes into further details, showing the differences between the adjusted numbers and the initial numbers: https://docs.google.com/spreadsheets/d/14l25NLvBOd9sk4mArK4k7dtV0MUwxr5GBuLHL5Sp8lo/edit?gid=957411191#gid=957411191.

[20] *Ibid.* See FTC spreadsheet supra comparing gifts reported by the justices and likely gifts.

[21] Joshua Kaplan, Justin Elliott, & Alex Mierjeski, *Clarence Thomas and the Billionaire*, ProPublica (Apr. 6, 2023), https://www.propublica.org/article/clarence-thomas-scotus-undisclosed-luxury-travel-gifts-crow [https://perma.cc/L8CL-C3AS].

[22] *Ibid.*

[23] *Ibid.*

Trump during his second term.) But perhaps this was an innocent gathering at Topridge of like-minded friends, if we assume that Thomas, Crow, and Leo were discussing the beauty of the Adirondack Mountains, not the business of the Supreme Court. Regardless of what they talked about, free airfare, lodging, and meals should have been disclosed.

Justice Thomas also failed to disclose tuition payments by Crow for Thomas's grand-nephew, whom Thomas, under his powers as legal guardian of a minor, enrolled in two private schools where he presumably was contractually obligated to pay the tuition.[24]

Health care industry executive Tony Welters assisted Justice Thomas with a $267,000 loan to purchase a recreational vehicle—a Prevost Le Mirage XL Marathon, to be exact—in 1999. This RV may have the best bus chassis in the world—the Prevost Coach. Add to this meticulous exterior and interior detail work and one has a recreational vehicle that 99 percent of Americans could never afford. In many parts of America, ordinary people paid less for their house than Welters paid for Justice Thomas's recreational vehicle.

Justice Thomas made very few payments on this "loan," and Welters ultimately forgave approximately $253,000 in principal and interest in 2008. Welters was the founder of AmeriChoice, the predecessor to United Health Group. Justice Thomas has not recused from a single healthcare-related case on the Supreme Court on account of this loan or his friendship with Welters. This includes the 2012 case, *National Federation of Independent Business v. Sebelius*,[25] in which Justice Thomas and three other justices dissented from a majority opinion upholding the individual mandate and other provisions of the Affordable Care Act (aka Obamacare).

Citizens for Responsibility and Ethics in Washington (CREW), a public interest organization, sent a letter to Chief Justice Roberts and Attorney General Garland requesting an investigation of these undisclosed gifts to Justice Thomas.[26] CREW did not receive a response. In July 2024, two US senators sent another letter to Attorney General Garland requesting an investigation.[27]

[24] Joshua Kaplan, Justin Elliott, & Alex Mierjeski, *Clarence Thomas Had a Child in Private School. Harlan Crow Paid the Tuition*, ProPublica (May 4, 2023), https://www.propublica.org/article/clarence-thomas-harlan-crow-private-school-tuition-scotus [https://perma.cc/73S3-N58H].

[25] *National Federation of Independent Business v. Sebelius*, 567 U.S. 519 (2012).

[26] *See* Letter from Noah Bookbinder, Virginia Canter, Norman L. Eisen, & Richard Painter to Chief Justice John Roberts & Attorney General Merrick Garland, dated Apr. 14, 2023 (requesting an investigation of Justice Clarence Thomas's failure to report gifts of private aircraft travel on his public financial disclosure report), https://www.citizensforethics.org/wp-content/uploads/2023/04/Justice-Clarence-Thomas-DOJ-Complaint-April-14-2023-1.pdf

[27] Letter from Senators Sheldon Whitehouse (D-RI) and Ron Wyden (D-OR) to Attorney General Garland, dated July 3, 2024, https://www.whitehouse.senate.gov/wp-content/uploads/2024/07/2024-07-03-Letter-to-AG-Garland-re-Special-Counsel-FINAL.pdf.

Justice Alito failed to disclose a 2008 fishing trip with billionaire and GOP donor Paul Singer. Singer flew Alito in a private plane to Alaska, where they were housed at the expense of another conservative donor.[28] In the years since, Singer's hedge fund has had cases before the court at least ten times, and Alito never recused himself.[29] The most prominent of these was a case in which Singer's hedge fund bought Argentine debt in a depressed trading market and then sued Argentina for payment of the entire amount at face value. The court, with Justice Alito joining the majority, sided with Singer and held that Argentina was required to pay.[30] Justice Alito should have recused from this case after having accepted such an expensive gift from Singer.[31] But each justice interprets the recusal statute for themselves, and sometimes they do not recuse in situations where their impartiality might reasonably be questioned.

Consider the impact this has on the international reputation of the court. Argentina has less than one-fifth the per capita income of the United States. The court may be correct that if Argentina borrows money by selling transferable bonds, and a US hedge fund buys them at a deep discount, Argentina must pay the entire amount due. But nonetheless, a Supreme Court justice should refrain from deciding this case after taking a free vacation with the US billionaire whose hedge fund bought the bonds. It doesn't matter that the fishing trip almost certainly had no impact on the outcome of the case. Appearances matter.

Justice Alito defended his 2008 fishing trip with Singer in a 2023 op-ed in the *Wall Street Journal*,[32] but his defense is weak. Alito argues that he did not need to recuse from cases involving Singer because he did not have a close relationship with Singer and that he had no reason to be aware of Singer's connection to any case.[33] He also claims that he did not need to report "personal hospitality" on his annual financial disclosure form and that his seat on Singer's plane "would have otherwise been vacant."[34]

[28] Joshua Kaplan, Justin Elliott, & Alex Mierjeski, *Justice Samuel Alito Took Luxury Fishing Vacation with GOP Billionaire Who Later Had Cases Before the Court*, ProPublica (June 20, 2023), https://www.propublica.org/article/samuel-alito-luxury-fishing-trip-paul-singer-scotus-supreme-court [https://perma.cc/MV9P-385E].

[29] *Ibid.*

[30] *See Rep. of Arg. v. NML Capital, Ltd.*, 573 U.S. 134 (2014). This was an 8–1 decision of the justices (Justice Ginsburg dissenting), so it is unlikely that Justice Alito's interactions with Paul Singer influenced the outcome. Still, we have no way of knowing how deliberations proceeded, and the appearance of conflict remains regardless of the votes of the other justices.

[31] *See* 28 U.S.C. § 455 (discussing recusal requirements for judges and justices).

[32] *See* Samuel A. Alito Jr., *Justice Samuel Alito: ProPublica Misleads Its Readers*, Wall St. J. (June 20, 2023), https://www.wsj.com/articles/propublica-misleads-its-readers-alito-gifts-disclosure-alaska-singer-23b51eda [https://perma.cc/HPL9-73NS] (The publication levels false charges about Supreme Court recusal, financial disclosures, and a 2008 fishing trip.).

[33] *Ibid.*

[34] *Ibid.*

Justice Alito's dubious "empty seat theory" of free luxury travel doesn't pass the smell test.

As discussed in Chapter 1, in 2006, the author of this book helped prepare Chief Justice Roberts and Justice Alito for Senate confirmation hearings and held regular meetings with White House staff and incoming cabinet members to explain ethics rules. Across the government, ethics lawyers emphasize repeatedly that free travel on a private plane is almost always an impermissible gift for a government official.[35] Even in the rare instance that it is permissible because the host is a close friend—the "personal hospitality" exception—it still must be disclosed.[36] But Alito says that he had spoken only a few times with Singer, meaning Singer was not a close friend, so Justice Alito should not have accepted a free trip on Singer's plane to begin with.

And in any event, the free travel to Alaska had to be disclosed. Justice Alito says he hitched a ride on Singer's plane that was headed to Alaska anyway, that it didn't cost Singer anything additional, and thus was not a gift that needed to be disclosed.[37] This focus on the marginal cost to the *gift giver* is nowhere in federal gift rules defining the value of a gift. It's the benefit to the *gift recipient* that matters. And that's for good reason: Marginal cost to the gift giver has nothing to do with the gift's potential to influence the recipient.[38] A seat on a private plane still has substantial value. Anyone who uses the empty seat theory to board a plane or a cruise ship without a ticket will quickly find that out.

Even less convincing is Justice Alito's assurance that "if there was wine it was certainly not wine that costs $1,000."[39] Most Americans splurge when they

[35] *See, e.g.*, Memorandum from US House Comm. on Ethics, Officers for all Members, Officers, and Employees re: Noncommercial Aircraft Travel, at 3–4 (Apr. 10, 2019), https://ethics.house.gov/wp-content/uploads/2019/04/Private-Plane-pinksheet-FINAL.pdf [https://perma.cc/4E5P-2FVG] ("When the value of a gift proposed to be accepted under the personal friendship provision exceeds $250, written approval of the Committee on Ethics is required before the gift can be accepted. Practically any flight on a non-commercial aircraft will exceed $250 in value and hence will require Committee approval.").

[36] *See* 5 U.S.C. § 102(a)(2)(A) (requiring disclosure of "[t]he identity of the source, a brief description, and the value of all gifts aggregating more than the minimal value . . . or $250, whichever is greater, received from any source other than a relative of the reporting individual during the preceding calendar year, except that any food, lodging, or entertainment received as personal hospitality of an individual need not be reported."). A free ride on a private plane is not "food, lodging, or entertainment received as personal hospitality" and therefore must be disclosed.

[37] Alito Jr., *supra*.

[38] The executive branch gift rules explicitly reject any approach to valuing gifts that focuses on marginal cost to the donor instead of value to the recipient. *See* 5 C.F.R. § 2635.203(c) Definitions (2023) ("Market value means the cost that a member of the general public would reasonably expect to incur to purchase the gift."). *See also Ibid.* Example 2 ("During an official visit to a factory operated by a well-known athletic footwear manufacturer, an employee of the Department of Labor is offered a commemorative pair of athletic shoes manufactured at the factory. Although the cost incurred by the donor to manufacture the shoes was $17, the market value of the shoes would be the $100 that the employee would have to pay for the shoes on the open market."). Nowhere does the Judicial Conference of the United States imply in its rules that gifts to judges would be valued any differently.

[39] Alito Jr., *supra*.

pay $20 for a bottle of wine, and $20 is the limit for permissible gifts in the executive branch.[40] If the trip was so simple and rustic, why didn't everyone, Justice Alito included, buy a ticket on a commercial airline and pay for their own wine?

In the executive branch, undisclosed personal travel on a private plane can result in criminal prosecution. In *United States v. Leonardo Silva*, for example, a senior Drug Enforcement Agency official accepted free personal trips between the United States and Mexico on private planes owned by two friends who were wealthy businessmen and failed to disclose these trips on his annual financial disclosure form.[41] He was indicted, pled guilty to violations of the false statements statute, 18 U.S.C. 1001(a), and was sentenced to two years of probation.[42] The annual financial disclosure filing for Supreme Court justices is nearly identical and is governed under the same statute, but when these rules are violated by the justices, nothing happens.[43]

The justices don't play by the same rules the rest of us do.

Real Estate Deals

Some Supreme Court justices aren't just good at enjoying free luxury vacations. They're good at buying and selling real estate too.

Justice Thomas sold his interest in three Savannah, Georgia, properties to Harlan Crow in 2014 for $133,363 without reporting the sales on his financial disclosure report.[44] One of the properties that Justice Thomas sold to Crow is a house in which Thomas's mother still lives.[45] Crow paid Justice Thomas for the property but for years has not been able to use it. He clearly doesn't want to.

[40] *See* 5 C.F.R. § 2635.204 (discussing exceptions to the prohibition for acceptance of certain gifts).

[41] *See United States v. Leonardo Silva*, Crim, 16–69 (D.D.C. 2016), Statement of Offense and Other Conduct, https://www.oge.gov/web/OGE.nsf/0/D80535E5A0FC14AA852585B6005A1C53/$FILE/Silva%20Statement%20of%20Offense.pdf [https://perma.cc/PEJ9-R9VQ]; 5 U.S.C. § 13104(a)(2)(A–B) (requiring gifts, including free transportation to be reported).

[42] *See* Memorandum from David Apol, Acting Director and General Counsel of the United States Office of Government Ethics to Designated Agency Ethics Officers, Re: 2016 Conflict of Interest Prosecution Survey (Aug. 7, 2017), https://www.oge.gov/web/oge.nsf/0/E15D086E908893B1852585BA005BEC3F/$FILE/FINAL%202016%20Prosecution%20Survey%20LA.pdf [https://perma.cc/KJ92-3M8U]; *United States v. Leonardo Silva*, Crim, 16–69 (D.D.C. 2016).

[43] *See* 5 U.S.C. § 13104(a)(2)(A–B) (describing the underlying reporting obligation for gifts).

[44] Justin Elliott, Joshua Kaplan, & Alex Mierieski, *Billionaire Harlan Crow Bought Property from Clarence Thomas. The Justice Didn't Disclose the Deal*, ProPublica (Apr. 13, 2023), https://www.propublica.org/article/clarence-thomas-harlan-crow-real-estate-scotus [https://perma.cc/EPF9-JDXA] ("The Crow company bought the properties for $133363 from three co-owners—Thomas, his mother and the family of Thomas' late brother according to a state tax document and a deed dated Oct. 15, 2014, filed at the Chatham County courthouse.").

[45] *Ibid.*

Shortly after he joined the court, Justice Gorsuch sold his $1.6 million jointly owned tract of land and house in Granby, Colorado. Gorsuch disclosed this sale but did not identify the buyer.[46] He left blank the field on his financial disclosure form asking the identity of the buyer, which may have been permissible because the property was sold through a limited liability company (LLC) in which Gorsuch owned a 20 percent interest rather than by Gorsuch himself. Even though the transaction was undertaken through an LLC, the identity of the buyer of real estate partly owned by a Supreme Court justice should be an important part of the disclosure. The undisclosed buyer was Brian L. Duffy, the chief executive of Greenberg Traurig, a large Washington, DC, law firm that has cases before the court.[47]

Gorsuch's failure to disclose this did not violate the law. (The Ethics in Government Act should be amended to require complete disclosure of the parties to transactions at the LLC level.)[48] Still, this undisclosed transaction by an LLC partially owned by a Supreme Court Justice with a powerful Washington, DC, lawyer does not increase public confidence in the court.

Meanwhile, Justice Amy Coney Barrett sold her home in South Bend, Indiana, for $905,000 to Brendan Wilson, a lawyer who moved from Washington, DC, to assume a leadership role at the Religious Liberty Initiative at Notre Dame University.[49] The Liberty Initiative is a socially conservative organization that files amicus briefs in religious liberty cases before the court. This information was obtained from real estate records and did not have to be disclosed on Justice Barrett's financial disclosure form because federal regulations do not require disclosure of the sale of a personal residence. Justice Barrett violated no existing ethics rule or other law, although the appearances are problematic.

Supreme Court justices seem to sell homes to people who are lawyers or billionaires. Just a coincidence.

[46] Charlie Savage, *Head of a Major Law Firm Bought Real Estate From Gorsuch*, N.Y. Times (Apr. 25, 2023), https://www.nytimes.com/2023/04/25/us/neil-gorsuch-property-sale.html [https://perma.cc/Q8ZT-P8VP].

[47] *See Ibid.*

[48] This author has previously urged Congress to amend the Ethics in Government Act to require disclosure of transactions at the corporate level. *See* Testimony of Richard W. Painter Before the Committee on Oversight and Government Reform United States House of Representatives, Hearing Entitled Legislative Proposals for Fostering Transparency (Mar. 23, 2017), https://oversight.house.gov/wp-content/uploads/2017/03/Painter-UMN-Statement-Legislative-Proposals-for-Transparency-3-23.pdf [https://perma.cc/7YEE-Q4BZ].

[49] *Amy Coney Barrett Faces Scrutiny over Real Estate Deal with Religious Group*, Newsweek (June 23, 2023). The author of this book has reviewed the property listing and concluded that the house was probably worth about what Mr. Wilson paid for it.

Spousal Income

Yet another source of conflict is spousal income. This is true of many government officials, not just Supreme Court justices, but with only nine justices on the court, and a single vote often deciding a case, perhaps the public interest in knowing about spousal income is more acute.

The financial disclosure rules of the Ethics in Government Act have bound the justices since 1978,[50] and cast some light on justices' financial affairs, but provide very little information about spousal income. A spouse's employer is disclosed, but not individual clients of the spouse. There is little transparency about sources of spousal income paid through an LLC or other entity owned by the spouse—only the entity itself is disclosed, not the identity of persons or entities who pay money into it.

We know, for example, that Virginia Thomas has a consulting firm called Liberty Consulting, but who are its clients?[51] Few people know. Virginia Thomas has done past work for companies and nonprofits connected with Leonard Leo, the conservative activist who controls billions in nonprofit money, much of it used to influence Supreme Court nominations and confirmation battles. Investigative journalists uncovered that financial information elsewhere,[52] not on Justice Thomas's disclosure forms, because it wasn't there. We don't know the total amount of income Virginia Thomas earns. Justice Thomas's 2021 financial disclosure form under "Spouse's Noninvestment Income" simply listed "Liberty Consulting, Inc.—salary and benefits."[53] This minimal disclosure, while insufficient to reveal conflicts of interest, apparently complied with the law.

Virginia Thomas insists that she and her husband have "separate careers" and don't discuss work with each other.[54] We have very little information about which of her clients have cases before the court, because we don't know who those clients are. Virginia Thomas is not in the legal profession—where

[50] The Ethics in Government Act of 1978 requires filing of financial disclosure reports by all federal judges, including justices of the Supreme Court. *See* 5 U.S.C. § 13103.

[51] *See* Brian Schwartz, *Inside the Consulting Firm Run by Ginni Thomas, Wife of Supreme Court Justice Clarence Thomas*, CNBC (Apr. 5, 2022, 6:43 p.m.), https://www.cnbc.com/2022/04/05/inside-the-consulting-firm-run-by-ginni-thomas-wife-of-supreme-court-justice-clarence-thomas.html [https://perma.cc/7489-7VKR] ("Very little is known about her company, Liberty Consulting, which is listed as an asset on her husband's Supreme Court disclosures.").

[52] See Schwartz, *Inside the Consulting Firm Run by Ginni Thomas*, *supra* (discussing partial disclosure of payments made to Thomas on individual nonprofit organization Forms 990, other tax filings, and similar reports).

[53] See Financial Disclosure Report Required by the Ethics in Government Act of 1978 for Calendar Year 2021 (5 U.S.C. app. §§ 101–111), filed by Associate Justice Clarence Thomas, May 16, 2022, https://www.scotusblog.com/wp-content/uploads/2022/06/Thomas-C-J3.-SC_SR_21.pdf.

[54] Schwartz, *supra*.

client confidentiality is essential—but there is no law requiring her or Justice Thomas to disclose the identity of her clients, and she won't.

Chief Justice Roberts also disclosed spousal income. Jane Roberts has earned about $1 million a year in commissions as a headhunter placing lawyers with top DC law firms, including firms with cases before the court.[55] But his disclosure form inaccurately labeled Ms. Roberts's income an "attorney search consultants—salary."[56] The term "salary" is misleading because it suggests a fixed income, whereas a legal recruiter is paid a commission earned only if a law firm decides to hire a candidate proposed by the recruiter.[57] Each law firm that hires a candidate proposed by Ms. Roberts increases her income from commissions, not her "salary." Although there is no law requiring Jane Roberts to find alternative employment, there is something unsavory about the spouse of the chief justice doing millions of dollars' worth of business with law firms having cases before the court.

Yet two decades ago Justice Ruth Bader Ginsburg's husband, Martin Ginsburg, was a prominent tax lawyer, leading to speculation about whether his clients could be impacted by cases before the court. He never argued a case before the court, but his partners at the law firm Fried Frank, Harris Shriver and Jacobson did, and Justice Ginsburg did not recuse from these cases.

In neither spousal income situation is recusal of a justice from a case the appropriate answer unless the spouse is a party or counsel in a case. Otherwise, a justice could have to recuse in too many cases. Furthermore, it would be too easy for a party to game the system by hiring the law firm employing a justice's spouse to force recusal. (In some cases, corporate clients of Fried Frank probably would have preferred that Justice Ginsburg not participate.) Recusal not being a valid option, the question is whether a judge should strongly encourage a spouse not to work for law firms that appear before the court. Both Martin Ginsburg, a tax lawyer, and Jane Roberts, an executive recruiter, could have worked for different employers, including smaller law firms without a Supreme Court practice, and appearances would have

[55] See Nicholas Reimann, "Chief Justice John Roberts' Wife Made Over $10 Million As Legal Consultant, Report Says," *Forbes*, April 28, 2023 (calculating Ms. Roberts' reported income over eight years) https://www.forbes.com/sites/nicholasreimann/2023/04/28/chief-justice-john-roberts-wife-made-over-10-million-as-legal-consultant-report-says/; *See* Steve Eder, *At the Supreme Court, Ethics Questions over a Spouse's Business Ties*, N.Y. Times (Jan. 31, 2023), https://www.nytimes.com/2023/01/31/us/john-roberts-jane-sullivan-roberts.html [https://perma.cc/7TTR-W975].

[56] *Ibid.*

[57] *See* Sworn affidavit of Kendal B. Price (Dec. 2, 2022), https://www.documentcloud.org/documents/23791123-2-of-8-sworn-affidavit-of-kendal-b-price-12-02-2022 [https://perma.cc/4XGX-EFYA] (affidavit of a former employee and co-worker of Jane Roberts discussing the commission structure at Major, Lindsey & Africa, Jane Roberts's legal recruiting firm).

been better if they had. Still, it is extremely unlikely that spousal employment affected the vote of either justice in a case.[58]

Spousal income presents special problems because married couples have their own professional lives, and the law cannot limit one spouse's options because the other is on the court. For most other government jobs, including the lower federal courts, these problems are usually dealt with by recusal, but recusal is much harder on the Supreme Court, where there are no substitute justices. (Chapter 9 explores the possibility of allowing retired justices to substitute for recused justices on the Supreme Court, but that proposal has downsides, including adding uncertainty to the court's case law.) It would be better if spouses sought employment with organizations not appearing as parties or counsel before the court, although this is probably more about appearances than the need to avoid actual improper influence.

There are no bright lines to be drawn here, and at a certain point, spousal employment could be sufficiently substantial to exert improper influence. A justice could not take money from a party with a case before the court without being accused of bribery, but should the justice's spouse be hired by that same party as a "consultant" without even public disclosure of that fact? Probably not. This is distinguishable from the scenario where Martin Ginsburg and Jane Roberts were employed by law firms, not by the parties to cases before the court, and were employed by these law firms before the cases came before the court.

More disclosure about spousal income would help. Justices probably should disclose their tax returns, including a breakdown of spousal income, although individual tax returns will not disclose payments made to a spouse's employer (e.g., a multipartner law firm, investment firm, or consulting firm). But justices don't disclose their tax returns and probably won't disclose unless they decide that safeguarding the credibility and reputation of the court requires it.

Supreme Court Book Deals

Supreme Court justices are also bestselling authors.

When it comes to book deals, the ethics rules for judges and justices are a lot more permissive than the rules for other public officials.

[58] See Ed Whelan, *Flimsy "Ethics Issues" Regarding Chief Justice Roberts's Wife*, Nat'l Rev. (Feb. 1, 2023) (comparing the Ginsburg and Roberts spousal employment scenarios and concluding that neither created a significant conflict of interest) (quoting Professor Amanda Frost saying of Chief Justice Roberts, "It feels hard to imagine how this would corrupt his vote.").

For employees of the executive branch, ethics rules on book royalties are strict. An employee "shall not receive compensation from any source other than the Government for teaching, speaking or writing that relates to the employee's official duties."[59] This regulation bans, among other things, royalties from books on topics related to official duties *or* where the book contract was extended in part because of official position.[60] A director of the Division of Enforcement at the Commodity Futures Trading Commission or another financial regulator may earn royalties from a book on stamp collecting or another hobby,[61] but may not earn royalties for a book on financial regulation.[62] Regardless of the topic of the book, no book royalties are permitted if the book contract was awarded because of the employee's official position.[63]

These rules, however, do not apply to federal judges, including the Supreme Court. No statute or regulation limits how much royalties or advances a justice can make from a book, regardless of the subject matter of the book.[64] This is one of several areas where federal law needs to be changed. Arguably the same rules should apply to the justices that apply to other federal officials, most of whom have far less impact than a justice does on federal law.

According to annual financial disclosure forms filed in 2022, Justice Amy Coney Barrett received $425,000 in 2021, her first full year on the court, as part of a book deal that may be worth as much as $2 million, while Justice

[59] 5 C.F.R. § 2635.807(a) (2023).

[60] *See, e.g.*, 5 C.F.R. § 2635.807(a)(2)(i)(B) (2023) ("[C]ircumstances indicate that the invitation to engage in the activity was extended to the employee primarily because of his official position."). A book deal signed after one is appointed to a high-ranking position would likely fit this definition, and that would include the Supreme Court but for the fact that these regulations do not apply to the Supreme Court.

[61] 5 C.F.R. § 2635.807(a), Example 1 (2023).

[62] *Ibid.* Example 4 (2023). *See also* Legal Advisory, LA-20-06, from the United States Office of Government Ethics' Director Emory Rounds to Designated Agency Ethics Officials, Subject: Recurring Book Deals Issues for Incoming and Outgoing Government Employees, (Sept. 24, 2020), https://www.oge.gov/web/oge.nsf/News+Releases/B7B3DC5398952B14852585EE004E2DE1/$FILE/LA-20-06%20Recurring%20Book%20Deals%20Issues%20for%20Incoming%20and%20Outgoing%20Government%20Employees.pdf [https://perma.cc/X5PP-8R7U].

[63] 5 C.F.R. § 2635.807(a)(2)(i)(B) (2023).

[64] Steve Eder, Abbie VanSickle, & Elizabeth Harris, *How Supreme Court Justices Make Millions from Book Deals*, N.Y. Times (July 27, 2023), https://www.nytimes.com/2023/07/27/us/politics/supreme-court-justices-book-deals.html#:~:text=The%20book%20deals%20are%20not,research%20and%20promote%20their%20books [https://perma.cc/5QTA-EAZM] (explaining that the "book deals are not prohibited under the law" although "income from the advances and royalties are reported on the justices' annual financial disclosure forms"). Earlier Supreme Court authors include Justice Joseph Story, author of the famous *Commentaries on the Constitution* (Brown, Shattuck, and Company 1833) and Justice William O. Douglas, who wrote over forty books including a book about environmental conservation, *Of Men and Mountains* (Harper & Brothers 1950). The first unusually high advance paid to a justice for a book targeting a large popular audience was for Justice Sandra Day O'Connor's book *Lazy B* (Random House 2002) about her childhood on a ranch in Arizona, followed by Justice Clarence Thomas's *My Grandfather's Son: A Memoir* (Harper Collins 2008).

Neil Gorsuch received over $250,000 in book royalties.[65] Justice Sotomayor received a more modest $115,000 in royalties from a book in 2021,[66] but as of 2023 had earned $3.6 million in book royalties and advances since joining the court in 2009.[67] Justice Sotomayor's Supreme Court staff have coordinated her speaking tours, on several occasions prodding universities and libraries hosting Justice Sotomayor to place large book orders for sale at book signings.[68] "Is there a reminder going out that people need to purchase a book at the event or bring a book to get into the signing line?" an assistant to Justice Sotomayor wrote to the Multnomah County Library in Oregon. "Most of the registrants did not purchase books."[69] Legal assistants to Supreme Court justices are federal employees with important responsibilities, but selling books should not be one of them.[70] The Supreme Court nonetheless released a statement saying ethics rules had been complied with, without explaining why Supreme Court staff, instead of the publisher, were involved in recommending the number of book orders at venues where the justice was speaking.[71]

It is conceivable that book royalties could influence how justices decide cases and write opinions. Some justices are heroes for millions of Americans on the left or the right of the political spectrum. This means that there's a steady market for their books sold to a loyal audience—loyal, that is, so long as the justice does not disappoint the audience. After voting in 2022 to overturn the nearly fifty-year-old constitutional right of a woman to get a first trimester

[65] Amy Howe, *Justices Earned Extra Money from Books and Teaching in 2021, Disclosures Show*, SCOTUSblog (June 9, 2022), https://www.scotusblog.com/2022/06/justices-earned-extra-money-from-books-and-teaching-in-2021-disclosures-show/ [https://perma.cc/W9LL-BDEN].

[66] *Ibid.*

[67] Nina Totenberg, *Supreme Court Justices, Minus Thomas, and Alito, File Financial Disclosure Reports*, NPR (June 7, 2023), https://www.npr.org/2023/06/07/1180896886/supreme-court-financial-disclosure-reports [https://perma.cc/K6LN-76XH].

[68] Brian Slodysko & Eric Tucker, *Supreme Court Justice Sotomayor's Staff Prodded Colleges and Libraries to Buy Her Books*, Assoc. Press (July 11, 2023), https://apnews.com/article/supreme-court-sotomayor-book-sales-ethics-colleges-b2cb93493f927f995829762cb8338c02 [https://perma.cc/XE6D-48RL] ("For an event with 1000 people and they have to have a copy of *Just Ask* to get into the line, 250 books is definitely not enough," the aide [to Justice Sotomayor], Anh Le, wrote staffers at the Multnomah County [Oregon] Library. "Families purchase multiples and people will be upset if they are unable to get in line because the book required is sold out.").

[69] *Ibid.* (quoting email dated August 27, 2019, from Anh Le, assistant to Justice Sotomayor, to Kate Chester, director of communications at Portland Community College).

[70] Executive branch ethics rules specifically prohibit use of official position to promote book sales or any other private gain. See 5 C.F.R. § 2635.702 Use of public office for private gain (2023) ("An employee shall not use his public office for his own private gain, for the endorsement of any product, service or enterprise, or for the private gain of friends, relatives, or persons with whom the employee is affiliated.").

[71] *See* Statement of the Supreme Court (July 11, 2023), https://s3.documentcloud.org/documents/23870397/supreme-court-statement.pdf [https://perma.cc/3KTK-B2G8] ("Asking whether attendees were reminded that they must either buy or bring a book in order to enter a signing line at an event would in no way conflict with the standard outlined above. . . . When [Justice Sotomayor] is invited to participate in a book program, Chambers staff recommends the number of books based on the size of the audience so as not to disappoint attendees who may anticipate books being available at an event.").

abortion, Justice Barrett published her 2025 book *Listening to the Law: Reflections on the Court and Constitution*, which in Chapter 11 defended her vote in *Dobbs v. Jackson Women's Health Organization* as an act of "judicial restraint," saying that the court in 1973 in *Roe v. Wade* "usurped the will of the American people" and got "ahead" of public sentiment.[72] Perhaps Justice Barrett's vote in this case was predictable, but it is unsettling to see a justice earn $2 million writing a book explaining, among other things, how she decided one of the most important cases in recent Supreme Court history.

But what if one of these justices were to defect to the "other side" on the court in a few high-profile cases? A solidly conservative justice siding with the liberal justices in an important case, or vice versa, could hurt book sales. Making up for it with sales to readers on the "other side" could be difficult, particularly if the book was pitched to the first side to begin with. Justices could be tempted to adjust their views or the way they express their views to increase book sales.

Cable news hosts also author books and sometimes go to extremes to pitch their shows to viewers on the left or right side of the political spectrum.[73] But we should have different expectations of Supreme Court justices. Their profession is interpreting the law, not writing books about it, even if their book royalties dwarf Supreme Court salaries. Allowing justices to earn royalties that depend in part on how popular they are with readers could conflict with official duties. Very high royalty earnings are hard to resist, and we do not know whether book sales affect justices' votes on cases or the way they write their opinions.

Book deals that involve advances, lump sum payments, or promotion services from publishers and agents are problematic in another way, particularly if the payors have an interest in cases before the court. Some literary agents working with Supreme Court justices are politically connected themselves. For example, Justice Barrett earned her initial $425,000 book advance through the Javelin Group, "a Virginia-based literary agency founded by Keith Urbahn, a former chief of staff to Secretary of Defense Donald Rumsfeld, and Matt Latimer, a former speechwriter for President George W. Bush."[74] There is no demonstrable link between any of these payments and an

[72] Amy Coney Barrett, *Listening to the Law: Reflections on the Court and Constitution*, Chapter 11 (Sentinel Press 2025). Sentinel is a conservative imprint of Penguin Random House.

[73] *See U.S. Dominion, Inc. v. Fox News Network, LLC.* A. N21C-03-257 EMD (Del. Super. Ct. Dec. 16, 2021) (denying defendant's motion to dismiss; reviewing evidence that Tucker Carlson and other FOX hosts, with encouragement from corporate management, reported news on the 2020 election to reflect what FOX viewers wanted to hear to increase advertising revenue, not what the news hosts knew to be the news).

[74] Howe, *supra*.

attempt to influence the outcome of decisions before the court. Still, allowing any one individual or company to be a source of such large payments to a Supreme Court justice is problematic and an invitation to mischief.

Contracts with book publishers also can lead to recusal problems. Justices Sotomayor and Gorsuch have lucrative book contracts with Penguin Random House, which was a party to two cases before the court, in both of which the court declined to grant certiorari, allowing lower court rulings favorable to Random House to stand.[75] Justice Sotomayor recused from neither case,[76] and Justice Gorsuch, who joined the court after the first case, failed to recuse from the second.[77]

Supreme Court justices are already authors of the most influential legal opinions in the country, perhaps the world. They are paid over $300,000 a year for this work (with the chief justice earning slightly more). That's enough. Perhaps the justices, like their counterparts in the executive branch, should not earn book royalties above a certain amount, perhaps half their Supreme Court salaries. After all, their published written opinions already are the last word in interpreting our Constitution and our laws.

Failure to Recuse

With all these potential conflicts of interest, Supreme Court justices presumably would recuse from a lot of cases. They don't.

The recusal statute provides: "Any justice, judge, or magistrate judge of the United States shall disqualify himself in any proceeding in which his impartiality might reasonably be questioned."[78]

In addition to this broad standard for recusal, the statute also enumerates specific instances in which recusal is required of a judge or justice:

(1) Where he has a personal bias or prejudice concerning a party, or personal knowledge of disputed evidentiary facts concerning the proceeding;

[75] *See Whitehead v. Netflix, Inc., cert. denied,* No. 20-1227 (2021). Justices Sotomayor and Gorsuch did not recuse. Justice Breyer recused. *See also Nicassio v. Viacom* International, Inc., *cert. denied,* No. 19-560 (2019). Justices Sotomayor did not recuse. Justice Breyer recused.

[76] *See* Madison Hall, *2 Supreme Court Justices Failed to Recuse Themselves from Cases Involving Their Publisher After Receiving Large Amounts in Book Advances and Royalties,* Business Insider (May 10, 2023), https://www.businessinsider.com/justices-didnt-recuse-themselves-from-cases-with-their-book-publisher-2023-5 [https://perma.cc/YQH9-E8V5].

[77] *See Nicassio v. Viacom Int'l and Penguin Random House,* No. 19-560, *cert. denied* (2019); *Jennie Nicassio v. Viacom Int'l Inc.,* No. 18-2085 (3d Cir. 2019) (dismissal of suit against Random House for infringement of copyright in a children's book).

[78] 28 U.S.C. § 455(a).

(2) Where in private practice he served as lawyer in the matter in controversy, or a lawyer with whom he previously practiced law served during such association as a lawyer concerning the matter, or the judge or such lawyer has been a material witness concerning it;
(3) Where he has served in governmental employment and in such capacity participated as counsel, adviser or material witness concerning the proceeding or expressed an opinion concerning the merits of the particular case in controversy;
(4) He knows that he, individually or as a fiduciary, or his spouse or minor child residing in his household, has a financial interest in the subject matter in controversy or in a party to the proceeding, or any other interest that could be substantially affected by the outcome of the proceeding;
(5) He or his spouse, or a person within the third degree of relationship to either of them, or the spouse of such a person: (i) Is a party to the proceeding, or an officer, director, or trustee of a party; (ii) Is acting as a lawyer in the proceeding; (iii) Is known by the judge to have an interest that could be substantially affected by the outcome of the proceeding; (iv) Is to the judge's knowledge likely to be a material witness in the proceeding.[79]

This chapter only addresses failure to recuse on account of financial interest. Chapter 3 addresses the separate and more complex problem that arises when justices refuse to recuse on account of apparent political bias or the political involvement of a spouse. The two types of conflicts can overlap—for example, if justices enjoy free vacations or other gifts from politically involved donors, or justices' politically involved spouses are also well paid for their work.

Recusal on the Supreme Court is more complicated than recusal on a court of appeals, where another judge on the circuit can be substituted for the judge who recuses. On the Supreme Court, there are no substitute justices, and the recusal of a justice might change outcomes, not just for the parties but for other persons, lawyers, and lower court judges who rely on Supreme Court decisions. Because of this, justices interpreting the recusal statute may be more reticent to recuse than they would have been on the courts of appeals. In close calls—cases where reasonable persons could differ as to whether a justice's impartiality might reasonably be questioned—a justice might decide not to recuse.

[79] 28 U.S.C. § 455(b).

The justice's reasons for not recusing might be good reasons. But just as important is the problem that justices, and their spouses, too often conduct themselves in a manner that gives rise to recusal issues to begin with. Many scenarios that suggest a need to recuse could be avoided in the first place. Justices and their spouses don't have to buy individual stocks and other investments that create conflicts, they don't have to accept free travel and other gifts from persons likely to have interests before the court, and they don't have to enter other arrangements likely to create conflicts. But too often they do.

As discussed above, Justice Alito did not recuse from any of the cases before the court involving businesses owned by Paul Singer, his host for the 2008 fishing trip to Alaska. If Singer was a good enough friend for Alito to be permitted to accept the free trip under the "personal friend" exception to gift rules,[80] Singer was a good enough friend that Alito needed to recuse himself from these cases. According to Justice Alito's account in the *Wall Street Journal*, they aren't friends at all, in which case Alito did not need to recuse, but he should not have gone fishing with Singer at Singer's expense. Alito could easily have avoided this recusal problem by not accepting the trip or by paying his own way.

There are dozens of other cases in which justices did not recuse, and reasonable arguments can be made that they should have recused, and probably reasonable arguments can be made that they need not recuse.[81] Ambiguity in the law on judicial recusal is a problem that may lead some justices to refuse to recuse even in cases where they should recuse.

Another problem is procedural. Presently, each justice makes recusal decisions on their own. The justices do not collectively rule on whether one of them must recuse. When the justices decide a case and apply the recusal statute to a lower court judge, all of the justices vote, and they have done this several times.[82] However, when the justices apply the same statute to

[80] Justice Alito was still required to disclose the trips even if Singer had been a friend.

[81] *See Recent Times a Justice Failed to Recuse Despite a Conflict of Interest*, Fix the Court (Jan. 12, 2024) (reporting eighteen cases since 2015 in which one or more justices had a conflict of interest that presumptively required recusal under the recusal statute, 28 U.S.C. § 455, but did not recuse), https://fixthecourt.com/2023/07/recent-times-justice-failed-recuse-despite-clear-conflict-interest/ [https://perma.cc/2TPY-JCSM].

This book will not analyze whether recusal was required in each of these cases, and some of them were close calls. Some of these missed recusals could have been avoided if the justice had taken steps to avoid the conflict of interest to begin with—for example, by divesting shares of stock in individual companies that could have future cases come before the court.

[82] *See, e.g., Liteky et al. v. United States*, 510 U.S. 540 (1994) (interpreting required recusal under § 455(a) using the "extrajudicial source" doctrine, under which a judge's bias generally must stem from a source *outside* the judicial proceedings to warrant recusal, and that opinions a judge forms based solely on facts during the course of a trial or appeal are ordinarily not grounds for disqualification); Liljeberg v. Health Svcs. Acq. Corp., 486 U.S. 847 (1988) (finding that federal district judge Robert Collins in New

themselves, each one decides for himself or herself with no intervention, and not even required consultation, with the other justices. This is yet one more way in which the court is a law unto itself.

Recusal will be discussed again in Chapter 3 of this book with regard to political conflicts of interest. It is in these cases involving elections and other political matters where justices' failure to recuse on account of their own political activity or that of their spouses has done even more damage to the integrity of the court.

Stock Holdings

Americans have heard much about stock trading by members of Congress who vote on bills that affect their stocks.[83] This problem dates to the founding of our Republic,[84] and 240 years later, Congress has yet to pass a law prohibiting stock trading or financial conflicts of interest in Congress. (The only prohibition is on insider trading on government information, and Congress did not even recognize that prohibition as applying to themselves until 2012.)[85]

The Supreme Court does not have as bad a problem with stock trading justices, but it does have a problem. Unlike Congress, where a single member usually does not cast the deciding vote on a bill, one or two justices often decide the outcome of a case. Also, unlike Congress, where there is no law prohibiting members from voting on legislation that affects their stocks, the very clear language of the recusal statute prohibits federal judges from participating in cases that affect their stock holdings.[86]

Orleans violated § 455, when he presided over a dispute between Health Services Acquisition Corp. and John Liljeberg, Jr. regarding ownership of a hospital project, at a time when Judge Collins was on the Board of Trustees of Loyola University, which could benefit significantly from his ruling in the case). In some cases, however, the court has refused to address recusal of a lower court judge. See e.g. *Ali Hamza Al Bahlul v. United States*, No. 23-1072, cert. denied, 604 U.S. ___ (2024) (seeking recusal of a DC court of appeals judge under § 455 on account of his prior government service connected to the defendant held at Guantanamo Bay).

[83] Donna Nagy & Richard W. Painter, *It's Time for Senators and House Members to Divest Stocks in Individual Publicly Traded Companies*, Bloomberg News (Jan. 6, 2021).

[84] See Richard W. Painter, *Ethics and Corruption in Business and Government: Lessons from the South Sea Bubble and the Bank of the United States* (discussing insider trading by members of the First Congress in individual state Revolutionary War bonds prior to voting on the Funding Act of 1790 in which the federal government agreed to pay these obligations in full) (published by the University of Chicago Law School as the 2006 Maurice and Muriel Fulton Lecture in Legal History).

[85] Stop Trading on Congressional Knowledge (STOCK) Act of 2012, Pub. Law 112-105, 126 Stat. 291 (enacted Apr. 4, 2012).

[86] *See* 28 U.S.C. § 455 (b).

As discussed in Chapter 1, some candidates for Supreme Court vacancies didn't make the short list because the White House ethics office found cases they had participated in as federal judges while they—or their spouses—owned stock in an interested party. No matter how inconsequential the violation of recusal rules, it would surely be exaggerated in a Senate confirmation hearing, a scenario best avoided by nominating someone else.

The *Wall Street Journal* in 2021 reported that many federal judges have not been careful—131 federal judges participated in cases involving companies in which they had a financial interest.[87] This is a problem that a judge can easily avoid by investing in diversified mutual funds and owning no individual stocks.

Once they are on the court, however, justices may not be so careful. Justices' ownership of individual stocks has created multiple conflicts of interest.[88] At least two justices currently own individual stocks—Chief Justice John Roberts and Justice Samuel Alito. Justice Breyer owned a significant number of individual stocks before he left the court. In 2021, these three justices had combined direct ownership interests in forty publicly traded companies, many of which frequently appear before the court, although Roberts and Alito appear to have reduced their holdings somewhat in 2022 and 2023.[89]

Recusal is an alternative to divesting,[90] but recusal on the Supreme Court is a worse option than on the lower courts, where substitute judges can be assigned to a case. There are no "replacement" justices on the Supreme Court. A recusal means that the case is decided by eight justices; two recusals mean the case is decided by seven justices.

Stock-based recusals disadvantage parties seeking certiorari review of a lower court's decision. The Supreme Court grants very few of the requests it receives, and it takes four votes for a grant, regardless of how many justices recuse. When fewer than nine justices consider a request for certiorari, the odds of certiorari being granted are lower.

[87] *See* James V. Grimaldi, Coulter Jones, & Joe Palazzolo, *131 Federal Judges Broke the Law by Hearing Cases Where They Had a Financial Interest*, Wall St. J. (Sept. 28, 2021), https://www.wsj.com/articles/131-federal-judges-broke-the-law-by-hearing-cases-where-they-had-a-financial-interest-11632834421?mod=searchresults_pos1&page=1 [https://perma.cc/D3GG-XLSH].

[88] *See* Richard W. Painter, *Supreme Court Justices' Stock Ownership Could Pose Conflict of Interest*, National L. J. (Oct. 12, 2021), https://www.law.com/nationallawjournal/2021/10/12/supreme-court-justices-stock-ownership-could-pose-conflict-of-interest/ [https://perma.cc/7JME-MTCV].

[89] *See* Spreadsheet of justices' individual stock ownership, https://docs.google.com/spreadsheets/d/11O9Kng2KQCGSobEWWP4aAIPKIeXlVQlWoL8T-w_U8Nw/edit?fbclid=IwAR3-DGYuPRefSramevH0sFh0AnL2mizbVdd_C2UakIXh0o4urVqk3z7sfzU#gid=0 [https://perma.cc/2LPS-PNBS].

[90] *See* 28 U.S.C. § 455 (discussing disqualification of justice, judge, or magistrate judge).

Stock-based recusals are also problematic when the court decides a case. Justices' recusals create a risk the court will split 4–4, leaving the legal issue unresolved. In *Warner-Lambert v. Kent*,[91] the court split 4–4 in a product-liability suit after Chief Justice Roberts recused because of his stock holdings in Pfizer, one of the parties to the case.[92]

As the court itself said in 1993, "Even one unnecessary recusal impairs the functioning of the court."[93] Recusals due to stock ownership are unnecessary. Justices can own mutual funds and similar investment funds without needing to recuse. (Judicial ethics rules do not look to the underlying stock holdings of diversified funds.) Congress has even exempted justices from capital gains taxes if they replace their stock holdings with mutual funds or other like investments to avoid potential conflicts of interest.[94] The justices should take advantage of that favorable tax treatment and divest their individual stock holdings.

But if a justice or the justice's spouse owns stock in a company that is a party to a case, or the parent company of a party, the justice must recuse. The law is clear on that point.[95] Justices who were extremely careful about recusals on account of stock ownership when they were on the court of appeals are not always as careful on the Supreme Court.

In 2021, for example, Chief Justice Roberts owned between $500,000 and $1 million of stock in both Texas Instruments and Thermo Fisher, and between $250,000 to $500,000 of stock in Charter Communication.[96] Just these three companies or their subsidiaries have appeared before the court many times in the past few years. In each case, Roberts should have recused himself from participating. Sometimes he recused and sometimes he didn't.[97]

[91] *Warner-Lambert Co., LLC v. Kent*, 552 U.S. 440 (2008).

[92] *See* Tony Mauro, *Roberts' Recusal Is Poison Pill for Drug Case Before Supreme Court*, National L.J. (Mar. 4, 2008), https://www.law.com/article/almID/900005504867/

[93] Statement of Recusal Policy, Supreme Court of the United States (Nov. 1, 1993), https://eppc.org/docLib/20110106_RecusalPolicy23.pdf [https://perma.cc/5XMH-D6T8].

[94] *See* 26 U.S.C. § 1043 (sale of property to comply with conflict-of-interest requirements).

[95] 28 U.S.C § 455(b).

[96] *See Financial Disclosure Report of Chief Justice John Roberts for Calendar Year 2020*, Fix the Court, https://fixthecourt.com/wp-content/uploads/2021/06/Roberts-JG-J3.-SC_SR_20.pdf [https://perma.cc/85X4-DRBC].

[97] *See* Greg Stohr, *U.S. Chief Justice Roberts Overlooked Stock Conflict in Case*, Bloomberg (Dec. 18, 2015), https://www.bloomberg.com/news/articles/2015-12-18/u-s-chief-justice-roberts-overlooked-stock-conflict-in-case [https://perma.cc/WT9S-SUUN] (discussing failure to recuse in a case involving Texas instruments); Lawrence Hurley, *U.S. Chief Justice Steps Aside in Patent Case over Stock Conflict*, Reuters (Jan. 4, 2017), https://www.reuters.com/article/idUSKBN14O2AX/ [https://perma.cc/C74E-PNFZ] (discussing Chief Justice Roberts's recusal from a case involving a unit of Thermo Fisher).

These missed recusals, perhaps inadvertent, probably did not affect the outcome of a case. But they are bad for the public image of the court, particularly when combined with its other ethics problems. Chief Justice Roberts participated in oral argument in a patent infringement case, *Life Technologies Corporation v. Promega Corporation*,[98] then recused himself due to his ownership of shares in one of the parties' parent companies.[99] Justice Alito missed a recusal in *Valentine v. PNC Financial Services, et. al.*,[100] when one of the parties was PNC Bank, whose shares he owned.

Lower federal courts have mandatory software that identifies conflicts with judges' stock holdings by cross-checking stocks owned by judges and their spouses, and subsidiaries of these companies, with names appearing in pleadings. If this software was used at the Supreme Court, it wasn't very effective, given the number of missed recusals. In February 2026 the court announced that it was upgrading its software used to detect conflicts of interest and adopted new rules requiring counsel to provide ticker symbols for publicly traded companies and other information to support the software.[101]

Selling a stock instead of recusing after a case comes before the court may not be a viable alternative either. It may be too late. If the justices have material nonpublic information about how the case might be decided, a justice who sells stocks that could be affected by the case could be charged with insider trading. At that juncture, holding on to the stock and recusing may be the only alternative. If the justices sold all the stocks in their portfolios and bought diversified mutual funds, they wouldn't be in this quandary.

Congress has taken limited steps to increase transparency, requiring federal courts to post judges' and justices' financial disclosure forms online, and requiring judges and justices to report larger stock transactions within forty-five days, but existing law does not ban judges and justices from trading

[98] *Life Techs. Corp. v. Promega Corp.*, 580 U.S. 140 (2017).

[99] *See* Adam Liptak, *The Hazards Justices Face by Owning Individual Stocks*, N.Y. Times (Jan. 9, 2017), https://www.nytimes.com/2017/01/09/us/politics/the-hazards-justices-face-by-owning-individual-stocks.html [https://perma.cc/HT7H-YLJT].

[100] *Valentine v. The PNC Fin. Servs. Grp., Inc.*, 141 S. Ct. 1100 (2021).

[101] *See* Supreme Court of the United States Press Release, February 17, 2026, announcing a revised version of the Rules of the Court ("Most of the changes are designed to support operation of newly developed software that will assist in identifying potential conflicts for the Justices, and the revisions impose a number of new requirements upon filers to support the software.") https://www.supremecourt.gov/publicinfo/press/pressreleases/pr_02-17-26; See Rules of the Supreme Court of the United States, Adopted February 17 2026, https://www.supremecourt.gov/filingandrules/2026RulesoftheCourt_WEB.pdf; *See* Judicial Conference of the U.S., Guide to Judiciary Policy, Vol. 2C: Codes of Conduct, Ch. 4: Financial Disclosures and Case-Related Financial Conflicts, § 410: Mandatory Conflict Screening Policy (2022) (describing mandatory automatic conflict checking system requiring input of judges' financial holdings), https://www.uscourts.gov/sites/default/files/guide-vol02c-ch04.pdf [https://perma.cc/Z9GF-LRMN].

stocks.[102] For the Supreme Court, at least, where recusal is a poor alternative, this is not enough.

Supreme Court justices should be required to divest individual stock holdings upon assuming office and to stay divested. Diversified mutual funds are suitable alternative investments. Indeed, if a Supreme Court justice is doing better at investing in individual stocks than professional fund managers, perhaps our ethics problems on the court are even worse than we thought.

The "Armada of Amici"

Individuals, and particularly organizations, frequently submit briefs as *amicus curiae*—or as a "friend of the court "—in cases where they are not a party. They do so because they may have some connection with the parties to the case or are interested in the precedent set by the case for other parties, including themselves. Trade associations, public policy organizations, university professors, churches and other nonprofits, labor unions, and other organizations file these briefs frequently. Some are "friends of the court" in name only; the justices have never heard of them. Some are literally friends with one or more of the justices or are affiliated with, or bankrolled by, people who are friends of the justices, although that is almost never disclosed in the brief.

Amici and their counsel are disclosed in an amicus brief, and the "interest of amici" is vaguely described. Who's funding organizations submitting the amicus brief is not disclosed. Many of these are nonprofits or trade associations that do not disclose their donors. Some of the justices may know who's paying for these amicus briefs and may know that their friends or acquaintances are involved, but other justices may not know. Parties to the case may know who's paying for amicus briefs on their side. (Lawyers for parties and amici often talk to each other although parties and their lawyers are not supposed to assist amici with brief writing.) Lawyers on the opposing side may not know who's paying for amicus briefs filed against them.

Senator Sheldon Whitehouse described an example of this phenomenon in his 2021 article, *A Flood of Judicial Lobbying: Amicus Influence and Funding*

[102] *See* Courthouse Ethics and Transparency Act, Pub. L. No. 117-125, § 2, 136 Stat. 1205, 1206 (2022), codified at 5 U.S.C. § 13107 (2025) (requiring federal courts to post judges' and justices' financial disclosures online) and 5 U.S.C. § 13105(l) (requiring judges and justices to report larger stock transactions within forty-five days).

Transparency, published in the *Yale Law Journal Forum*. Ironically, the case before the court involved the very issue these organizations care about most—nonprofit organizations' "right" not to disclose their sources of funding. Whitehouse writes:

> *Americans for Prosperity Foundation v. Bonta* [594 US _ (2021)] provides a recent and extreme example of the "flotilla" phenomenon. Plaintiff Americans for Prosperity Foundation (AFPF), the 501(c)(3) arm of the Koch network's right-wing 501(c)(4) political-advocacy group Americans for Prosperity, objected to a California state regulation that required 501(c)(4) nonprofits to confidentially disclose their largest donors. The nonprofits had to provide the state Attorney General with a copy of their IRS Form 990 Schedule B—information the organizations must already, of course, provide to the IRS. The case proceeded through the federal courts with little fanfare or media attention. But at the Supreme Court cert stage, a veritable armada of amici supporting AFPF barraged the Court, urging it to grant cert.
>
> This was a highly coordinated effort made possible only by the money and connections of the Koch political enterprise. At least fifty-five of the cert-stage amici in support of the petitioner had taken money either from the Koch political network or from a Koch-linked anonymous account at Donors Trust, an administrator of "donor-advised" funds that has been described as "the dark-money ATM of the right." Subsequently, at the merits stage, at least forty-five filers had apparent financial ties to the Koch network and/or Donors Trust. Additionally, the Center for Media and Democracy found that eleven prominent right-wing groups gave close to $222 million to sixty-nine of the organizations filing amicus briefs in support of AFPF.
>
> It is difficult—if not impossible—to credibly argue that such amici are independent of the plaintiff, because AFPF is itself a central political organization of the Koch network. Yet none of these groups disclosed their financial ties to the plaintiff.[103]

Dark money funding of amicus briefs is a question of judicial ethics. This is particularly true if the same special interests deploy other means of influencing justices (e.g., gifts of luxurious travel or payment of spousal income). Some gift donors omitted from justices' financial disclosure forms—including

[103] Sheldon Whitehouse, *A Flood of Judicial Lobbying: Amicus Influence and Funding Transparency*, Yale L.J. F. (Oct. 24, 2021), https://www.yalelawjournal.org/forum/a-flood-of-judicial-lobbying-amicus-influence-and-funding-transparency [https://perma.cc/8J6C-9NDQ].

Harlan Crow[104] and Paul Singer[105]—are involved with organizations filing amicus briefs. This is in addition to whatever "friend of the court" briefing may or may not take place in private conversations, perhaps during a justice's free travel on yachts or private planes. The two problems are interrelated, and the common theme is the failure to disclose the money paying for the justices' free luxury travel and other gifts and the money paying for amicus briefs. In some instances, the source of that money may be the same.

The Enforcement Problem

Rules promulgated by federal courts, including by the Supreme Court, must be consistent with acts of Congress[106] Federal law establishes the Judicial Conference of the United States for the purpose of reviewing, modifying, or abrogating rules for courts other than the Supreme Court "for consistency

[104] The National Multifamily Housing Council, an apartment building trade group that through 2024 was chaired by Ken Valach, CEO of Crow Holdings Inc., has filed a series of friend-of-the-court, or amicus, briefs in cases related to racial discrimination in housing, the Clean Water Act and rent control, according to research from Accountable US. *See* Paul Blumenthal, *Clarence Thomas Said His Billionaire Friend Didn't Come Before the Court—But His Business Interests Did: A Real Estate Trade Group Now Chaired by Crow Holdings' CEO Has Filed Briefs in Supreme Court Cases Relevant to Harlan Crow's Financial Interests*, Huff. Post (Apr. 26, 2023), https://www.huffpost.com/entry/clarence-thomas-harlan-crow-business-interests_n_64494a12e4b0d840388c2935 [https://perma.cc/E3UQ-NKCS]. Harlan Crow also since 1996 has been a member of the American Enterprise Institute's board of trustees. *Board of Trustees*, Am. Enterprise Inst., https://www.aei.org/about/board-of-trustees/ [https://perma.cc/SYE4-7ETQ]. AEI has supported and published Supreme Court amicus briefs written by scholars affiliated with AEI during Thomas's tenure on the court. *See, e.g.*, John E. Calfee, Robert W. Hahn, Tomas J. Philipson, & Ernst R. Berndt, *Supreme Court Amicus Brief Regarding Wyeth v. Diana Levine* (June 3, 2008), https://www.aei.org/research-products/testimony/supreme-court-amicus-brief-regarding-wyeth-v-diana-levine/ [https://perma.cc/SHH6-2GZ6]; Peter J. Wallison, *Supreme Court Amicus Brief Seeking Certiorari in AT Corp. v. Lila T. Gavin* (Feb. 8, 2007), https://www.aei.org/research-products/speech/supreme-court-amicus-brief-seeking-certiorari-in-at-corp-v-lila-t-gavin/ [https://perma.cc/SM8F-T24E].

[105] Paul Singer until 2025 was chairman of the board of the Manhattan Institute. *Paul Singer*, Manhattan Inst., https://manhattan.institute/person/paul-singer [https://perma.cc/GFA7-ZZCE]. The Manhattan Institute has submitted amicus briefs to the court repeatedly, including two in March 2023. *See* Amicus brief in *Roberts v. McDonald*, No. 22-757, https://media4.manhattan-institute.org/sites/default/files/amicus-brief-roberts-v-mcdonald.pdf [https://perma.cc/M9CH-EDB3] (asking the Supreme Court to review a case involving the ability to challenge government directives instructing medical providers to allocate Covid-19 treatments on the basis of race.); *see also* Amicus brief in *Moore v. United States*, No. 22-800, https://duyrl8j74t5sy.cloudfront.net/wp-content/uploads/amicus-brief-moore-v-united-states.pdf [https://perma.cc/BEW6-LXTF] (asking the Supreme Court to hold that Congress does not have the power to tax citizens on their ownership of shares in a corporation without realization of income under the 2017 Tax Cuts and Jobs Act, which assessed a one-time "deemed repatriation tax" on investments in some corporations abroad).

[106] 28 U.S.C. § 2071(a) (discussing rule-making power generally) ("The Supreme Court and all courts established by Act of Congress may from time to time prescribe rules for the conduct of their business. Such rules shall be consistent with Acts of Congress and rules of practice and procedure prescribed under section 2072 of this title.").

with Federal law."[107] Federal law, however, does not give the Judicial Conference the power to enforce federal statutes that apply to the Supreme Court or to discipline the justices.[108] The Supreme Court justices are accountable only to themselves.

Congress, by not giving the Judicial Conference jurisdiction over the Supreme Court, apparently assumes that the court will make sure that its rules and practices adhere to federal law. But nowhere does Congress or the Constitution say that the Supreme Court is exempt from federal law. As discussed in Chapters 4 and 5 of this book, the court could, on separation of powers grounds, rule that it is unconstitutional to apply any federal statute to the justices of the court. They are above the law. As discussed further in Chapter 5, a representative democracy is not likely to survive such an assertion of political power coupled with absolute immunity, whether for the president[109] or for justices of the Supreme Court.

Ethics laws are binding on Supreme Court justices, including laws governing financial disclosure filings, gifts, and recusal. Enforcement of existing ethics rules at the Supreme Court is the most serious problem. There are too many violations of gift rules, disclosure rules, and recusal rules, suggesting that enforcement is weak or nonexistent.

That is why this book proposes in Chapters 6 and 7 that Congress pass laws tightening up the substantive ethics rules for the Supreme Court and requiring the court to have an ethics lawyer and an inspector general. But we must also keep in mind that the court, on its current trajectory, may decide that even if Congress passes such laws, the justices are free to ignore them. In that case, more drastic reform of the court, including possibly a constitutional amendment, may be needed.

[107] 28 U.S.C. § 331 ("The Judicial Conference shall review rules prescribed under section 2071 of this title by the courts, other than the Supreme Court and the district courts, for consistency with Federal law. The Judicial Conference may modify or abrogate any such rule so reviewed found inconsistent in the course of such a review.").

[108] *Ibid.* ("The Judicial Conference shall review rules prescribed under section 2071 of this title by the courts, *other than the Supreme Court* and the district courts, for consistency with Federal law." [emphasis added]).

[109] *See* discussion in Chapter 5 of *Trump v. United States*, 603 U.S. 593 (2024).

3
Political Conflicts of Interest

Chapter 1 discussed the highly political process of nomination and confirmation to the federal bench. Successful nominees to the Supreme Court have mastered this process. Most of them spent their careers intimately involved in partisan politics, and close to the special interest groups that invest millions in judicial nomination and confirmation battles, while at the same time appearing sufficiently impartial to perform the functions of a judge.

As explained in Chapter 1, there is a balancing act between partisanship and judicial independence, and getting that balance right is crucial to a judge having a realistic chance of getting on the Supreme Court. A judge with too few connections in partisan political circles or too little commitment to the judicial philosophy of the president's political party won't make the short list. A judge who appears to be too partisan probably won't get nominated because Senate confirmation would be an uphill fight. With the votes of only fifty senators needed to confirm a justice (the vice president can cast a tie-breaking vote), however, this balance shifts toward partisanship provided the president's political party controls the Senate.[1]

Once on the court, or any court, a judge or justice, should avoid the appearance of partisanship as much as possible. Otherwise, litigants and lawyers before the court will perceive its decisions to be biased based on politics and not law. Some people believe law and politics are inseparable, a topic discussed later in this chapter, but most Americans still expect a judge to be different from a politician, with impartiality being the core principle distinguishing the two.

Federal judges are bound by the Code of Conduct for United States Judges. Canon 1 states, "An independent and honorable judiciary is indispensable to justice in our society. A judge should maintain and enforce high standards of conduct and should personally observe those standards, so that the integrity and independence of the judiciary may be preserved. The provisions of this

[1] Chapter 7 addresses the question of whether the Senate returning to a supermajority requirement to confirm judges and justices would reduce partisanship in the nomination and confirmation process and on the court itself.

Conduct Unbecoming. Richard W. Painter, Oxford University Press. © Oxford University Press (2026).
DOI: 10.1093/9780197832301.003.0004

Code should be construed and applied to further that objective." The commentary to Canon 1 reads, "Deference to the judgments and rulings of courts depends on public confidence in the integrity and independence of judges."

This point is discussed again at the close of this chapter—deference to the judgments and rulings of courts cannot be assumed; it must be earned through public confidence in the courts. Ordinary citizens can perhaps be compelled to obey court orders. But elected officials, including presidents, members of Congress, and governors, among others, are uniquely positioned to mobilize public opinion against the courts. Judges who in their conduct do not demonstrate integrity and independence play right into the hands of politicians who want to ignore the orders of courts, including the Supreme Court.

Canon 2 of the Code of Conduct provides that "[a] judge should avoid impropriety and the appearance of impropriety in all activities." More specifically, "A judge should respect and comply with the law and should act at all times in a manner that promotes public confidence in the integrity and impartiality of the judiciary." Also, "[a] judge should not allow family, social, political, financial, or other relationships to influence judicial conduct or judgment."[2]

Again, the phrase "act at all times" is worth emphasizing. Judges might work a forty-hour to sixty-hour week, but with respect to conduct that "promotes public confidence in the integrity and impartiality of the judiciary," judges are on duty 24/7. There are things a judge simply cannot do or say that other people can do or say. The arguments that judges have private lives, which are nobody's business, or that judges also have the right to free speech like everybody else, undermine confidence in the judicial decision-making process if what a judge is doing or saying implies bias, whether it be political bias or any other type of bias.

Canon 5 states that "[a] judge should refrain from political activity." Its subsection A provides:

> (A) A judge should not: (1) act as a leader or hold any office in a political organization; (2) make speeches for a political organization or candidate, or publicly endorse or oppose a candidate for public office; or (3) solicit funds for, pay an assessment to, or make a contribution to a political organization or candidate, or attend or purchase a ticket for a dinner or other event sponsored by a political organization or candidate.

[2] *Ibid.*

Subsection (B) requires a judge to resign from office to become a candidate for elective office. Subsection (C), however, provides more broadly that "[a] judge should not engage in any other political activity."[3] In the commentary, Canon 5 defines the term "political organization" to refer to "a political party, a group affiliated with a political party or candidate for public office, or an entity whose principal purpose is to advocate for or against political candidates or parties in connection with elections for public office." The term "political activity" is not defined.

Campaigns, political parties, political action committees (PACs), and super PACS meet the definition of a "political organization." Judges must stay away from those. But many other organizations engage in political activity. Indeed, the Supreme Court in *Citizens United v. Federal Election Commission*[4] held that corporations have the constitutional right to fund organizations that make electioneering communications. Under federal election law, these organizations are not supposed to be affiliated with or to coordinate with political parties and candidates, but they are intensely "political" in a broader sense. Some organizations have a principal purpose to advocate for or against candidates, while others orient toward public policy issues and only spend some resources supporting or opposing candidates. Organizations such as the Heritage Foundation and the American Civil Liberties Union do not formally support or oppose candidates, which could jeopardize their tax status, but they strongly support or oppose the policies of candidates. For example, proposals in Heritage's Project 2025 were incorporated into President Trump's 2024 campaign. Some of these organizations also have affiliate organizations, using the same name and established under Section 501(c)(4) of the Internal Revenue Code, that do support and oppose candidates. Others such as the Federalist Society do not have corporate affiliates that openly support or oppose candidates, making it easier for judges to participate in their programming without the appearance of political bias, even if senior officers and board members of these organizations are actively involved in supporting or opposing candidates.

These organizations engage with issues that come before the courts such as immigration, criminal justice, antitrust law, intellectual property protection, and free speech. Some of these organizations also get involved with amicus briefs before the court, forming part of the "armada of amici" that Senator Sheldon Whitehouse (D-RI) referred to in his *Yale Law Journal Forum* article

[3] Subsection (C) also has a broad carve out for lectures, symposia, teaching, and similar activities described in Canon 4: "This provision does not prevent a judge from engaging in activities described in Canon 4."

[4] *Citizens United v. Federal Election Commission*, 558 U.S. 310 (2010).

on conflicts of interest before the Supreme Court.[5] Judges affiliating with such organizations, or participating in the programming of these organizations, can create an appearance of political bias even when it is not clear whether judicial ethics rules expressly prohibit it.

Drawing lines under Canons 1, 2, and 5 is not always easy. The test most appropriately applied is subjective: Could a judge's involvement with an organization appear to be political or partisan to an extent that it would lead a reasonable private citizen to question the impartiality of a judge or justice? If so, it should be avoided.

One approach, the better approach, would be for judges and justices to broadly construe the definition of a "political organization" for purpose of Canon 5. This would mean staying away from organizations that do not strictly meet that definition but still appear to support candidates, or policies associated with candidates, particularly if those policies are likely to come before the court. If the judge's or justice's relationship with an organization that appears to be political is such that a reasonable person could think the judge is being influenced, perhaps that is enough that the judge should establish a distance from the organization.

But, as explained in Chapter 1, these same organizations are often involved with judicial nominations. A judge or justice may already have a preexisting relationship with one or more of them. Detaching from social ties with these organizations may be difficult.

A different approach would be to assume that a judge's or justice's involvement in an organization, even if it were political, is not likely to change case outcomes, so the judge should participate in the activities of any organization not clearly prohibited by a rule such as Canon 5. The problem with this approach is that the public still may think an organization is changing case outcomes, and the public may also not readily distinguish between two different ways outside organizations try to change case outcomes: first, by influencing who gets on the federal bench to begin with, the process described in Chapter 1, and second, by influencing judges' decisions after they are on the bench, which more likely conflicts with judicial ethics rules. As explained in Chapter 1, lawyers play tit for tat with outside organizations to get appointed to the bench, but for a judge to continue that pattern violates the impartiality principle that we expect to be binding on the judiciary.

Yet another approach would be to assume that politics has already affected case outcomes through the nomination and confirmation process described

[5] Sheldon Whitehouse, *A Flood of Judicial Lobbying: Amicus Influence and Funding Transparency*, Yale L.J. F. (Oct. 24, 2021), https://www.yalelawjournal.org/forum/a-flood-of-judicial-lobbying-amicus-influence-and-funding-transparency [https://perma.cc/8J6C-9NDQ].

in Chapter 1, and judges and justices continuing to participate in political organizations makes only an incremental difference or has no impact at all. An extreme iteration of this theory is that politics and law are inseparable, and law is merely an instrument of politics. Under this view, Canon 5 and similar rules are merely window dressing, and poor window dressing at that, trying to cover up what the public already knows—that judges and justices are intensely political.

It is true that law and politics are connected. Politics shapes statutory law when voters choose Congress and the president. Elections also determine outcomes in the process for nominating and confirming federal judges and justices, and even more directly influence outcomes in contests for judicial office in many states. Politics, in turn, is influenced by economics. (Those with more money have more political say than those with less money.) There's nothing new about these observations, no grand theory of political economy that anyone has not talked about before.

The country witnessed the intersection of politics and Supreme Court nominations in 1916 when banks, railroads, and other commercial interests allied themselves with antisemites to try to defeat President Wilson's nomination of progressive Louis Brandeis to the court.[6] President Franklin Roosevelt became so frustrated with an archconservative Supreme Court striking down his New Deal legislation in the 1930s that he tried to get Congress to authorize him to appoint additional justices. The court became more liberal in the 1950s and 1960s, and then, as presidents and senators campaigned on promises to install more conservative justices, the court became more conservative from the 1970s to the present. As discussed in Chapter 1, Supreme Court nominations and confirmations are highly political, perhaps more so today than ever before.

But it is also simplistic to overstate the relationship between law and politics or to refuse to recognize that fundamental principles of law supersede politics. It is also dangerous when judges do that. Politicization of the judiciary can all too easily become a self-fulfilling prophecy. Just because there is some of it doesn't mean we should tolerate all of it. And the point of this chapter is that there should be a lot less than there is now, particularly for justices sitting on the Supreme Court.

For judges and justices to embrace a politicized vision of law, regardless of whether it changes case outcomes, will undermine the credibility of the courts. Once on the bench, a judge or justice should interpret the

[6] *See* John T. Noonan Jr. & Richard W. Painter, *Professional and Personal Responsibilities of the Lawyer*, Chapter 6 (1997), Second Edition (2001), and Third Edition (2011) (including transcripts and other documents from the Brandeis nomination in 1916).

Constitution, laws and treaties of the United States, and state law according to that judge's or justice's best good faith assessment of what the law is, not according to a political ideology or with a view toward getting the political result the judge or justice would prefer.

By way of analogy, some referees in sporting matches may have favorites teams, but they don't show it. Americans would not accept the result of a football or basketball game in which the referees were not neutral but wore the jersey of one of the competing teams. When fundamental rights and liberties are at stake instead of a sporting trophy, we cannot accept such partisanship in our courts either. We can never entirely rid adjudication from politics, but judges and justices should try their utmost to avoid the appearance or the reality that they are partisans.

The Supreme Court has not lived up to that obligation. Some of the more egregious examples follow.

Justice Thomas

Justice Thomas's difficulties with partisanship are twofold. First are his close personal, and financial, relationships with wealthy individuals who have also donated large sums of money to Republican candidates and conservative organizations. These relationships are discussed in Chapter 2 in the context of judicial ethics rules prohibiting most gifts to judges regardless of the party affiliation of the donor and requiring disclosure of others. It should be kept in mind, however, that the political activity of these same donors introduces an appearance of political partisanship on top of the appearance of financial conflict of interest discussed in Chapter 2. Second, are complications arising out of the political activity of Justice Thomas's spouse, Virginia Thomas, and his failure to recuse from cases in which her activity creates an appearance of bias. That second aspect of the problem is addressed in this chapter.

Virginia Thomas has long been involved in conservative public policy organizations. For over a decade, she was employed by the Heritage Foundation. As discussed in Chapter 1, the Heritage Foundation is active in supporting nominations and confirmations to the Supreme Court in Republican administrations and opposing them in Democratic administrations. As discussed in Chapter 2, Ms. Thomas later formed her own consulting company that serves clients not identified on Justice Thomas's financial report, but that probably includes conservative and business organizations with interests before the court.

Virginia Thomas supported President Trump in seeking to overturn the 2020 election. She attended the January 6, 2021, Stop the Steal rally[7] and strategized with President Trump's White House chief of staff, Mark Meadows.[8] In text messages between Ms. Thomas and Meadows, she said Trump was the victim of election fraud.[9] When the House January 6 Committee subpoenaed White House records, and former President Donald Trump asked the Supreme Court to stay that subpoena, the Supreme Court heard that case. Justice Thomas should have recused because this was a case "in which his impartiality might reasonably be questioned."[10] His wife's texts with Meadows could be among the documents responsive to the subpoena. Yet, in *Trump v. Thompson*,[11] Justice Thomas did not recuse. In fact, he was the only justice to vote in favor of staying the subpoena.[12] This is about as clear a violation of the recusal statute as can be.

In 2022, Justice Thomas refused to recuse from yet another case involving the efforts to overturn the 2020 election. It was publicly known that Ms. Thomas had sent letters to twenty-nine Arizona legislators asking them to fight back against "fraud" and select a "clean slate of Electors."[13] In September 2022, Ms. Thomas had a "voluntary" meeting with the US House January 6 Committee in lieu of a subpoena.[14] In November 2022, in *Ward v. Thompson*,[15] the court refused to block a January 6 Committee subpoena of records of Arizona's GOP chair.[16] Justices Thomas and Alito dissented, saying that

[7] Kevin Daley, *Exclusive: Ginni Thomas Wants to Set the Record Straight on January 6*, Wash. Free Beacon (Mar. 14, 2022), https://freebeacon.com/courts/exclusive-ginni-thomas-sets-the-record-straight-on-january-6/ [https://perma.cc/MB46-5PWT].

[8] Caroline Linton, Ellis Kim, & Melissa Guinn, *Ginni Thomas Tells January 6 Panel Her Husband Was Completely Unaware of Texts with Mark Meadows*, CBS News (Sept. 30, 2022), https://www.cbsnews.com/news/ginni-thomas-jan-6-committee-interview/ [https://perma.cc/9XER-7VS6].

[9] Bob Woodward & Robert Costa, *Virginia Thomas Urged White House Chief of Staff to Pursue Unrelenting Efforts to Overturn the 2020 Election, Texts Show*, Wash. Post (Mar. 24, 2022), https://www.washingtonpost.com/politics/2022/03/24/virginia-thomas-mark-meadows-texts/ [https://perma.cc/EHJ4-8SRQ].

[10] 28 U.S.C. § 455(a).

[11] *Trump v. Thompson*, No. 21A272 (on application for stay of mandate and injunction pending review) (decided Jan. 19, 2022).

[12] *Ibid.* (discussing how "Justice Thomas would grant the application"). In a 2024 law review article this author addressed this and other instances in which Justice Thomas, and Justice Alito, failed to recuse from cases involving the 2020 election in which their impartiality might reasonably be questioned on account of political partisanship. See Richard W. Painter, "SCOTUS House: Can A Supreme Court Ethics Lawyer and Inspector General Help Get This Fraternity Under Control?," *Georgetown Journal of Legal Ethics* 37, no. 1 (2024): 347.

[13] Emma Brown, *Ginni Thomas Pressed 29 Ariz. Lawmakers to Help Overturn Trump's Defeat*, Wash. Post (June 10, 2022), https://www.washingtonpost.com/investigations/2022/06/10/ginni-thomas-election-arizona-lawmakers/ [https://perma.cc/25WS-U45K].

[14] See Caroline Linton, *Ginni Thomas Will Meet with House Jan. 6. Committee, Lawyer Says*, CBS News (Sept. 22, 2022), https://www.cbsnews.com/news/ginni-thomas-agrees-to-january-6-house-committee-interview-public-hearing-september-28/ [https://perma.cc/6H2D-75EC].

[15] *Ward v. Thompson*, 22A350 (Nov. 14, 2022), https://www.supremecourt.gov/orders/courtorders/111422zr_4gc5.pdf [https://perma.cc/GAQ5-4NPB].

[16] *Ibid.*

they would grant the Arizona GOP's application for stay and injunction.[17] This was an order decided on the court's shadow docket, so few people heard about it. But, as Professor Amanda Frost has pointed out, this was a clear violation by Justice Thomas of Section 455.[18] The other eight justices all knew about it, yet they did nothing to prevent it nor said anything publicly about it.[19]

In 2024, two more cases came before the court that also arose out of the January 6 insurrection. The first was an appeal of a Colorado Supreme Court order disqualifying Donald Trump from the presidential primary ballot under the Fourteenth Amendment, Section 3, because of his attempt to overturn the 2020 election. The Supreme Court in *Trump v. Anderson*[20] reversed that decision, holding that Colorado could not itself decide whether Trump's conduct in connection with the events of January 6 amounted to "rebellion" against the United States, and required Colorado to put Trump back on the ballot. Justice Thomas voted with the majority. The second case was the "immunity case" *Trump v. United States*,[21] ruling on a motion to dismiss criminal charges in the District of Columbia against Trump in connection with the attempt to overturn the 2020 election. Justice Thomas sided with the majority, holding that the president is immune from criminal prosecution for acts within core constitutional powers. Given Virginia Thomas's active involvement in this same attempt to overturn the election, Justice Thomas should have recused from these two cases as well.

Of these cases, the *Trump v. United States* ruling was the most consequential. President Trump and the spouse of a Supreme Court justice were, with thousands of others, involved with an effort to overturn the 2020 election. Many people involved in this effort did not commit crimes, but some did. Virginia Thomas was never accused of a crime and was treated as a witness in the investigation.[22] President Trump, however, was indicted on multiple felony counts in federal court in the District of Columbia and in state court in Georgia. The court, by a 6–3 vote, bestowed on him absolute immunity from

[17] *Ibid.*

[18] Amanda Frost, *Why the Other Eight Justices Must Censure Clarence Thomas: A Justice Who Does Not Respect the Rules Around Conflict of Interest Will Further Undermine This Court*, Slate (Dec. 5, 2022), https://slate.com/news-and-politics/2022/12/clarence-thomas-conflict-of-interest-consequences.html [https://perma.cc/WDH6-W8EH].

[19] *Ibid.*

[20] *Trump v. Anderson*, 601 U.S. 100 (2024).

[21] *Trump v. United States*, 603 U.S. 593 (2024).

[22] Deirdre Walsh & Claudia Grisales, *Ginni Thomas, Wife of Supreme Court Justice, Testifies Before Jan. 6 Panel*, NPR (Sept. 29, 2022), https://www.npr.org/2022/09/29/1125886442/ginni-thomas-wife-supreme-court-justice-testifies-jan-6.

criminal prosecution for acts within his core constitutional powers as president, including instructions he gave to the Justice Department to investigate fraud in the 2020 election, and a strong presumption of immunity for other official acts. In addition to the other problems with this ruling, and the dangerous incentives it creates for future presidents to use criminal means to hold on to power,[23] the spouse of one of the Supreme Court justices voting for presidential immunity was involved in the underlying events that were one of the most traumatic experiences for American democracy since the Civil War.

Justice Alito

Justice Thomas was not the only justice conflicted in *Trump v. United States.*

After President Trump lost the 2020 election, demonstrators, some carrying the American flag upside down, descended on the US Capitol, on January 6, 2021, to disrupt counting of the electoral votes. Some broke into the building, inflicting violence on Capitol police officers and threatening violence against members of Congress and the vice president.

On January 17, 2021, the American flag briefly flew upside down outside the home of Justice Samuel Alito. Justice Alito said the flag was flown that way because of his wife's dispute about the election with a neighbor.

Then, from 2021 through 2024, the court heard a series of cases arising out of President Trump's attempt to overturn the results of the 2020 election. Justice Alito, like Justice Thomas, participated in all these cases. First came the cases involving subpoenas from the January 6 Committee of the US House, and then came criminal cases against the Capitol rioters, and finally the criminal case against President Trump, which led to the court's landmark immunity decision in *Trump v. United States.* While the upside-down flag alone might not be sufficient grounds for Justice Alito to recuse from these cases, it was precisely the type of political gesture that judges and justices are supposed to avoid under Canon 5. Justice Alito surely knew this, and his wife, Martha, must have known it as well.

Justice Alito has also been drawn into private conversations where he made remarks that are more political than judicial. A left-leaning filmmaker posing as a religious conservative at a Supreme Court Historical Society reception lured him into a conversation where he appeared to agree with her that there

[23] This author discusses the dangerous ramifications of the court's ruling in *Trump v. United States* in another recent book. E. Thomas Sullivan and Richard W. Painter, *The U.S. Presidency: Power, Responsibility and Accountability* (Cambridge University Press 2025), 254-64.

can be no compromise between left and right. Then she said, "People in this country who believe in God have got to keep fighting for that, to return our country to a place of godliness." Justice Alito responded saying, "I agree with you, I agree with you."[24]

Chief Justice Roberts was approached by the same person, who suggested to him that the United States was a "Christian nation," and his response was a model of what a member of the judiciary should say in this type of situation: "Yeah. I don't know that we live in a Christian nation. I know a lot of Jewish and Muslim friends who would say, maybe not. And it's not our job to do that. It's our job to decide the cases as best we can."[25]

Putting aside the dubious ethics of someone using deception to lure Supreme Court justices into private conversations, one would think Justice Alito would be more careful in what he said to someone he didn't know. It appears that even eighteen years after his joining the court he was still eager to ingratiate himself with the conservative groups that helped him get there.

Justice Kagan

Justice Kagan has not been the focal point of many Supreme Court ethics controversies, except one. In 2012, she joined the 5–4 majority of the court in *National Federation of Independent Businesses v. Sebelius*,[26] upholding the constitutionality of the individual health insurance mandate in the Affordable Care Act (ACA). As solicitor general in the Obama administration, Kagan had not formally appeared for the government in litigation over the ACA, but she had been involved in preparing a legal defense of the ACA as soon as it passed Congress on March 23, 2010. Kagan was nominated for the court on May 10, 2010. If she had not been appointed to the court, she likely would have argued the case defending the ACA for the government. Instead, she decided it.

The recusal statute requires that a judge recuse herself if the judge "has served in governmental employment and in such capacity participated as counsel, adviser or material witness concerning the proceeding or expressed an opinion concerning the merits of the particular case in controversy."[27]

[24] Pierre Thomas, *Justice Alito, in Secretly Recorded Audio, Apparently Agrees Nation Needs to Return to Place of "Godliness,"* ABC News (June 11, 2024), https://abcnews.go.com/Politics/justice-alito-secretly-recorded-audio-apparently-agrees-nation/story?id=111014360.

[25] *Ibid.*

[26] *National Federation of Independent Businesses v. Sebelius*, 567 U.S. 519 (2012) (holding that the ACA's individual mandate penalty is a tax for the purposes of the Constitution's Taxing and Spending Clause and is a valid exercise of congressional authority).

[27] 28 U.S. Code § 455—Disqualification of justice, judge, or magistrate judge.

The *NFIB v. Sebelius* case technically was not a "proceeding" when Kagan was at the Justice Department, yet the department was preparing for the proceeding that it knew would come when a case challenging the ACA reached the Supreme Court. Kagan had been on an email exchange between Justice Department lawyer Neal Katyal and Associate Attorney General Tom Perrelli about a meeting to discuss ACA litigation, although she may not have attended the meeting. She attended at least one meeting where the litigation was discussed.[28] This was sufficient under the recusal statute. She should have recused from the ACA case.

Why didn't she recuse? One can make an argument, however technical, that because there was no ACA "proceeding" in the Justice Department in which Kagan had participated, her work preparing to defend the ACA did not come within the ambit of the recusal statute. But, probably even more important, she might never have been nominated to the court if President Obama had believed she would recuse from the ACA case. This was no ordinary case. This was an extremely important case politically, and Kagan's vote was needed to uphold the ACA (the portion of the court's opinion upholding the individual health insurance mandate turned out to be a 5–4 decision). President Obama's re-election in 2012 very likely depended on the ACA, his most important piece of legislation, surviving intact. Obama, like every president, sought to appoint justices who would agree with him philosophically and advance his agenda. By nominating Kagan, he did not intend to give up a key vote on a case so critically important if a credible argument against Kagan's recusal could be made.

Kagan didn't recuse. There was nobody to tell her she had to recuse; each justice gets to decide for herself whether to recuse. When she was nominated and confirmed to the court, the Senate knew about this issue, and she made no firm commitment to recuse.

In her Senate confirmation hearings, Kagan was asked about recusal. This was her written response:

> First, I would recuse myself from any case in which I served as counsel of record. Second, I would recuse myself from any case in which I played a substantial role. This category would include cases in which I approved or denied a recommendation for action in the lower courts and cases in which I reviewed a draft pleading or participated in formulating the government's litigating position. Third, in all

[28] Eric Segal, *A Liberal's Lament on Kagan and Health Care. Should Elena Kagan Recuse Herself in the ACA Case?* Slate (Dec. 8, 2011) (concluding that Justice Kagan should have recused), https://slate.com/news-and-politics/2011/12/obamacare-and-the-supreme-court-should-elena-kagan-recuse-herself.html.

> other circumstances I would consider recusal on a case-by-case basis. In *Florida v. U.S. Department of Health and Human Services* [another case challenging the constitutionality of the ACA], I neither served as counsel of record nor played any substantial role, as defined above. Therefore, I would consider recusal on a case-by-case basis, carefully considering any arguments made for recusal and consulting with my colleagues and, if appropriate, with experts on judicial ethics.[29]

This answer left just enough wiggle room for Kagan not to recuse from at least some cases challenging the ACA, and in fact she mentioned one of these cases in which she did not play a substantial role, suggesting that she would not recuse from that case. Arguably, she "participated in formulating the government's litigating position" to defend the ACA in future cases but the rest of her written answer refers to specific cases. By emphasizing a "case by case" approach to applying the recusal rule and saying that she did not participate in the Florida case, she left open the possibility that there would be some ACA cases from which she would not recuse.

But does interpretation of the recusal statute, or any other Supreme Court ethics rule, turn on what the Senate knows about at the time a justice is confirmed? Under the terms of the statute, clearly not. The Senate does not dispense "ethics waivers" to Supreme Court justices at their confirmation hearings. Yet when interpretation of the recusal statute is arguably ambiguous, politics does become a factor. (This is true of the court's opinions in general, and there is no reason to think that the justices approach the recusal statute differently.) Justice Kagan surely knew that the president who appointed her did not want her to recuse, and the Senate confirmed her without insisting on an iron-clad promise to recuse from cases concerning the ACA. This would be a political rationale—not an ethics rationale—for her not recusing, and we do not know whether it factored into the calculus of Justice Kagan.

And yet Justice Kagan did not entirely do the bidding of the president who appointee her. She joined a 7–2 majority of the justices in ruling *against* the Obama administration, holding that the ACA's Medicaid expansion was unconstitutionally coercive toward the states.[30] Regardless of the merits of her decision not to recuse, which in this author's view was the wrong decision, it

[29] US Senate Committee on the Judiciary, Responses [of Elena Kagan] to Supplemental Questions from Senators Jeff Sessions, Orrin Hatch, Charles Grassley, Jon Kyl, Lindsey Graham, John Cornyn, and Tom Coburn at 2–3 (2010) https://www.judiciary.senate.gov/imo/media/doc/ElenaKagan-QFRs.pdf.

[30] *National Federation of Independent Business v. Sebelius*, 567 U.S. 519 (2012) (holding that the ACA's Medicaid expansion provisions exceeded Congress's enumerated powers and violated principles of federalism).

would be simplistic to say that her calculus on the case was mostly political. When she believed the law went the other way, against the president who appointed her, she said so.

Justice Ginsburg

Some justices on the liberal wing of the court have worn their politics on their sleeves. The late Justice Ruth Bader Ginsburg, an icon of liberals and of liberal women's groups, was probably the most outspoken, and at times she went too far.

Justice Ginsburg commented publicly about Donald Trump the summer before the 2016 election. In an interview with the *New York Times*, Ginsburg said of Trump, "I can't imagine what this place would be—I can't imagine what the country would be—with Donald Trump as our president. For the country, it could be four years. For the court, it could be—I don't even want to contemplate that." Referring to what she thought her late husband would have said about Trump being elected, she said, "Now it's time for us to move to New Zealand."[31] Trump responded by saying she should resign from the court for these "very dumb political statements about me" and because "her mind is shot."[32] At this point, Justice Ginsburg should have disengaged with him, but she retorted to CNN calling him a "faker": "He has no consistency about him. He says whatever comes into his head at the moment. He really has an ego. . . . How has he gotten away with not turning over his tax returns? The press seems to be very gentle with him on that."[33] Justice Ginsburg later apologized for these remarks, acknowledging that judges should stay out of partisan politics.[34]

Justice Ginsburg's remarks about Trump could have spelled disaster for the Supreme Court had it been called upon to rule on the 2016 election.

[31] Adam Liptak, *Ruth Bader Ginsburg, No Fan of Donald Trump, Critiques Latest Term*, N.Y. Times (July 10, 2016), https://www.nytimes.com/2016/07/11/us/politics/ruth-bader-ginsburg-no-fan-of-donald-trump-critiques-latest-term.html? rref=collection%2Ftimestopic%2FGinsburg%2C%20Ruth%20Bader&action=click&contentCollection=timestopics&region=stream&module=stream_unit&version=latest&contentPlacement=1&pgtype=collection&_r=1.

[32] Tweet from @RealDonaldTrump, dated July 12, 2016, 11:54 p.m., https://x.com/realDonaldTrump/status/753090242203283457?ref_src=twsrc%5Etfw%7Ctwcamp%5Etweetembed%7Ctwterm%5E753090242203283457%7Ctwgr%5E0ec17a4e69bf32cdd998c69f2268c52c90b31775%7Ctwcon%5Es1_&ref_url=https%3A%2F%2Fwww.npr.org%2F2016%2F07%2F14%2F486012897%2Fginsburg-apologies-for-ill-advised-trump-comments.

[33] Joan Biskupic, *Justice Ruth Bader Ginsburg Calls Trump a "Faker." He Says She Should Resign*, CNN (July 13, 2016), https://www.cnn.com/2016/07/12/politics/justice-ruth-bader-ginsburg-donald-trump-faker/.

[34] Jessica Taylor, *Ginsburg Apologizes For "Ill-Advised" Trump Comments*, NPR (July 14, 2016), https://www.npr.org/2016/07/14/486012897/ginsburg-apologies-for-ill-advised-trump-comments.

At the time of Justice Ginsburg's remarks, the 2016 election was projected to be very close. Only sixteen years earlier, the court had decided the extremely close 2000 election in the highly contentious 5–4 decision in *Bush v. Gore*.[35] In 2016, Hillary Clinton won the popular vote, like Al Gore in 2000, but this time Trump clearly won the electoral college, a situation far from Bush's 400 plus vote margin in Florida in 2000. The Supreme Court did not have to decide the 2016 election. But if Clinton had done a little better in a few swing states, and if the election had been contested, Justice Ginsburg's public remarks about Trump would have been a lightning rod. If there had been a very close election and another case like *Bush v Gore*, there surely would have been demands that she recuse. If Justice Ginsburg had not recused, one can imagine how Trump and his supporters would have lashed out at the court, and the chaos that would have ensued on January 6, 2017. Fortunately, that did not happen.

Furthermore, all the justices of the court, Justice Ginsburg included, should have been aware that after the controversy following *Bush v. Gore*, even the appearance of partisanship on the court would make it very difficult for them to decide any future election law cases without public backlash.

Justice Ginsburg also had a history of intense involvement in politicized legal issues off the bench. She did a lot for the women's movement before she was on the court and wanted to continue her support. But the best way for her to do that was to be an exemplary justice, including deciding cases that involved women's rights. Her speaking on these same issues for law schools and bar associations risked undermining the aura of objectivity needed to maximize the impact of her judicial opinions, particularly on an increasingly conservative court. Ginsburg's public comments probably went overboard, mirroring from the left the almost incessant appearances before the Federalist Society and other conservative groups of Justice Scalia, her intellectual antagonist, and close friend, on the court.[36]

Justice Scalia

Justice Scalia, like Justice Ginsburg, enjoyed debate and discussion outside the court, sometimes too much so. For example, Justice Scalia made controversial comments about the law and homosexuality at an appearance at

[35] *Bush v. Gore*, 531 U.S. 98 (2000).

[36] Jennifer Senior, *The Ginsburg-Scalia Act Was Not a Farce. There Is a Lot for Us to Learn, Not Just from Their Friendship, but from Their Intellectual Combat.* N.Y. Times (Sept. 22, 2022), https://www.nytimes.com/2020/09/22/opinion/ruth-bader-ginsburg-antonin-scalia.html.

Princeton University in 2012.[37] Scalia was explaining his 2003 dissent from the court's ruling striking down state sodomy laws by comparing them to laws prohibiting murder, an analogy both logically flawed and hurtful to people in his audience, an audience that expanded well beyond Princeton when Scalia's remarks were publicized.[38] Some observers might dismiss these remarks as unimportant because Scalia was only being honest about his views on homosexuality and with extrajudicial statements revealing his own thought processes, going beyond what he had already said in his dissent. What's wrong with such transparency?

Potentially a lot. These public remarks did not reflect the impartiality expected of a justice, particularly when the legal rights of same sex couples would again come before the court. In 2015, Justice Scalia would dissent again, this time from the court's ruling that same sex marriage is a constitutional right.[39] Had that case gone the other way, and Justice Scalia joined a majority upholding state laws prohibiting same sex marriage, his Princeton remarks three years earlier would have come back to haunt him. His remarks would have done considerable damage to the credibility of the court's ruling, inviting criticism that the court was simply homophobic rather than deciding such questions on constitutional grounds.

By way of comparison, after Justice Scalia passed away, the court in 2022 in *Dobbs v. Jackson Women's Health*[40] overturned forty-nine-year precedent in *Roe v. Wade*[41] and took away the constitutional right to abortion. Speculation about the justices' motives has been rampant, and there was a leak of the draft opinion. The court's credibility would have suffered even more, however, if a justice had given a public speech comparing abortion to murder. Fortunately for the court, no justice is on record having said that. Observers for whom transparency is the only important value may believe one of the justices should have compared abortion to murder publicly, provoking even more political pressure on both sides of the debate before and after the

[37] See Cara Marasca, *Scalia: Opposing Homosexuality Like Opposing Murder*, NBC News (Dec. 11, 2012), https://www.nbcnews.com/id/wbna50164683; Elisha Fieldstadt, *Supreme Court Justice Antonin Scalia's Most Controversial Remarks and Opinions*, NBC News (Feb. 13, 2016) ("While speaking at Princeton in 2012, Scalia was asked by a student why he would compare laws banning homosexuality with laws against murder. 'It's a form of argument that I thought you would have known, which is called the "reduction to the absurd"' Scalia answered. 'If we cannot have moral feelings against homosexuality, can we have it against murder? Can we have it against other things? I'm surprised you aren't persuaded,' Scalia told the student, who identifies as gay.") https://www.nbcnews.com/news/us-news/supreme-court-justice-antonin-scalia-s-most-controversial-remarks-opinions-n518246.

[38] *Lawrence v. Texas*, 539 U.S. 558 (2003).

[39] *Obergefell v. Hodges*, 576 U.S. 644 (2015). Justice Scalia's 2012 remarks at Princeton were not directed to the issue of same-sex marriage, which had not yet been decided by the court, but instead to explaining his dissent from the court's ruling striking down sodomy laws in *Lawrence v. Texas*, 539 U.S. 558 (2003).

[40] *Dobbs v. Jackson Women's Health*, 597 U.S. 215 (2022).

[41] *Roe v. Wade*, 410 U.S. 113 (1973).

Dobbs decision. But once again, the job of a judge is to adjudicate, not to make extrajudicial statements that provide fodder for other branches to respond.

Justices Scalia, like Justice Ginsburg, had First Amendment rights like everyone else, and perhaps they were such good friends because they both enjoyed intellectual debate, both inside and outside the court. But litigants have rights too, and these types of public statements can be grounds for motions for a justice to recuse. Recusal on the Supreme Court is a poor remedy, however, as discussed in Chapter 2. The best course of action would be for the justices to refrain from making controversial remarks to begin with and save their opinions for a written opinion. That is not too much to ask of the only nine judges in the entire country whose opinion on many of these legal issues may be the only opinion that really makes a difference.

Finally, Justice Scalia crossed another boundary important to our system of checks and balances in which the court has constrained the power of the executive branch since *Marbury v. Madison*. After the 9-11 terrorist attacks and U.S. invasions of Afghanistan and Iraq, cases involving presidential power in wartime once again came before the court. Vice President Richard Cheney was instrumental in shaping the Bush administration's war on terror. On January 9, 2004, the Supreme Court granted certiorari in *Hamdi v. Rumsfeld*,[42] a case involving a US citizen detained as a suspected combatant for the Taliban. Only one month earlier, Justice Scalia had gone duck hunting with Vice President Cheney.[43] While there is no evidence that they talked about any cases pending in the federal courts, it is not inconceivable that they would have talked about the conduct of the war on terror, which was on everyone's mind in the years after 9-11.

Furthermore, their December 2003 duck hunting trip was weeks after the court granted certiorari in *Cheney v. United States District Court for the District of Columbia*,[44] a case involving Vice President Cheney's energy task force. When the Sierra Club moved for Justice Scalia's recusal from this case, he wrote a memo explaining his decision not to recuse:

> A rule that required Members of this Court to remove themselves from cases in which the official actions of friends were at issue would be utterly disabling. Many Justices have reached this Court precisely because they were friends of the incumbent President or other senior officials–and from the earliest days down to modern

[42] *Hamdi v. Rumsfeld*, 542 U.S. 507 (2004).

[43] Dan Collins, *Scalia-Cheney Trip Raises Eyebrows*, CBS News (Dec. 15, 2003), https://www.cbsnews.com/news/scalia-cheney-trip-raises-eyebrows/.

[44] *Cheney v. United States District Court for the District of Columbia*, 542 U.S. 367 (2004), cert granted Dec. 15, 2003.

times Justices have had close personal relationships with the President and other officers of the Executive.[45]

All this is true, and indeed such is the point of Chapter 1 of this book: Judges get on the Supreme Court because of who they know. Friendships with powerful politicians are part of the calculus, and it would be unreasonable to require a justice to recuse on the court merely because of the relationships that got him there in the first place. Scalia's memo made a mostly convincing argument for his decision not to recuse from the case, which if he had recused would have led to demands that he recuse from other cases involving the Bush administration's policies in which Vice President Cheney had an important part. (It is no secret that Cheney was one of the more influential vice presidents in American history.)

But none of this explains the duck hunting trip and whether Justice Scalia should have declined the opportunity to go with the vice president. Scalia went duck hunting with a named party to a case pending before the court. Cheney also had a substantial interest in other cases likely to come before the court. This was a problem even if there were no *ex parte* discussions about any case and even if Justice Scalia was right to insist that their close friendship would not change his decisions.[46] Even if Scalia and Cheney only talked about ducks, the appearances aren't right.

A fundamental duty of the court for over 200 years has been to define the boundaries of permissible use of presidential power under the Constitution and laws of the United States. There are often several presidential powers cases before the court during each term. A justice cognizant of this immense responsibility should go hunting, and on other excursions, with someone other than the president, vice president, or another high-ranking member of the incumbent administration.

The Court's Election Cases

The appearance of justices being partisan is even worse when the court decides a wide range of election law cases. This book has already discussed the

[45] *Cheney v. District Court, supra*, No. 03–475. Decided Mar. 18, 2004, Memorandum of Justice Scalia.

[46] *See* Steve Twomey, *Scalia Angrily Defends His Duck Hunt with Cheney*, N.Y. Times (Mar. 18, 2004) ("Justice Antonin Scalia of the United States Supreme Court today bluntly rejected demands that he step aside in a case involving Vice President Dick Cheney, mocking criticism that a duck hunting trip the two were on in January suggested he would be biased toward his longtime friend."), https://www.nytimes.com/2004/03/18/politics/scalia-angrily-defends-his-duck-hunt-with-cheney.html.

court's 5–4 decision in *Bush v. Gore* determining the winner of the 2000 election and the cases arising out of President Trump's attempt to overturn the 2020 election. Other Supreme Court cases do not focus on specific elections but will have a big impact on the outcome of future elections.

First are the campaign finance cases. The court's 2009 decision in *Citizens United v. FEC* giving First Amendment protection to corporate funded electioneering communications is one of the most famous, or infamous, of these cases, but there are others that are more recent. In 2022, the court, in *FEC v. Ted Cruz for Senate*,[47] struck down Section 304 of the Bipartisan Campaign Reform Act, which limited the amount of money Cruz and other candidates could repay themselves on personal loans to their campaigns from money raised from donors after an election. Additionally, the court has not yet fully decided the status of super PACs. The court may be asked to decide the constitutionality of a 2024 Maine ballot measure that imposes caps on individual contributions to super PACs.[48] The District of Columbia Circuit Court has held that the constitutional protection afforded to electioneering communications in *Citizens United v. FEC* also applies to super PACs,[49] but the Supreme Court has not yet decided that issue.

Second, the gerrymandering and voter ID cases are very contentious, and partisan. In 2015, the court upheld an Arizona ballot measure that reversed gerrymandering by the state legislature.[50] But in 2019, the court also ruled that while state legislatures' gerrymandered maps of legislative districts may be "incompatible with democratic principles," federal courts should not intervene because such practices involve nonjusticiable political questions.[51] In 2008, the court upheld state law requiring voters to present government-issued ID,[52] but some states are seeking to make these laws even more

[47] *See FEC v. Ted Cruz for Senate*, 596 U.S. 289, 305 (2022).

[48] See *Dinner Table Action et el. v. Maine Commission on Governmental Ethics and Election Practices, et al.*, No. 1:24-cv-00430-KFW., (July 15, 2025), *Dinner Table Action v. Schneider*, Nos. 25-1705 & 25-1706 (1st Cir.) (oral argument January 2026), appealing an order of a federal magistrate judge enjoining enforcement of Maine ballot measure limiting contributions to Super PACs. ; https://freespeechforpeople.org/wp-content/uploads/2025/07/dinner-table-action-district-court-ruling-071525.pdf. The author of this book is chairman of the board of Equal Citizens, a public interest group supporting litigation of this case in the federal courts.

[49] *See SpeechNow.org v. FEC*, 599 F.3d 686 (D.C. Cir. 2010) (en banc) (interpreting the *Citizens United* holding to allow unlimited spending on Super PACs), cert. denied, 562 U.S. 1003 (2010), *Lieu v. FEC*, No. 19-5072, 2019 WL 5394632, at ∗1 (D.C. Cir. 2019), (dismissing suit asking the circuit court to overturn its decision in *SpeechNow*).

[50] *Arizona State Legislature v. Arizona Independent Redistricting Commission*, 576 U.S. 787 (2015) (holding that under the Elections Clause of the US Constitution states may transfer authority over the process of redrawing congressional districts from the legislature to an independent committee formed by ballot initiative).

[51] *Rucho v. Common Cause*, 588 U.S. 684 (2019).

[52] *Crawford v. Marion County Election Board*, 553 U.S. 181 (2008).

onerous—for example, requiring proof of US citizenship. Such cases may also reach the Supreme Court.[53]

A related issue is the precarious status of the 1965 Voting Rights Act. The court eliminated a central component of the Voting Rights Act in *Shelby County v. Holder*[54] by invalidating Section 5 of the act requiring states with a history of racial discrimination to obtain federal preclearance for changes in their voting laws. Then, in 2021, in *Brnovich v. Democratic National Committee*,[55] the court narrowly construed Section 2 of the Voting Rights Act and allowed Arizona to ban both out-of-precinct voting and collection of absentee ballots by third parties. As states enact increasingly stringent voting laws, with arguably disproportionately impact on racial minorities, more such cases may soon reach the Supreme Court.

These are only a sampling of the election law issues that already have come before the court and will likely be revisited.[56] Most of the court's rulings over the past two decades have made it more difficult, if not impossible, for Congress and the states to regulate the role of money in elections, while making it easier for states to gerrymander legislative districts and to enact new laws that make it harder for some people to vote. It is already bad enough for justices handing down these decisions to be accepting free yacht and plane excursions from politically active billionaires, the problem addressed in Chapter 2. The point in this chapter is that Supreme Court justices also should not be wearing partisanship on the sleeves of their judicial robes.

[53] *See, e.g., Equality State Policy Center v. Chuck Gray, Wyoming Secretary of State*, (D. Wyo. 2025), Civil Case No. 25-cv-00117-SWS (lawsuit challenging state law requiring proof of citizenship to vote).

[54] *Shelby County v. Holder*, 570 U.S. 529 (2013) (holding Section 4 of the Voting Rights Act is unconstitutional, and cannot be used as a basis for subjecting jurisdictions to preclearance).

[55] *Brnovich v. Democratic National Committee*, 594 U.S. 647 (2021).

[56] See *Alexander v. South Carolina State Conference of the NAACP*, 602 U.S. ___ (2024) (trial courts should draw an adverse inference from a plaintiff's failure to submit an alternative map in a redistricting case); *Moore v. Harper*, 600 U.S. ___ (2023) (Elections Clause does not vest authority in state legislatures to set rules for federal elections); *Allen v. Milligan*, 599 U.S. ___ (2023) (striking down Alabama redistricting map that diluted Black voters impact on elections); *Brnovich v. Democratic National Committee*, 594 U.S. ___ (2021) (upholding Arizona law that disregards votes cast at the wrong precinct and that make it a crime for any person other than a postal worker, an elections official, or a voter's caregiver, family member, or household member to collect an early ballot); *Chiafalo v. Washington*, 591 U.S. ___ (2020) (a state may enforce an elector's pledge to support their party's nominee for president); *Rucho v. Common Cause*, 588 U.S. ___ (2019) (partisan gerrymandering claims present political questions that cannot be adjudicated by the federal courts); *Abbott v. Perez*, 585 U.S. ___ (2018) (in redistricting cases, the good faith of the state legislature must be presumed); *Cooper v. Harris*, 581 U.S. ___ (2017) (a state may not use race as the predominant factor in drawing district lines unless it has a compelling reason); *Evenwel v. Abbott*, 578 U.S. ___ (2016) (under the Fourteenth Amendment and the one-person, one-vote principle states properly create legislative districts with equal total populations, rather than equal voter populations); *McCutcheon v. FEC*, 572 U.S. 185 (2014) (striking down Federal Election Campaign Act provision restricting aggregate contributions to political campaigns); *Crawford v. Marion County Election Board*, 553 U.S. 181 (2008) (a state can require residents to present government-issued photo IDs in order to vote).

If Elected Justices Are Politicians, Why Should Elected Politicians Do What They Say?

In *Marbury v. Madison*, Chief Justice John Marshall in 1803 famously wrote, "It is emphatically the province and duty of the judicial department to say what the law is."[57] The court made it clear that the president, Thomas Jefferson, was obligated to follow the court's interpretation of the law, not his own.

But if courts are just political bodies, why shouldn't other political bodies directly elected by the people just ignore the courts?

The president only obeys the court's orders because he respects its authority to interpret the law, an American tradition over 200 years old going back to *Marbury*. Alternatively, the president obeys because Congress through threat of impeachment would hold him accountable if he did not.

The court has no army to enforce its orders. If force were to decide who interprets the law, the president would be the decision maker. If direct election by the people were to be the deciding factor, the president and Congress would interpret the laws and the Constitution, not the Supreme Court.

No president has defied a Supreme Court order since Andrew Jackson refused to assist with enforcing the court's order that the State of Georgia release a missionary held prisoner in *Worcester v. Georgia*,[58] an 1832 case where the court held that the Cherokee Indians were a nation holding sovereign powers that could not be intruded upon by Georgia. Jackson ignored the court and allowed, indeed encouraged, the Georgia militia to keep Worcester and other missionaries as prisoners and to forcibly removed the Cherokee from their land.

It has been suggested that President Lincoln ignored a Supreme Court order when he suspended habeas corpus, but this is not true. Chief Justice Roger Taney, a Confederate sympathizer[59] sitting by designation as a federal district judge in *Ex parte Merryman*,[60] held that Lincoln suspending habeas corpus without consent of Congress was unconstitutional. Lincoln continued to do it anyway, although Congress eventually authorized it. This was not, however, an order of the Supreme Court. Lincoln disobeying a federal district court order was an extreme action, and was not justified, but it was during the extreme circumstances of the Civil War.

[57] *Marbury v. Madison*, 5 U.S. (1 Cranch) 137 (1803).
[58] *Worcester v. Georgia*, 31 U.S. (6 Pet.) 515 (1832)
[59] Chief Justice Taney was also the author of one of the court's most infamous pro-Southern opinions, *Dred Scott v. Sandford*, 60 U.S. (19 How.) 393 (1857), holding that persons of African descent were not US citizens and could not avail themselves of the rights and privileges of citizens.
[60] *Ex parte Merryman*, 17 F. Cas. 144 (C.C.D. Md. 1861) (No. 9487).

In the 1950s, after *Brown v. Board of Education*,[61] some southern governors defied the orders of federal courts, but President Eisenhower insisted that judicial orders must be obeyed. Eisenhower used his commander in chief power to deploy federal troops to enforce federal court orders in Little Rock, Arkansas.

But a series of decisions by the liberal-leaning Warren court then sparked a political backlash against the court, and President Nixon began what became a decades-long intense political effort by the Republican Party to appoint more conservative justices to the court.

In this increasingly politicized environment, there have been calls on the left as well as the right for presidents to ignore orders of the federal courts, even the Supreme Court. Two credible academics—Samuel Moyn of Yale Law School and Ryan Doefler of Harvard Law School—in 2024 made the incredible argument that President Biden and Congress should consider ignoring the orders of the Supreme Court, suggesting among other things that Biden ignore the court's order invalidating his student loan forgiveness program, which had not been approved by Congress.[62] After President Trump won the 2024 election, Vice President JD Vance suggested Trump could ignore the Supreme Court.[63] Yale Law School professor Jed Rubenfeld[64] agreed with the vice president, his former law student.

In a democracy, politics, to some extent, will shape the content of law. But if law is nothing more than politics, why should an elected head of state, or Congress for that matter, submit to the rulings of an unelected Supreme Court?

The American constitutional framework assumes otherwise and depends upon deference to judicial review of actions taken by the elected branches of government. For this system to be credible, there must be some concept of law that is not purely political and somebody to adjudicate it. If the Supreme Court does not to have the final say in what the law is, then who does?

[61] *Brown v. Board of Education*, 347 U.S. 483 (1954).

[62] Samuel Moyn & Ryan Doefler, *We Are Already Defying the Supreme Court. The Risks of Calling on Politicians to Push Back Against the Court Must Be Weighed Against the Present Reality of a Malign Judicial Dictatorship*, Dissent (Winter 2024). There is no indication that the Biden administration took this suggestion seriously, although the administration implemented a scaled-back version of the student loan forgiveness program that also ran into trouble with federal courts.

[63] Charlie Savage & Minho Kim, *Vance Says "Judges Aren't Allowed to Control" Trump's "Legitimate Power": The Declaration by the Vice President Came as Court Orders Have Temporarily Blocked Parts of the Trump Administration's Agenda*, N.Y. Times (Feb. 9, 2025), https://www.nytimes.com/2025/02/09/us/politics/vance-trump-federal-courts-executive-order.html.

[64] Asher Boiskin, *"Yale Law School should be embarrassed": Vance Law '13 Clashes with Legal Scholars over Judicial Power*, Yale Daily News (Feb. 19, 2025) (reporting that Yale law professor Jed Rubenfeld defended Vance, writing on X that Vance was "correct" and that "judges cannot constitutionally interfere" in areas where the executive branch has "sole and plenary power under the Constitution," such as "in commanding military operations or exercising prosecutorial discretion.").

An extreme iterations of the "law as politics" concept came to prominence in the early twentieth century when German legal philosopher Carl Schmitt wrote his famous 1932 essay *The Concept of the Political*.[65] Schmitt argued that the executive branch, which was embodied in the president and the chancellor of Germany could rewrite the Weimar Constitution to override checks and balances from the legislature and judges. The executive, Schmitt argued, was chosen by all the people of Germany and embodied the will of the people who existed prior to the relatively recent constitutional document. (Under the 1919 Weimar Constitution, the elected president of Germany appointed the chancellor.) Schmitt's theory of the executive as "the exception" was that a sovereign who expresses the political will of the people may set aside the legal and constitutional order. The real sovereign under Schmitt's theory was not the law, or any judge's interpretation of the law, but the will of the people embodied in the executive.[66]

What happened next in Germany explains why an apolitical and independent judiciary with the power of judicial review is so important.

Schmitt was not just a political philosopher; he was also a lawyer for the German government in the early 1930s, the last years of the Weimar Republic. Schmitt advocated for an expansive interpretation of Article 48 of the Weimar Constitution,[67] a provision allowing the president of Germany to suspend civil liberties and use military force inside states that did not fulfil their obligations to the national government. In a famous—and tragic—1932 case, *Reich v. Prussia*,[68] Schmitt successfully argued before the Supreme Court of Germany that President Paul von Hindenburg and Chancellor Franz von Papen had the constitutional power to send federal troops into the State of Prussia over the objections of the government of Prussia to put down allegedly violent protests. Germany's Supreme Court caved in to the executive, and the federal troops remained in Prussia.

[65] Carl Schmitt, *The Concept of the Political* (George Schwab trans., 2007) (1932). More broadly speaking, the jurisprudential question Schmitt posed was about the relationship between law and politics. Schmitt argued law is so firmly rooted in politics that law is inseparable from politics, and politics in turn is grounded in the power of the state to define the distinction between friend and enemy of the collective group.

[66] *See generally* Carl Schmitt, *Political Theology* 6 (George Schwab trans., 1985) (1922). In this book, Schmitt articulates the doctrine of "Sovereignty" with the opening line "Sovereign is he who decides on the exception." *Id.* at 5.

[67] Die Verfassung des Deutschen Reichs [Constitution], Aug. 11, 1919, art. 48 (Ger.).

[68] *See* Lars Vinx, *Kelsen on the Judgment of the Staatsgerichtshof of 25 October 1932. In* The Guardian of the Constitution: Hans Kelsen and Carl Schmitt on the Limits of Constitutional Law, 228–253 (2015). See Aziz Z. Huq, *The January 6 Insurrection and the Problem of Constitutional Guardianship*, 37 Const. Comment. 365 (2022) (discussing the 1932 decision in *Reich v. Prussia* and also doubt that the US Supreme Court can be an effective guardian of the constitution).

With the judiciary caving in to the executive branch, another crisis soon ended judicial review altogether. In 1933, newly appointed Chancellor Adolf Hitler, after an unexplained fire in the Reichstag, urged President Hindenburg to declare an emergency and deploy federal troops for law enforcement throughout the county.[69] Hitler then removed politically unreliable judges and prosecutors, among other civil servants, and replaced them with Nazi Party loyalists.[70] That was the same year Carl Schmitt joined the Nazi Party. After World War II, some of these same Nazi Party judges stood trial at Nuremberg for war crimes, in cases prosecuted by US Supreme Court Justice Henry Jackson.[71] Germany's Nazi-era judges exemplified Schmitt's "concept of the political" in its most extreme form.

Politicization of law in the United States—including the politicization of the Supreme Court discussed in this chapter—does not come remotely close to what happened there. We are still a constitutional republic. But public confidence in the judiciary is undermined well short of that point. The problem begins when the public believes that party politics has infected the courts to such an extent that law depends on politics. Once the "concept of the political" takes root, it is hard to eradicate and can grow like a cancer on the judiciary, and on the elected branches of government, until the constitutional order is destroyed.

Pushing back on the idea that judges are merely political actors is vital to preserving an independent judiciary. Politics will shape law in a healthy democracy, but when the branch of government that interprets the law does not maintain a distance from politics, its functions are folded into those of the political branches to an extent that it can no longer be a check on their excesses.

Imagine a case like *Reich v. Prussia* arising in the United States, where the Supreme Court considers whether the president must withdraw federal troops he has sent into a major US city to put down allegedly violent protests, and that the president did so over the objections of the governor of the State and in violation of federal law prohibiting use of federal troops for domestic law enforcement.[72] Perhaps our Supreme Court would make the same tragic

[69] Verordnung des Reichspräsidenten zum Schutz von Volk und Staat, Feb. 28, 1933, Reichsgesetzblatt [RGB1] I at 83 (Ger.) (Decree of the Reich President for the Protection of the People and State).

[70] Gesetz zur Wiederherstellung des Berufsbeamtentums, Apr. 7, 1933, Reichsgesetzblatt [RGB1] I at 175 (Ger.) (Law for the Restoration of the Professional Civil Service).

[71] *See U.S. v. Altstoetter* (Military Tribunal III 1947), from *Trials of War Criminals Before the Nurenberg Military Tribunals*, Volume III ("The Justice Case"), excerpted and discussed in John T. Noonan Jr. & Richard W. Painter, *Professional and Personal Responsibilities of the Lawyer*, Chapter 11 (1997), Second Edition (2001), and Third Edition (2011).

[72] In *Trump v. Illinois*, 607 U.S. ___ (2025) (Docket No. 25A443), the Supreme Court declined to stay a lower court order that barred the President from federalizing and deploying the National Guard within

error that Germany's Supreme Court did in *Reich v. Prussia* and cave in to the president. But if the court instead ordered federal troops to be withdrawn, would the president obey the court's order and withdraw the troops? If the justices are merely political actors, and behave as such, why should he?

Today, some academics continue to explore the boundaries of Schmitt's notion that law is the same as politics (Schmitt is cited by admirers of his philosophy if not his politics on both the left and right).[73] But for judges to lend credibility, through their words or conduct, to the concept that law is only political is dangerous.

The Supreme Court insists that its work is not political, but the public is skeptical. Politicians have joined the chorus of criticism. As Chief Justice Roberts noted in his 2024 year-end report, "Public officials, too, regrettably have engaged in recent attempts to intimidate judges—for example, suggesting political bias in the judge's adverse rulings without a credible basis for such allegations."[74] Some of these criticisms of judges are unfair, and as Chief Justice Roberts also points out in his report, they are nothing new; he recounts the horrific intimidation of federal judges over civil rights rulings in the 1950s.

But Supreme Court justices are not doing enough to discredit criticism that the judiciary is too political. Part of the problem is the highly politicized judicial nomination and confirmation process discussed in Chapter 1. But when the justices themselves become political actors, by appearing to take sides in elections and making public statements on politically contentious issues, they make the problem worse. The justices cannot argue that law stands apart from politics, and that their decisions should be respected and obeyed by politicians when they act like politicians.

If judicial review is to survive in the long run, the justices should distance themselves from partisan politics more than they now do. They should act like the guardians of the law and the Constitution they purport to be, and under our system of law are required to be.[75]

Illinois. The justices in a 6–3 decision held that the Trump Administration failed to prove it had the legal authority under 10 U.S.C. § 12406(3) to deploy the Guard troops for domestic law enforcement. *See* also *Governor Newsom and the State of California v. Donald Trump, President of the United States* (N D Cal.) (complaint filed June 9, 2025) alleging that deployment of federal troops in Los Angeles was prohibited under federal law.

[73] *See The Oxford Handbook of Carl Schmitt* (Jens Meierhenrich & Oliver Simons eds., 2017) (containing thirty essays giving different perspectives on Schmitt's theory on law and politics).

[74] John G. Roberts Jr., Chief Justice of the United States, 2024 Year End Report on the Federal Judiciary at 7. *See Id.* at 6 (photo of a cross "burned on the lawn of Chief Justice Warren's apartment building early in the morning on July 14, 1956"), https://www.supremecourt.gov/publicinfo/year-end/2024year-endreport.pdf.

[75] "Judicial independence is not conferred so judges can do as they please. Judicial independence is conferred so judges can do as they must." Roberts, 2024 Year-End Report, *supra* at 4 quoting Justice Anthony M. Kennedy, Testimony in Senate Judiciary Committee Hearing on Judicial Independence, 2007.

Concluding Thoughts

This chapter, and indeed this book, is not about the ethics of judging, and how political considerations should or should not factor into deciding cases. Such an inquiry goes down the path of distinguishing "political" judging in a good or at least neutral sense from the bad sense. A judge considering political values in interpreting the law—for example, a conservative judge embracing originalism in constitutional interpretation, or a liberal judge emphasizing due process—is not only accepted but encouraged. However, a judge deciding in favor of a party because of a personal political relationship or deciding a disputed election case in favor of the candidate the judge would have voted for, most people would think unacceptable, perhaps unethical. But there are more complex cases in between, where a judge appears to have abandoned objectivity, neutrality, and impartiality in interpreting a law to reach the result that the judge wants to reach. Perhaps this is the result the judge would have supported had he been in the legislature voting for the law he is now interpreting, even if the judge's task is not to vote for or against a law, but to interpret the language of the law and the intent of the legislature that enacted it. These questions concern the ethics of judging.

The subject addressed in this chapter, however, is different. The relevant question is at what point judges should step back from partisan actions and words, often off the bench, that create the appearance that their decisions on the bench are political more than judicial. This was the issue in Justice Chase's impeachment trial in 1805[76] and is at least as serious an issue today. A related question is when, in rare instances, such as with Justice Kagan and the ACA case, a justice's recent involvement with the political branches of government means that recusal from a case is the better course of action.

Some would say that the "appearance of impropriety" standard does not matter and should be abandoned, and that critics of the courts should focus only on how politics affect judicial decisions. Such an approach is wrong, however, and potentially dangerously so when the role of the courts is considered in a polarized political climate. Public confidence in the courts, and particularly in the Supreme Court, is most critical when the integrity and

[76] "Controversial and irascible, Chase's temperament and rulings landed him at the center of a power struggle between the Federalists and the Democratic-Republicans that culminated in his impeachment by the House and acquittal in the Senate in 1805. Chase prevailed at trial, despite a supermajority of Democratic-Republicans in the Senate, because many Senators concluded that disapproval of a judge's decisions provided an invalid basis for removal from office." John Roberts, "2025 Year End Report on the Federal Judiciary," citing and quoting William H. Rehnquist, *Grand Inquests* (1992) (Chief Justice Rehnquist's historical account of Justice Chase's impeachment)

power of the courts and fundamental principles of judicial review are challenged by partisans on the left and right. Supreme Court justices should recognize this and, for their own sake if not the country's sake, focus on the appearances that their conduct leaves with the public. After all, in the political process, the public has a role in determining both the composition and the power of the judiciary. If the left and right agree on only one thing, that they don't like judges and that the role of the courts should be reduced, it is only a matter of time before that happens. Appearances matter, and justices who do not understand that and are excessively political endanger the very institution that defines their role in the political process.

4

Why Can't the Supreme Court Fix Its Ethics Problem?

There was a time when the Supreme Court appeared capable of policing itself.

Until recently, the court's most well-known ethics scandal was fifty-seven years ago, in 1969.

The court was a political lightning rod then as it is today. School desegregation had inflamed racial tensions after the court's 1954 decision in *Brown v. Board of Education*,[1] followed by the court striking down schemes school boards used to get around *Brown*.[2] Religious conservatives were angry at the court's ruling that teacher-led prayer was unconstitutional in public schools.[3] The court in 1965 struck down state laws restricting the sale of birth control,[4] raising the possibility that abortion laws would soon follow. (*Roe v. Wade*[5] was not decided until 1973.) The court's rulings in the late 1950s and 1960s angered conservatives as much as the court's rulings today often anger liberals.

Road signs posted by the ultra-conservative John Birch Society called for the impeachment of Chief Justice Earl Warren,[6] a Republican and Eisenhower appointee perceived as too liberal, particularly in the segregationist South. Justice Abe Fortas, a close confidant of former President Lyndon Johnson, a Democrat, was even more liberal. President Richard Nixon, a Republican, had been in the White House only a few months and was eager to name more conservative justices to the court.

[1] *Brown v. Board of Education of Topeka*, 347 U.S. 483 (1954).

[2] *See, e.g., Griffin v. County School Board of Prince Edward County*, 377 U.S. 218 (1964), holding that a school board's decision to close all local public schools and provide vouchers to attend private schools violated the Equal Protection Clause of the Fourteenth Amendment; *Green v. County School Board of New Kent County*, 391 U.S. 430 (1968), ruling that a "freedom of choice" plan intended to circumvent the court's ruling in *Brown* did not comply with the constitutional requirement that admission to public schools not be based on race.

[3] *Engel v. Vitale*, 370 US 421 (1962).

[4] *Griswold v. Connecticut*, 381 U.S. 479 (1965).

[5] *Roe v. Wade*, 410 U.S. 113 (1973), overruled in *Dobbs v. Jackson Women's Health Organization*, No. 19-1392, 597 U.S. ___ (2022).

[6] *See* Bob Fitch, *John Birch Society Billboard Calls for the Impeachment of Earl Warren*, Bob Fitch Photography Archive (June 1966), https://exhibits.stanford.edu/fitch/catalog/bg116nt5712 [https://perma.cc/BA6A-XN8Z].

Conduct Unbecoming. Richard W. Painter, Oxford University Press. © Oxford University Press (2026).
DOI: 10.1093/9780197832301.003.0005

Then, in 1969, *Life Magazine* revealed that Justice Fortas had a serious ethics problem. Shortly after joining the court in 1965, he entered an agreement to accept payment of $20,000 ($176,000 in 2024 dollars) every year for life for consulting services from the Wolfson Family Foundation, established by Louis Wolfson, a financier Fortas had met in private practice.[7] There were no mandatory financial disclosure laws for federal judges at the time, and ethics rules did not prohibit a justice from receiving outside income from charitable boards. Indeed, Justice William O. Douglas served as president and director of the Albert Parvin Foundation for compensation of $12,000 a year until he resigned from the foundation in May 1969.[8] Justice Warren Burger served on the Mayo Clinic board for compensation of $2,000 a year until he resigned that position in October 1969 a few months after being elevated to chief justice.[9] But those board memberships were publicly known; Fortas's arrangement with Wolfson was secret until 1969.[10] Additionally, Fortas would receive a lot of money from Wolfson *for life*.

Wolfson had a horrible business reputation. He had been indicted for securities law violations in 1966.[11] Fortas resigned his Wolfson Foundation post when Wolfson's legal difficulties first emerged, and Fortas returned all the money to the foundation when Wolfson was referred by the Securities Exchange Commission to the Justice Department for criminal prosecution.[12] But this was too late, and a political firestorm erupted three years later when the payment was revealed. Fortas said that he did nothing wrong (there was probably no law that he violated), but he acknowledged that the controversy adversely affected the court and said that protecting it as an institution was his priority.

On May 11, 1969, shortly after the Fortas news broke, Minnesota Senator Walter Mondale became the first Democrat to call upon Fortas to resign, soon followed by Joseph Tydings of Maryland, a liberal Democrat "who had been one of Fortas's biggest supporters."[13] Republicans were eager to replace Fortas as well, knowing that Nixon would appoint his successor. Fortas probably

[7] *See The Texts of Letters and Statements Involving the Resignation of Justice Fortas*, N.Y. Times (May 16, 1969), letter from Justice Fortas to Chief Justice Earl Warren (describing Fortas's arrangement with Wolfson and his foundation).

[8] *Douglas Resigns Foundation Post, Cites His Health*, N.Y. Times (May 24, 1969); Albert Parvin "was named as a co-conspirator," but was never tried in a securities fraud case involving Louis Wolfson. *Ibid.*

[9] *Justice Burger Resigns Mayo Foundation Post*, N.Y. Times (Oct. 4, 1969).

[10] *See The Texts of Letters and Statements Involving the Resignation of Justice Fortas, supra.*

[11] *United States v. Wolfson*, 405 F.2d 779 (2d Cir. 1968) (upholding criminal conviction for sale of unregistered securities in violation of the 1933 Securities Act).

[12] *See The Texts of Letters and Statements Involving the Resignation of Justice Fortas, supra.*

[13] Adam Cohen, *54 Years Ago, a Supreme Court Justice Was Forced to Quit for Behavior Arguably Less Egregious Than Thomas's*, N.Y. Times (Apr. 11, 2023).

would have been impeached by the House and convicted in the Senate if he had not resigned.

Fortas resigned from the court on May 14, 1969.[14] In a letter addressed to Chief Justice Warren, he explained:

> There has been no wrongdoing on my part. There has been no default in the performance of my judicial duties in accordance with the high standards of the office I hold. So far as I am concerned, the welfare, and maximum effectiveness of the court to perform its critical role in our system of government are factors that are paramount to all others, It is this consideration that prompts my resignation. which, I hope, by terminating the public controversy, will permit the court to proceed with its work without the harassment of debate concerning one of its members.[15]

It is difficult to imagine a Supreme Court justice today resigning so quickly in the face of scandal. But both Congress and the court were different in 1969, and the reaction to Supreme Court ethics scandals then was different. One factor may have been that conservative Democrats (the South was still solidly Democratic at the time) disliked Fortas at least as much as the Republicans, although that does not explain why some liberal Democrats, including Senators Mondale and Tydings, also demanded Fortas's resignation as a matter of principle. These Democrats called for Fortas's resignation even though it meant giving President Nixon an opportunity to fill another vacancy on the court.

Recall that a few years later Congress was also capable of standing up to obstruction of justice by President Nixon, first pushing back on his firing of Watergate Special Prosecutor Archibald Cox in 1973 and then insisting that Nixon resign in 1974 after the White House tapes revealed that he had obstructed justice in the Watergate investigation. Several Republican senators also urged Nixon to resign.

That was an era when ethics, although politicized, was not strictly viewed through a political lens. Both parties recognized that there were some limits on what the public would tolerate, and Fortas's resignation demonstrates that in the case of the court expectations were high. He had not taken a bribe, and Wolfson did not have a case before the court while Fortas was on the court, but nonetheless Fortas should not have taken the money, and he had to go.

Fast forward to the 2020's. Despite many recent ethics scandals on the court, not a single member of the House or Senate has called for resignation,

[14] *See The Texts of Letters and Statements Involving the Resignation of Justice Fortas supra; see also Fortas Is First Justice To Resign Under Fire*, N.Y. Times (May 16, 1969).

[15] *See Ibid.*

or even a congressional investigation, of a justice appointed by a president of their own political party. As explained in the previous chapters, several of the justices have had ethics lapses, but Justice Thomas is the justice whose misconduct has been the most serious. This means Republicans in Congress have been put to the test, which they have failed. But one wonders whether, if a liberal justice were in a similar predicament, the reaction of today's Democrats in Congress would be any different.

Even more shocking, the justices do not call on each other to be accountable. Assuming they cared about the reputation and prestige of the court, one would expect them to be more vigilant about matters of ethics. They aren't.

Some of the reasons why the court is in such an ethics mess are explained in this chapter.

The Court Has Legalized Corruption

In a series of cases, the justices have carved out exceptions to public corruption laws analogous to the exceptions to ethics rules they carve out for themselves. The justices have read into statutory and even constitutional law a narrow definition of *quid pro quo* corruption at the same time as justices benefit from undisclosed gifts from billionaires, multi-million-dollar book contracts, and substantial spousal income from law firms and other organizations with business before the court.

In the criminal prosecution of Enron Corporation Chief Financial Officer Jeffrey Skilling, the court in 2010 ruled for Skilling, limiting the reach of the federal theft of honest services statute to bribery and kickback schemes, not other types of self-dealing and conflicts of interest. The court believed the language of the criminal statute would be unconstitutionally vague if applied to Skilling's corrupt conduct, which was a big factor in the collapse of Enron in 2002.[16] Undisclosed conflicts of interest and breaches of corporate ethics codes are not criminal. That holding should be comforting for justices of the court who have difficulty following their own ethics code.

Next came the governor of Virginia, Robert McDonnell, who was convicted of having exchanged official meetings for gifts to himself and his wife. In *McDonnell v. United States*,[17] the court in 2016 held that an "official act" for purposes of the federal bribery statute is an action that "involves a specific exercise of formal governmental power."[18] Agreeing to a meeting in

[16] *Skilling v. United States*, 130 S. Ct. 2896 (2010).
[17] *McDonnell v. United States*, 136 S. Ct. 2355 (2016).
[18] *Ibid.*

exchange for a gift is insufficient to be an "official act" under the bribery statute. Under *McDonnell* exchange of a thing of value (e.g., a yacht vacation in the Caribbean, a fishing trip to Alaska, or even a quarter-million-dollar recreational vehicle) in return for access to a public official (e.g., a Supreme Court justice) is not a bribe unless the official also agrees to a specific official act (e.g., a vote in a case) in return.

Finally, in 2024, during intense public controversy over gifts to Supreme Court justices, the court ruled in favor of James Snyder, the former mayor of Portage, Indiana, who had been convicted for receiving a large payment from a city contractor after he approved the contract. The court bent over backward to distinguish bribery, which is criminalized in every jurisdiction, from a gratuity (i.e., a "thank you" gift to a public official after an official act), which is a lesser crime in some jurisdictions and is not a crime at all in others.[19] The current federal criminal code, 18 U.S.C. § 201(b), provides that the crime of bribery occurs whenever anyone "directly or indirectly, corruptly gives, offers or promises anything of value to any public official . . . with intent to influence any official act." 18 U.S.C. § 201(c), by contrast, prohibits "gratuities," which is the acceptance of a reward after an official act even if there was no corrupt intent before the official act, but is considered a lesser crime. But those statutes don't apply directly to state and local government officials. The court in *Snyder v. United States* ruled that a separate federal criminal statute that does apply to state and local officials, 18 U. S. C. §666(a)(1)(B), only prohibits bribes and not gratuities, which are left to regulation under state laws.[20] The fact that some states don't prohibit gratuities at all did not seem to bother the justices.

Of course, none of the justices would admit to receiving a gratuity, which is still illegal for federal officials, but they did emphasize in *Snyder* that such a "thank you" present is nowhere near as serious a matter as a bribe—a gift given in advance explicitly in exchange for an official act. Whether gifts justices receive from their benefactors are motivated by appreciation for their rulings on the court is a matter for speculation, even more so when the benefactors are ideologically aligned with a justice. But it does not look good for the justices to narrowly interpret the application of federal law to gratuities for state and local officials while as the same time treading close the federal ban on gratuities themselves.

[19] 18 U.S.C. § 201.

[20] *Synder v. United States*, 603 U. S. ____ (2024). Slip Op. at 4: "Importantly, because bribery can corrupt the official act, Congress treats bribery as a far more serious offense than gratuities. For example, if a federal official accepts a bribe, federal bribery law provides for a 15-year maximum prison sentence. See 18 U. S. C. §201(b). By contrast, if a federal official accepts a prohibited gratuity, federal gratuities law sets a 2-year maximum prison sentence. See §201(c)."

The court has gone beyond criminal law in imposing its narrow definition of public corruption. In *Citizens United v. Federal Election Commission*,[21] the court in 2010 struck down an act of Congress that unconstitutionally interfered with corporations' First Amendment right to spend money on electioneering communications. The court held that corporations, just like billionaires, are people too and have the constitutional right to spend as much money as they want influencing elections. The court held there was insufficient evidence of quid pro quo between political spending and politicians benefiting from such largess to show a compelling state interest in regulating this form of "speech."[22]

The court's point in *Citizens United* is that quid pro quo must be proven, not assumed, to regulate spending on electioneering communications. *Citizens United* was a First Amendment case concerning elections to the executive and legislative branches of government, but as discussed in Chapter 5 of this book, the justices could apply a similarly narrow definition of quid pro quo corruption to themselves if Congress tries to impose more stringent ethics rules on the court. Where is the quid pro quo when justices accept free yacht excursions, rides on private jets, million-dollar book contracts, or interest-free/principal-free "loans" from billionaires? The court might hold that if Congress can't demonstrate quid pro quo, an evidentiary showing like that needed to prosecute a criminal bribery case, in the justices personal and financial relationships with persons having interests before the court, Congress can't tell the justices what to do on First Amendment grounds (justices have freedom of association with billionaires) and on separation of powers grounds. We are not at that point yet because Congress for other reasons explained in Chapter 8 has failed to act to tighten Supreme Court ethics rules, but it is not inconceivable that the justices believe the narrow definition of corruption as quid pro quo bribery also applies to themselves.

There Is No External Oversight

Nobody—not Congress, nor an independent ethics agency, nor an inspector general (IG), nor other federal judges—oversees the ethics of the Supreme Court. The justices do it themselves. Or they say they do.

[21] *Citizens United v. FEC*, 558 U.S. 310 (2010).

[22] *See* Richard W. Painter, *Taxation Without Representation: The Conservative Conscience and Campaign Finance Reform (Take Back our Republic* (2016); Edmond and Lily Safra Center for Legal Ethics, Harvard University, Seminar 2014–2015 (criticizing the *Citizens United* decision), https://ethics.harvard.edu/richard-painter-taxation-only-representation-conservative-conscience-and-campaign.

In a law review article and media appearances, the author of this book likened the Supreme Court to an out-of-control fraternity without supervision by a college dean.[23] If the court is the "animal house" of ethics, where is Dean Wormer (the college dean from the *Animal House* movie)? He's nowhere to be found. The chief justice surely does not want that role. There is no IG for the court. And Congress, to the extent it has power to do anything about the court's ethics, won't.

But perhaps we expect Supreme Court justices to observe a higher standard of voluntary compliance and self-enforcement than we expect of a college fraternity. After all, they are at the highest rank of their profession and supposedly would value their individual reputations as well as the reputation of the institution in which they serve.

Perhaps, but it doesn't work that way. Simply because people hold prestigious positions does not mean they police themselves.

Professionals in many fields are not good at self-regulation. Prestigious Wall Street banks and stock exchanges once resembled tightly knit social clubs and were disastrous self-regulatory organizations, necessitating federal regulation in the 1930s.[24] Effective self-regulation on Wall Street again was assumed to be the norm by the deregulation movement of the 1980s and 1990s, only to be followed by the 2008 financial crisis; the most prestigious firms, such as Lehman Brothers, Merrill Lynch, and Bear Stearns, all of which failed in 2008, could not regulate themselves.[25]

The bar also has failed to regulate its most powerful law firms, leading Congress to insist upon federal regulation of securities lawyers in the Sarbanes–Oxley Act after the collapse of Enron and WorldCom in 2002.[26]

Congress is yet another example of an institution held in low public esteem because of ethics scandals and members' refusal to submit to external oversight. How long did it take Democrats in Congress to insist that Senator

[23] Richard W. Painter, "SCOTUS House: Can a Supreme Court Ethics Lawyer and Inspector General Help Get This Fraternity Under Control?," *Georgetown Journal of Legal Ethics* 37, no. 3 (2024): 347.

[24] *See generally* Richard W. Painter, *The Dubious History and Psychology of Clubs as Self Regulatory Organizations, reprinted in* Restoring Trust in America's Business (Jay Lorsch et al., eds., 2004).

[25] The failure of Wall Street firms to regulate their own financial and legal risk is a result of distorted financial incentives as well as a mindset that equates money with power and even with moral virtue. *See* Claire A. Hill & Richard W. Painter, *Better Bankers, Better Banks: Promoting Good Business Through Contractual Commitment* (2015).

[26] *See* Sarbanes–Oxley Act, § 307, 15 U.S.C. § 7245 (2002); Final Rule: Implementation of Standards of Professional Conduct for Attorneys, Securities Act Rel. No. 8185 (Sept. 26, 2003), 17 C.F.R. §§ 205.1–205.7. SOX 307 was based on a proposal in a letter written by the author of this book and signed by forty law professors. *See* Letter from Professor Richard Painter and professors of securities regulation and/or professional responsibility to Harvey Pitt, chairman of the Securities and Exchange Commission (Mar. 7, 2002); *see also* Richard W. Painter & Jennifer E. Duggan, *Lawyer Disclosure of Corporate Fraud: Establishing a Firm Foundation*, 50 SMU L. Rev. 225 (1996) (suggesting that Congress mandate that lawyers representing public companies report known securities law violations to boards of directors or a designated committee of the board).

Robert Menendez (D-NJ) resign after he was indicted (twice) for bribery? Too long. Only when he was convicted of multiple counts of bribery—evidenced by among other things gold bars stashed in his home—did Senator Menendez finally leave the Senate in 2024. Republicans are no better at policing ethics of members of their own caucus, much less a president or former president of their party.

It should not be a surprise that we have a similar phenomenon at the Supreme Court. Nobody enforces ethics rules, because there is no external supervision.

This is very different from lower court judges, who are subject to the jurisdiction of the Judicial Conference. Not only can lower court judges be disciplined for violating ethics rules, but their decisions can also be overturned when they fail to recuse from a case despite an appearance of bias.[27] State court judges can also be disciplined by courts in their states, and their decisions can be reversed by federal courts on due process grounds if conflicts of interest create an appearance of bias.[28] Only nine judges in the United States are never held accountable by any other judges, and those nine sit on the Supreme Court.

The justices also reject attempts at external oversight of the court. As discussed earlier in this book, Chief Justice Roberts, in refusing Senator Durbin's (D-IL) invitation to testify before the Senate Judiciary Committee, apparently had the backing of all eight associate justices, who signed the accompanying statement attesting to their compliance with ethics rules.

The only recourse Congress has is a subpoena fight with the Supreme Court, with an uncertain outcome, or impeachment of a justice by the House and trial and removal by the Senate. For reasons explained separately at the end of this chapter, that is almost certainly not going to happen.

Going back to the college fraternity analogy, we know what probably would happen if a fraternity president refused even to meet with the college dean to talk about the rules. Arguments about "separation of powers" or that the college dean had "no jurisdiction" over what happens in the fraternity house, probably wouldn't go very far. (Yes, a lot of fraternities try making these arguments, but they rarely get away with it.).

But the Supreme Court justices are different. They're special. Or at least they are until somebody does something about the court's ethics problem rather than just talk about it.

[27] *Liljeberg v. Health Services Acquisition Corp.*, 486 U.S. 847 (1988) (reversal of federal district judge's ruling in case because of failure to recuse under 28 U.S.C. 455).

[28] *Caperton v. Massey Coal*, 556 U.S. 868 (2009) (reversing West Virginia Supreme Court holding on Fourteenth Amendment due process grounds because of a justice of that court failed to recuse after receiving substantial campaign contributions from a party to the case).

Colleagues Cover for Colleagues

The justices cover for each other.

This is a phenomenon in many workplaces. In police departments, the "thin blue line" too often means a "blue wall of silence."[29] The Church is another example, as sexual abuse investigations worldwide have revealed.[30] Academic departments are another parallel. In many departments, sexual harassers are an "open secret," yet are rarely sanctioned.[31]

The underlying problem is that colleagues cover for colleagues. It's not that much different on the Supreme Court.

Not a single justice has openly criticized breaches of ethics by another justice. Even Justice Thomas's multiple violations, discussed in Chapter 2 and Chapter 3 of this book, are not criticized by any of his colleagues. Some of the justices (e.g., Justice Kagan) are more open to ethics reform than others (e.g., Justice Alito), but none of the justices criticize each other's violations by name. Colleagues cover for colleagues.

The fewer colleagues there are in an organization, the more likely they may have close personal relationships and cover for each other. Of the active justices, there are only nine.

And the circle of colleagues providing cover extends well past the nine justices. The justices are at the center, but adjacent rings of colleagues circle the wagons around them. The first ring includes appellate court judges, some of whom previously were colleagues of Supreme Court judges on the courts of appeals and may not want to get involved in controversy over Supreme Court ethics. (This is a potential drawback to proposals to rely on appellate judges to review Supreme Court ethics, discussed later in this book.) Second, Supreme Court clerks and active members of the Supreme Court bar have much to lose by criticizing the court, and, in fact, much to gain by ingratiating themselves with the justices. Former clerks and members of the Supreme Court bar socialize with justices *and* argue cases before them. These lawyers are not colleagues in the sense of being professional

[29] *See* Matthew L. M. Fletcher, *Erasing the Thin Blue Line: An Indigenous Proposal*, 2021 Mich. St. L. Rev. 1447 (2020) (drawing on political theories of indigenous nations to recommend proposals for judicial oversight of policing). See Richard W. Painter, "SCOTUS House" supra, comparing such workplace cover ups to the conduct of justices and clerks on the court who cover for their colleagues.

[30] *See* Office of the Maryland Attorney General, Attorney General's Report on Child Sexual Abuse in the Archdiocese of Baltimore, Interim Public Release (Apr. 2023), https://www.andersonadvocates.com/wp-content/uploads/2023/04/MarylandAGReport.pdf [https://perma.cc/DDV3-466R]. "Time and again, members of the Church's hierarchy resolutely refused to acknowledge allegations of child sexual abuse for as long as possible." *Id.* at 9.

[31] Nancy Chi Cantalupo & William C. Kidder, *A Systematic Look at a Serial Problem: Sexual Harassment of Students by University Faculty*, 2018 Utah L. Rev. 671, 709 (2018).

equals of the justices, yet inequality goes the other way too, as many lawyers make far more money than the justices and have clients who make even more.

Colleagues cover for colleagues at the very top of a professional hierarchy against the backdrop of an economic hierarchy that is intrinsically intertwined.

Lifetime Tenure Emboldens Some and Intimidates Others

Lifetime tenure reinforces the "colleagues covering for colleagues" phenomenon. (Senior university professors, bishops and cardinals in the Church, and many public servants have the equivalent of lifetime tenure.) Nobody is going anywhere, and people with tenure know that they will be working with each other for a long time.

Law clerks and others who are aware of ethics violations on the court also will think twice before saying anything, fearing retaliation not only from a justice on the court but also from other former clerks.

Consider the problem of sexual harassment and assault. In academia and in the Church, lifetime tenure too often is abused in this way. One reason victims do not come forward is fear of retaliation by colleagues of the perpetrator. When Harvard's Title IX office found a tenured professor guilty of violating its sexual harassment policy, other tenured professors at Harvard defended him.[32] Three graduate students sued for harassment and retaliation,[33] and then Harvard drew a rebuke from the US Department of Education and the Justice Department in a 2022 Statement of Interest filed with the court siding with the plaintiffs.[34] Tenure in prestigious institutions is a privilege all too easily abused.

[32] Isabella B. Cho & Ariel H. Kim, *38 Harvard Faculty Sign Open Letter Questioning Results of Misconduct Investigations into Prof. John Comaroff*, Harv. Crimson (Feb. 4, 2022), https://www.thecrimson.com/article/2022/2/4/comaroff-sanctions-open-letter/ [https://perma.cc/H3CQ-ZLNM]. After the students filed their lawsuit, most of these faculty retracted their support for Comaroff. Ariel H. Kim & Meimei Xu, *35 Harvard Professors Retract Support for Letter Questioning Results of Comaroff Investigations*, Harv. Crimson (Feb. 10, 2022), https://www.thecrimson.com/article/2022/2/10/comaroff-faculty-letter-retraction/ [https://perma.cc/Z9HR-EJXD].

[33] *Czerwienski, v. President and Fellows of Harvard Coll.*, Case 1:22-cv-10202 (D. Mass. 2022). Graduate students sued under Title IX, alleging harassments by Harvard anthropology Professor John Comaroff.

[34] *Ibid.*; United States Department of Justice, Statement of Interest (filed Sept. 7, 2022), https://www.justice.gov/crt/case-document/file/1553801/download [https://perma.cc/7VXQ-VNHZ]. "Harvard argues that Plaintiffs' retaliation claims should be dismissed because they allege that Harvard employees, rather than 'Harvard itself,' engaged in retaliatory conduct. Def's Memo in Supp. at 22. This argument not only ignores that retaliation is typically carried out by individuals employed by the recipient, but also conflicts directly with Supreme Court and other relevant case law." *Id.* at 3.

The courts have similar problems. No Supreme Court justice has been accused of sexual harassment or assault while on the court, although two of the justices (Thomas and Kavanaugh) were accused at their confirmation hearings before they joined the court.[35] On the Ninth Circuit, two high-profile judges, Judge Stephen Reinhardt[36] and Judge Alex Kozinski,[37] were accused of sexually harassing law clerks, and in both cases, law clerks and perhaps other judges were aware of the alleged behavior for a long time.[38] Judge Reinhardt's conduct was not made known publicly until after he died.[39] Judge Kozinski eventually faced a disciplinary process that persuaded him to resign from the Ninth Circuit.[40] Had he been on the Supreme Court, however, he might have stayed, knowing that the disciplinary process used by the Ninth Circuit (referral of his case to an independent investigation by the Second Circuit) would not be used for a justice of the Supreme Court, and that impeachment by the House and removal by two-thirds of the Senate probably wouldn't happen.

If there is sexual harassment and assault at the Supreme Court, we won't hear about it. The appellate court clerks who stayed silent for so long in the cases of Judges Reinhardt and Kozinski likely would not have spoken out any sooner had they been on the Supreme Court. Indeed, the impetus to stay silent would be more powerful given the value of a Supreme Court clerkship to the career of a former clerk who remains in good graces of the justice and other former clerks.

[35] Michael S. Rosenwald, *"A High-Tech Lynching": How Brett Kavanaugh Took a Page From the Clarence Thomas Playbook*, Wash. Post (Sept. 27, 2018), https://www.washingtonpost.com/history/2018/09/25/high-tech-lynching-how-clarence-thomass-fury-saved-his-supreme-court-nomination/ [https://perma.cc/NNU2-MUXM].

[36] Catie Edmondson, *Former Clerk Alleges Sexual Harassment by Appellate Judge*, N.Y. Times (Feb. 13, 2020), https://www.nytimes.com/2020/02/13/us/politics/judge-reinhardt-sexual-harassment.html [https://perma.cc/EK6J-9CFF] ("Detailing her experience working for Judge Reinhardt in 2017 and 2018, Olivia Warren, the former clerk, testified before a subcommittee of the House Judiciary Committee that Judge Reinhardt openly commented on his female clerks' physical appearances and on her sexual relationship with her spouse").

[37] Niraj Chokshi, *Federal Judge Alex Kozinski Retires Abruptly After Sexual Harassment Allegations*, N.Y. Times (Dec. 18, 2017), https://www.nytimes.com/2017/12/18/us/alex-kozinski-retires.html [https://perma.cc/ZXU8-3KBZ].

[38] Dylan Hedtler-Gaudette & Sarah Turberville, *Sexual Harassment by Judges Operating with Impunity Shows Courts Need Their Own #MeToo: The Branch of Government Charged with Enforcing Federal Discrimination and Harassment Laws Does Not Police Its Own*, NBC News THINK (Feb. 15, 2020), https://www.nbcnews.com/think/opinion/olivia-warren-s-testimony-sexual-harassment-judges-shows-courts-need-ncna1137321 [https://perma.cc/8QGC-WTFJ].

[39] Edmondson, *supra* ("The former clerk told a House committee that Judge Stephen R. Reinhardt, a prominent liberal judge who died in 2018, routinely sexually harassed her and other women who worked for him.").

[40] On December 14, the chief judge of the Ninth Circuit referred the allegations for investigation and assigned them to the Second Circuit. On December 18, 2017, after additional allegations were made, Kozinski announced his retirement from the Ninth Circuit. *See* Chokshi, *supra*.

Judicial misconduct, of course, goes well beyond sexual harassment, yet the shield of tenure ensures that a justice will be in a position of power indefinitely. The fear of retaliation discourages law clerks from reporting misconduct. Even the justices themselves know that they probably will serve much of their term on the court with a colleague whom they criticize. Lifetime tenure for justices ensures that all these relationships reinforcing silence will remain intact for a very long time.

Overachievement Can Mean Overconfidence

A robust literature of psychology studies evaluates the problem of overconfidence of high-status decision makers.[41] High-status decision makers may tend to be more overconfident than others, perhaps because they attribute their status to their presumed ability to make good decisions. As Jennifer Robbennolt and Jean Sternlight observed in their 2013 article *Behavioral Legal Ethics*, "Social status tends to be negatively associated with ethics, with those in higher status positions tending to engage in more unethical behavior."[42] In sum, highly successful people may be overconfident in their own judgment, including their judgment about ethics.

Never mind that the justices, while probably qualified for their positions, are not demonstrably more qualified jurists than judges on district courts, courts of appeals, and state courts. They are able jurists, but they got on the Supreme Court through personal relationships and politics, the process described in Chapter 1. This is true of many prestigious appointments, including in government, in academia,[43] and on other courts. Most people who hold such appointments are qualified, but not demonstrably more qualified than others. The fact that lots of people envy a job, for example, an

[41] *See, e.g.*, Hyoseok (David) Hwang et al., *The Blind Power: Power-Driven CEO Overconfidence and M&A Decision Making*, 52 N. Am. J. Econ. and Fin. 1 (2020) (finding that increased CEO power increases the probability of a CEO being overconfident).

[42] Jennifer K. Robbennolt & Jean R. Sternlight, *Behavioral Legal Ethics*, 45 Ariz. St. L. J. 1107, 1143 (2013) (providing overview of behavioral ethics and psychology concepts applied to lawyers' ethics) (citing Don A. Moore & Paul J. Healy, *The Trouble with Overconfidence*, 115 Psych. Rev. 502, 502 (2008)); Paul K. Piff et al., *Higher Social Class Predicts Increased Unethical Behavior*, 109 Proc. Nat'l Acad. Sci. 4086, 4088 (2012); Bella L. Galperin et al., *Status Differentiation and the Protean Self: A Social-Cognitive Model of Unethical Behavior in Organizations*, 98 J. Bus. Ethics 407, 416 (2011); Joris Lammers et al., *Power Increases Hypocrisy: Moralizing in Reasoning, Immorality in Behavior*, 21 Psych. Sci. 737, 742 (2010).

[43] Adam Bonica et al., *The Legal Academy's Ideological Uniformity*,47 J. Legal Studies 1, 32 (2017) (finding based on analysis of political donations that 15 percent of law professors, compared to 35 percent of lawyers, are politically conservative).

appointment to the Supreme Court, and many people tried to get it, does not mean that the person who gets it is necessarily more qualified.[44]

But the justices probably don't see it that way. Their sense of superiority has been reinforced by years of high-profile appointments, promotions, and other indicia of professional success.

The badge of superiority worn by today's Supreme Court justices goes back to law school. Four of the justices sitting on the court in 2025 attended Harvard Law School (Chief Justice Roberts and Justices Kagan, Gorsuch, and Jackson) (Justice Kagan also was formerly the Dean of Harvard Law School), and four of the justices attended Yale Law School (Justices Alito, Thomas, Sotomayor, and Kavanaugh). Of these eight Harvard and Yale justices, only one (Justice Thomas, Bachelor of Arts degree, Holy Cross) earned an undergraduate degree outside the Ivy League. The outlier is the ninth and newest justice, Amy Coney Barrett, who is a graduate of another prominent law school, Notre Dame, and of Rhodes College, another highly respected private institution.

None of the justices earned either a law degree or an undergraduate degree at a public university. Over 70 percent of American college students attend public universities.[45]

The educational background of the justices, particularly chief justices, used to be somewhat more diverse. Chief Justice Warren Burger was a graduate of the St. Paul School of Law, a night school in St. Paul, Minnesota, now called the Mitchell-Hamline School of Law, an excellent law school, but not a pretentious school. His predecessor, Chief Justice Earl Warren, was a graduate of the University of California Berkely Law School, a prestigious law school, but a public law school. Warren's predecessor, Chief Justice Fred Vinson, was a graduate of the Centre College Law School in Kentucky, which has since been closed. Some other well-known justices of the mid-twentieth-century court went to highly regarded regional law schools, including Hugo Black (University of Alabama Law School) and Robert Jackson (Albany Law School).

Until the appointment of Justice Thurgood Marshall (Howard University Law School) in 1967, the justices had, since the founding, all been white men. But still, the justices came from more diverse educational backgrounds than today.

[44] *See* Thomas H. Noe & Dawei Fang, *Superstars: Talented or Merely Lucky? The Effect of Competition on Rank-Based Talent Attribution* (July 22, 2021), https://papers.ssrn.com/sol3/papers.cfm?abstract_id=3456646, [https://perma.cc/SU3V-GSFA] (observing that increasing the number of competitors in a competition presumably based on talent does not tend to increase the chance of the winner being more talented than with fewer competitors).

[45] Malanie Hanson, College Enrollment & Student Demographic Statistics, Education Date Initiative, last updated on Jan. 10, 2024, https://educationdata.org/college-enrollment-statistics.

The reasons for the bias today toward ultra-elite credentials in appointment of Supreme Court justices are not entirely clear, but it may have to do with the contentious confirmation process described in Chapter 1. Each side, Democratic and Republican, looks for nominees whose credentials can refute any possible question about their qualifications. Other than Justice Kagan, who was solicitor general of the United States as well as former dean of Harvard Law School, every current justice also was previously a US court of appeals judge. This is yet another characteristic distinguishing this court from the court in an earlier era, when at least some of the justices had previously served as state supreme court judges or held elected office as senators, governors, or in the case of Justice William Howard Taft, president.

Although there is no demonstrable evidence associating an Ivy League law degree or service on the US court of appeals with qualification to serve on the Supreme Court, public opinion may still associate these credentials with professional accomplishment, making these the safest nominees for the Supreme Court.

The immediate question here is whether today's justices have over many years developed the notion that they somehow have better judgment than other people. Their professional success in most instances has been uninterrupted, and for many of the justices their experience on the bench has been remarkably the same.

For whatever reason, some of the justices may "look down" on others in less-prestigious positions, as well as equally prestigious positions without lifetime tenure. Even presidents are accountable to the voters and have term limits. Not so the Supreme Court.

Chief Justice Roberts's refusal to testify before the Senate Judiciary Committee is premised on separation of powers concerns,[46] but this is also intrinsically linked to his status as head of the judicial branch and perhaps his knowledge that he may still be chief justice years from now when some of the senators who want him to testify will no longer be there. Justices' sense of professional superiority is also reinforced over time. After years of having the power to define the Constitution and law, justices may assume that they are inherently better jurists than other people, sufficiently so that they can interpret their own ethics rules.

If the psychology studies associating prestige of position with overconfidence in ethical decision-making are correct, that could be part of the reason the court fails to recognize the seriousness of the ethics violations, discussed in Chapters 2 and 3 of this book.

[46] *See* Roberts' April 25, 2023 letter to Senator Durbin.

Groupthink Prevails in Washington's Most Exclusive Club

It is difficult to imagine a more closely knit club of professionals than the US Supreme Court. The members of this club—only nine with active memberships—may disagree about the law, but they see each other and work together all the time.

And, like most private clubs, there is a "club table" for lunch where members only are seated. Nonmembers, including members of the Supreme Court bar, go to the basement cafeteria. The justices lunch alone in a dining room with oak paneling and a high ceiling. Their food, of course, is brought to them. (Don't expect to see a justice in the downstairs cafeteria line.)[47]

Justice John Paul Stevens once commented that "[t]he lunch break is both a pause in the action and a chance for collegiality," and Justice Sonia Sotomayor said "[i]t's a wonderful experience."[48]

What do they talk about? Apparently not cases, but subjects such as sports, grandchildren, art exhibits, movies, and books. Justice Sotomayor observed, "We try to avoid controversy," and that the justices "are very guarded about raising topics that might create hostility in the room. That does not mean we do not talk about politics, but not in the great depth we might do in the privacy of our homes. . . . We tell funny stories. Someone will tell about an experience with a child or grandchild. There is just the normal type of conversation that people have who want to get to know each other as individuals rather than justices."[49]

This is a bonding experience for an otherwise fractured court. With sharp ideological differences among the justices, it is important for them to socialize together, talk about things other than cases, and avoid personal attacks on each other.

That makes sense. But when justices ignore each other's ethics issues, they take collegiality overboard.

Chief Justice Roberts's main concern about the court appears to be collegiality, perhaps more so than its ethics. In writing for the majority in *Biden v. Nebraska*, he went out of his way to emphasize that disagreement among the justices should not mean disparagement and to remind his colleagues that they should write their opinions accordingly.[50] The justices often ignore

[47] Clare Cushman, *Table for Nine*, 102 Judicature 3 (2018).
[48] *Ibid.*
[49] *Ibid.*
[50] The Chief Justice wrote:

> It has become a disturbing feature of some recent opinions to criticize the decisions with which they disagree as going beyond the proper role of the judiciary. . . . We have employed the traditional tools of judicial decisionmaking in doing so. Reasonable minds may disagree with our analysis—in fact, at least three do (citation omitted). We do not mistake

such instructions and disparage each other's opinions on jurisprudential and ideological grounds, but they try to remain collegial in other ways. They do not extend the acrimony further by criticizing each other's approach to ethics in areas such as personal conflicts of interest, gifts, financial reporting requirements, and recusal.

Also, in matters concerning the court itself, the justices' views are closely aligned. None of the justices, for example, has supported expanding the court, term limits for justices, public dissemination of draft opinions, or even allowing television cameras in the courtroom. (Justices Kagan and Sotomayor were open to cameras in the courtroom before joining the court, but they apparently changed their minds afterward.)[51] Additionally, the 2023 statement signed by all nine justices that was attached to Chief Justice Roberts's letter to Senator Durbin implied that the justices *unanimously* believe that the court does *not* have an ethics problem.[52]

Only in July 2024 did one justice, Elena Kagan, publicly acknowledge that the court lacks an ethics code with an enforcement mechanism. She said that it is difficult to determine who should enforce ethics rules for the justices and how, but that there *should* be an enforcement mechanism.[53] Justice Kagan also said it *might* work to have lower court judges review ethics matters pertaining to the Supreme Court. A small step—by a single justice—in the right direction.

But where are the others? The Supreme Court club, like many social clubs, apparently has a lot of "groupthink."

Psychologist Irving Janis identified groupthink as

> [A] mode of thinking that people engage in when they are deeply involved in a cohesive ingroup, when the members striving for unanimity, override their motivation to realistically appraise alternative courses of action. Groupthink refers to a deterioration of mental efficiency, reality testing, and moral judgment that results from in-group pressures.[54]

> this plainly heartfelt disagreement for disparagement. It is important that the public not be misled either. Any such misperception would be harmful to this institution and the country.

Biden v. Nebraska, 143 S. Ct. 2355, 2375–2376 (2023).

[51] *See Sotomayor, Kagan Backtrack on Cameras in the Supreme Court*, CBS News (Feb. 3, 2015), https://www.cbsnews.com/news/sotomayor-kagan-backtrack-on-cameras-in-the-supreme-court/ [https://perma.cc/ES7Z-BNUJ]; Gavin Broady, *Kagan, Sotomayor Backtrack on Cameras in the Courtroom*, Law360 (Feb. 2, 2015), https://www.law360.com/articles/617541/kagan-sotomayor-backtrack-on-cameras-in-the-courtroom [https://perma.cc/9J8W-FGNA].

[52] *See* Roberts's letter to Durbin, *supra*, attachment (statement of ethics) signed by all nine justices.

[53] Josh Gerstein, Elena *Kagan Calls for Better Enforcement of Supreme Court's Ethics Code. At a Legal Conference in California, the Liberal Justice Suggested That Lower-Court Judges Could Review Alleged Violations*, Politico (July 25, 2024), https://www.politico.com/news/2024/07/25/elena-kagan-supreme-court-ethics-reform-00171317

[54] Irving L. Janis, *Groupthink: Psychological Studies of Policy Decisions and Fiascoes* 9 (2nd ed. 1982).

Social identity is a factor in reinforcing groupthink.[55] Social identity built around being members of the most elite club of jurists in the country—the nine members of the Supreme Court—is a powerful impetus for groupthink.

This groupthink may bring some measure of cohesion on an otherwise badly fractured court and reinforce the collegiality that seems to be an important priority for the chief justice, more important than ethics. But groupthink around lower standards of ethics, or ignoring colleagues' ethics problems, does long-term damage to the reputation of the court.

We do not know whether the justices are willing to discuss ethics seriously with each other. But if they do, it appears that even after consulting with one another, they usually conclude that their fellow club members are doing nothing wrong.

Justices Have Special Friends

Supreme Court justices make a lot of "special friends," and there is temptation on both sides of those relationships. From Justice Abraham Fortas in the 1960s to Justice Clarence Thomas and Justice Samuel Alito today, these special friends are almost invariably wealthy or have close ties to wealthy people. Some of these special friends have created ethical problems for the court.

As discussed in Chapter 1, some of these friendships existed before a justice joined the court. In other instances, justices make new friends, which is probably quite easy given who they are.

The social network that helps justices get on the Supreme Court—the social network described in Chapter 1 of this book—thus continues to interact with them after they join the court. Justice Fortas's colleagues and clients from private practice, including Louis Wolfson, continued their relationship with him after he joined the court. Today, ideological affinity—and the money and organizations behind it—defines justices' social networks.

For example, as discussed in Chapter 1, the Federalist Society, a well-known and well-funded organization of conservative and libertarian lawyers and judges, provides networking opportunities for aspiring judges and plays an ad hoc role in advising the White House and Justice Department on judicial nominations in Republican administrations.[56] They also help with the

[55] *See* Michael A. Hogg, *Social Identity Theory, in* Understanding Peace and Conflict Through Social Identity Theory: Contemporary Global Perspectives 3, 6 (Shelley McKeown, Reeshma Haji & Neil Ferguson eds., Springer Cham 2016).

[56] *See* Jeffrey Toobin, *The Conservative Pipeline to the Supreme Court*, New Yorker (Apr. 10, 2017), https://www.newyorker.com/magazine/2017/04/17/the-conservative-pipeline-to-the-supreme-court [https://perma.cc/PZB8-2VDP].

confirmation battles. Friends during nomination and confirmation remain friends afterward.

Leonard Leo of the Federalist Society reportedly arranged the 2008 fishing trip that Justice Alito took with billionaire Paul Singer two years after he joined the court.[57] (Both Singer and Robin Arkley II, the owner of the lodge where the fishing expedition was hosted, were major donors to Leo's political groups.[58]) The court's more conservative justices often attend the Federalist Society's annual dinner in Washington.[59] Then, as pointed out in Chapter 2, comes the "armada of amici," various organizations submitting amicus briefs to the court.[60] Some amici are funded by people who are friends of justices or by their organizations. Sometime friends of justices and acquaintances of justices, like Paul Singer,[61] are involved with parties in cases before the court.

This is not one sided. As discussed in Chapter 1, liberal justices have their own social networks grounded in progressive organizations, elite universities, and think tanks. These friends also do not go away after they join the court.

Many of justices' "special friends" are wealthy or well connected with wealthy people. Harlan Crow was recently interviewed by the *Dallas Morning News*, and the reporter asked him whether he would be friends with Thomas if he were not a Supreme Court justice. Crow's answer: "It's an interesting, good question. I don't know how to answer that. Maybe not. Maybe yes. I don't know."[62]

The "friendship paradox" has been observed across society—on average, an individual's friends have more friends than that individual.[63] People tend to gravitate toward friendships with people who have a lot of friends—more friends than they do. This may be even more true for Supreme Court justices,

[57] *See* Jake Johnson, *Alito's WSJ Op-Ed Didn'tMmention SCOTUS Takeover Architect Leonard Leo's Key Role in Ethics Scandal*, Salon (June 21, 2023), https://www.salon.com/2023/06/21/alitos-wsj-op-ed-didnt-mention-scotus-takeover-architect-leonard-leos-key-role-in-ethics-scandal_partner/ [https://perma.cc/8VVP-8WT3] ("According to ProPublica, Leo 'invited Singer to join' and asked the hedge fund tycoon 'if he and Alito could fly on the billionaire's jet.'").

[58] *Ibid.*

[59] *See* Mark Sherman, *Justices Cheered at Conservative Group's Anniversary Dinner*, Assoc. Press (Nov. 11, 2022), https://apnews.com/article/abortion-voting-rights-us-supreme-court-samuel-alito-donald-trump-f0926d7b4a8bbaf7b698ada1a791ab25 [https://perma.cc/BDP3-EYQE] ("Four of the five Supreme Court justices who overturned the constitutional right to abortion showed up at the conservative Federalist Society's black-tie dinner marking its 40th anniversary.").

[60] *See* Senator Whitehouse's (D-RI) article, discussed in Chapter 2, *supra*, (describing the "armada of amici" flooding the court).

[61] *See* Chapter 2 (detailing Justice Alito's fishing trips with Singer).

[62] Cheryl Hall, *Harlan Crow: There's Nothing Wrong with My Friendship with Clarence Thomas*, Dallas Morning News (Apr. 17, 2023), https://www.dallasnews.com/news/2023/04/17/harlan-crow-theres-nothing-wrong-with-my-friendship-with-clarence-thomas/ [https://perma.cc/7HM6-2A38]. Scott L. Feld, *Why Your Friends Have More Friends than You Do*, 96 Am. J. Socio. 1464, 1477 (1991).

[63] Scott L. Feld, *Why Your Friends Have More Friends than You Do*, 96 Am. J. Socio. 1464, 1477 (1991).

who are on the court in part because they effectively cultivated a network of friends who, in turn, could enlist other friends to advance the justices' careers. Some of these friends, including lawyers or parties appearing before the court, may seek advantage from the friendship.

Friendship also has a powerful emotional pull that has been shown to change political opinions,[64] and friendship probably impacts judgment about ethics as well. Friends aren't likely to believe that friends do anything wrong. When a justice's ethics are called into question, people who think of themselves as friends with the justice can be depended upon to rush to his defense.

On top of these natural emotional ties of friendship are the obvious material benefits that ensue when justices have friendships with the very wealthy. Saying "no" to a trip on a private plane or yacht of a friend is difficult. Even if the owner of the plane or yacht is not a friend of the justice, if the person who arranged the trip is, that's probably enough.

A justice may not believe a friend is misusing the relationship. Friendship thus becomes its own value, perhaps even a moral principle, blinding the justices to the bias that friendship creates and rendering them incapable of complying with ethics rules or holding each other to account for doing the same.

Closing this loop of friendship are the friendships that justices have with each other, meaning they are not likely to hold each other to account for doing anything wrong.

Friends all too often let friends ignore the law. Lawyers who are close friends with directors and officers of corporate clients usually are not effective gatekeepers.[65] The author of this book—a frequent critic of high-ranking officials working for multiple presidents—more than once has been told that he should not publicly criticize the ethics of a friend holding high political office, or even the ethics of a friend of a friend. Others have surely experienced this as well. That includes Supreme Court justices. As close friends with their colleagues on the court, justices are not likely to be good ethics gatekeepers for the court.

[64] A survey of French university students' political opinions demonstrated that after six months, friendship caused a reduction of differences in opinions by one-quarter of the mean difference; friendship caused politically similar students to join political associations together, reinforcing political similarity. Yann Algan et al., *Friendship Networks and Political Opinions: A Natural Experiment Among Future French Politicians*, SSRN (May 31, 2019), https://ssrn.com/abstract=3397092 [https://perma.cc/MZ3B-L28H].

[65] Lawyers who see themselves as friends for managers of institutional clients are not likely be effective gatekeepers. *See* Sung Hui Kim, *Inside Lawyers: Friends or Gatekeepers?*, 84 Fordham L. Rev. 1867, 1895 (2016). The same is likely true for Supreme Court justices.

The Supreme Court Is Exceptional

The justices have the power to interpret the law, and this includes the power to overturn statutes passed by Congress if they are unconstitutional.[66] Short of amending the Constitution, the justices' rulings cannot be reversed by anyone but themselves.

But does this mean the justices get to decide their own ethics rules and when they will be enforced? For the justices to assert "ethical exceptionalism" under Article III of the Constitution would be analogous to presidents asserting their power under Article II to redefine laws and carve out exceptions for themselves. But the court largely has allowed presidents to do just that.[67] In 2024, the Supreme Court, in *Trump v. United States*, bestowed on the president sweeping immunity from criminal prosecution for official acts. It is not surprising that the justices would use some of their power in interpreting the law to carve out exceptions for themselves as well. This topic is explored in more depth in Chapter 5.

This exceptionalism is most problematic when justices exempt themselves from ethics laws and regulations that apply to other judges. The interpretive guidance of the Judicial Conference of the United States is not binding on the justices, and neither is the enforcement mechanism that applies to lower court justices. If the justices don't believe a free yacht excursion, private plane ride, or stay in a luxury resort needs to be disclosed on a financial disclosure form, and that they also don't need to disclose a mostly forgiven loan from a "friend" for a recreational vehicle worth over a quarter of a million dollars, there is nobody to tell them otherwise.

Indeed, some of the justices firmly believe that Congress lacks the power to pass *any* laws that govern the conduct of the justices of the court. Justice Alito recently told the Wall Street Journal: "I know this is a controversial view, but I'm willing to say it. No provision in the Constitution gives them the authority to regulate the Supreme Court—period."[68] This constitutional separation of powers question is discussed more thoroughly in Chapter 5 of this book, but the ramifications of Justice Alito's comment are frightening. Chapter 5 also explores the even more dangerous flip side of Alito's argument: a president

[66] *See Marbury v. Madison*, 5 U.S. 137 (1803) (establishing the principle of judicial review).

[67] Professor Claire Finkelstein and this author have examined the intersection of criminal law with assertions of presidential privilege and power. *See, e.g.*, Claire O. Finkelstein & Richard W. Painter, *"You're Fired": Criminal Use of Presidential Removal Power*, 25 N.Y.U. J. Legis. & Pub. Pol'y 307 (2023); *Presidential Accountability and the Rule of Law: Can the President Claim Immunity if He Shoots Someone on Fifth Avenue?*, 24 U. Pa. J. Const. L. 93 (2022).

[68] David B. Rivkin Jr. & James Taranto, *Samuel Alito, the Supreme Court's Plain-Spoken Defender*, Wall St. J. (July 28, 2023).

who says, "No provision in the Constitution gives them [the Supreme Court or Congress] the authority to regulate the president—period."

The court's professed admonition, repeated in *Trump v. Vance*,[69] but hollowed out significantly four years later in *Trump v. United States*,[70] is that no person is above the law.[71] This should apply equally to the justices themselves. It doesn't. Exceptionalism says justices are above the law, that they can do what they want, and that there is nothing anybody can do about it.

Defending the Court Transcends Ideological Division

The nine justices agree on one thing: protecting the court's independence as an institution. All nine justices apparently supported Chief Justice Roberts's refusal of Senator Durbin's invitation to testify before the Judiciary Committee, and all nine signed the statement affirming that the justices were complying with ethics rules.

This resistance to oversight fits a pattern where all three branches of government guard their power and privilege against encroachment by the other two. Presidents, regardless of party, often defend each other's executive privilege; the Biden administration, for example, defended privileged communications of the Trump administration from discovery by Democrats in Congress.[72] Prosecuting a former president also is a rarity, never done until Donald Trump was indicted by a special prosecutor in June 2023.[73] Congress also jealously guards its evidentiary privileges under the Speech and Debate Clause

[69] *Trump v. Vance*, 140 S. Ct. 2412, 2431 (2020) (upholding a state grand jury subpoena of a president's personal financial records).

[70] *Trump v. United States*, 603 U.S. 593 (2024) (holding the president presumptively immune from criminal prosecution for official acts)

[71] *Trump v. Vance* at 2432 (Kavanaugh, J., concurring) ("In our system of government, as this Court has often stated, no one is above the law.").

[72] Up through 2023, the Biden administration continued the Trump administration's opposition to requests from Congress for General Services Administration documents concerning a lease with the Trump Hotel. *See* Nina Totenberg, *Supreme Court Will Hear a Subpoena Case That—Surprise—Trump and Biden Agree On*, NPR (May 15, 2023), https://www.npr.org/2023/05/15/1163241734/supreme-court-subpoena-case-congress-trump-biden [https://perma.cc/WYC6-4BCW]. 5 U.S.C. § 2954 allows individual members of Congress to request information from executive branch agencies without a formal subpoena. The Court of Appeals for the District of Columbia Circuit ruled that members of Congress have standing under Article III to enforce this right to information. *Maloney v. Murphy*, 984 F.3d 50, 54 (D.C. Cir. 2020). The Biden administration disagreed and sought review by the Supreme Court. After the Supreme Court agreed to hear the case, House Democrats dropped the lawsuit in June 2023. *Carnahan v. Maloney*, 143 S. Ct. 2653 (2023), vacated and remanded for dismissal.

[73] This is also a reason why, absent special counsel, it may be difficult to get the Justice Department to prosecute any former president. *See* Claire O. Finkelstein & Richard W. Painter, *Restoring the Rule of Law through Department of Justice Reform, in* Overcoming Trumpery: How to Restore Ethics, the Rule of Law, and Democracy (Norman Eisen ed., Brookings Institution 2022) (discussing reluctance of the Justice Department, even under a different political party, to investigate or prosecute officials from a previous administration).

of the Constitution[74]—for example, successfully suing to enjoin a warrant for an FBI search of a congressman's office.[75]

The justices of the Supreme Court, regardless of their sharp disagreements on cases before them, will join to defend the court from encroachment by the president or Congress.

But there needs to be checks and balances. An unaccountable Supreme Court is as dangerous to democracy as an unaccountable president or Congress that does anything it wants. As discussed in Chapters 6 and 7 of this book, Congress passing ethics laws that apply to the Supreme Court (including installing an IG, as this book will later suggest), and Congress asking the chief justice to testify about Supreme Court ethics are both reasonable oversight measures. Such oversight is not fairly compared with more extreme and constitutionally problematic measures such as Congress subpoenaing drafts of Supreme Court opinions or requiring justices to testify under oath to explain their opinions. The court's resistance to excessive oversight of the judicial branch is understandable, but resistance to any oversight at all is not reasonable; furthermore, such resistance is inconsistent with the court's own rulings subjecting the legislative and executive branches to measured oversight by the courts, one of three coequal branches of government.[76] The Supreme Court cannot be the only part of the federal government that is not accountable to anyone.

Chapter 5 of this book explores the outer limits of constitutionally permissible congressional oversight of the Supreme Court. But the constitutional views of this author, and the views of experts on constitutional law, such as Laurence Tribe and Michael Dorf,[77] may not be of concern to this court. The constitutionality of applying any ethics law, or any other law, to the justices of the court is a question about which the justices themselves, despite their obvious conflict of interest,[78] may decide.

[74] The Speech or Debate Clause, U.S. Const. art. I, § 6, cl. 1, protects Members of Congress from being questioned about their deliberations in Congress. There is no similar clause in the Constitution creating an express evidentiary privilege for either the president or for the Supreme Court.

[75] *See* United States v. Rayburn House Office Bldg., Room 2113, Wash., D.C. 20515, 497 F.3d 654, 656 (D.C. Cir. 2007).

[76] *See, e.g.*, *Marbury v. Madison*, 5 U.S. 137 (1803) (establishing the principle of judicial review); *Youngstown Sheet & Tube Co. v. Sawyer*, 343 U.S. 579 (1952) (enjoining President Truman's executive order seizing privately owned steel mills during a wartime strike); *United States v. Nixon*, 418 U.S. 683 (1974) (ordering the president to comply with a subpoena from the Department of Justice special prosecutor for White House tapes).

[77] *See, e.g.*, Laurence H. Tribe, *How the US Supreme Court Shredded The Constitution and What Can Be Done to Repair It*, The Guardian (July 8, 2024), https://www.theguardian.com/commentisfree/article/2024/jul/08/us-supreme-court-presidential-immunity; Michael Dorf, *Justice Alito Is Wrong: Congress Can and Does Regulate the Supreme Court*, Verdict (Aug. 16, 2023). https://verdict.justia.com/2023/08/16/justice-alito-is-wrong-congress-can-and-does-regulate-the-supreme-court.

[78] Arguably, Supreme Court justices ruling on the constitutionality of a statute passed by Congress to regulate Supreme Court ethics might violate an existing statute, 28 U.S.C. § 455, requiring a judge or justice

It's Secret

Justice Louis Brandeis, writing about Wall Street and the titans of finance before he joined the court, said, "Publicity is justly commended as a remedy for social and industrial diseases. Sunlight is said to be the best of disinfectants; electric light the most efficient policeman."[79] The same is true for the Supreme Court.

But there is little transparency at the court. If a justice decides not to recuse from a case, we rarely hear the reasons why. (As discussed in Chapter 3, an exception was Justice Scalia's explanation in 2004 of why he would not recuse from a case after he went duck hunting with Vice President Cheney, a named party in the case.) If a justice interprets ethics rules to allow acceptance of a gift, including free travel on a yacht or plane, or failure to disclose that gift, we do not learn the reasons why until years later, if at all. As discussed in Chapter 2, Justice Alito explained in an op-ed in the *Wall Street Journal* his reasons for accepting without disclosing an all-expenses-paid fishing trip after it was discovered over a decade later.

There are good reasons for confidentiality rules in the court, if those rules are designed to protect the justices' deliberations about cases. In 1998, this author strongly criticized the publication of a former Supreme Court clerk's book that quoted from leaked emails, drafts, and other materials improperly obtained from the court.[80] Chief Justice Roberts was rightly concerned about the leak of the *Dobbs* opinion in 2022,[81] although the investigation he ordered has not yet revealed who did it. These confidentiality concerns, however, pertain to deliberations about cases before the court. The argument for confidentiality is less persuasive when the subject involves conflicts of interest and other ethical issues for the justices themselves.

The financial disclosure rules of the Ethics in Government Act have bound the justices since 1978,[82] casting some light on justices' affairs, but these rules are ineffective if they are not enforced. Presently, there is nobody to make sure they are enforced. Also, the financial disclosure rules are incomplete.

to recuse in a case in which their impartiality might reasonably be questioned. However, given that the court has asserted the power to overturn acts of Congress, the court might still use that power to protect itself if the justices truly believed a statute regulating the court to be unconstitutional.

[79] Louis D. Brandeis, *Other People's Money and How the Bankers Use It* 92 (1914).

[80] *See generally* Richard W. Painter, *Open Chambers?*, 97 Mich. L. Rev. 1430, 1430–1471 (1999) (reviewing Edward Lazarus, *Closed Chambers* (1998)).

[81] *See* Painter, *SCOTUS Draft Opinion Leak Is a Breach of Legal Ethics*, Bloomberg News (May 6, 2022, 4:00 a.m.), https://news.bloomberglaw.com/us-law-week/scotus-draft-opinion-leak-is-a-breach-of-legal-ethics [https://perma.cc/DR8U-XNGK].

[82] The Ethics in Government Act of 1978 requires filing of financial disclosure reports by all federal judges, including justices of the Supreme Court. *See* 5 U.S.C. § 13103.

There is too little transparency, for example, about sources of spousal income. Who are Virginia Thomas's clients?[83] Which law firms paid Jane Roberts a headhunter's fee for placing new lawyers? Who bought the property Justice Gorsuch partially owned in Colorado, and why? (We only learned this information from the property records, not from Justice Gorsuch's financial disclosure form.)

Most importantly, however, there is no public report on allegations of ethics breaches on the court. In an executive branch agency, allegations of wrongdoing are forwarded to an IG, who investigates, writes a report, and upon request submits it to Congress. The Supreme Court does not have that. One might argue that Supreme Court justices are not the same as executive branch agencies because they, like the president, head an entire branch of government. But that means they have more power, and that is perhaps a reason for more accountability and transparency, not less.

The Chief Knows Nothing

Sargent Schultz, the iconic bungling World War II German POW camp guard on the 1970s TV show *Hogan's Heroes*, repeatedly summed up a very familiar stance toward other people breaking the rules: "I see nothing, know nothing."[84]

See no evil, hear no evil.

The justices, including the chief justice, do not know everything the other justices are doing. Some information is shared with other justices and some is not. And there is some information—particularly concerning each other's ethical lapses—that the justices may not want to know.

The chief justice is supposed to oversee the administrative aspects of the court, but ensuring that other justices comply with ethics rules apparently is not among his duties.[85] He does not review their financial disclosure reports, and he apparently does not interfere with their decisions about whether to

[83] *See* Brian Schwartz, *Inside the Consulting Firm Run by Ginni Thomas, Wife of Supreme Court Justice Clarence Thomas*, CNBC (Apr. 5, 2022, 6:43 p.m.), https://www.cnbc.com/2022/04/05/inside-the-consulting-firm-run-by-ginni-thomas-wife-of-supreme-court-justice-clarence-thomas.html [https://perma.cc/7489-7VKR] ("Very little is known about her company, Liberty Consulting, which is listed as an asset on her husband's Supreme Court disclosures.").

[84] Des Hammond, *The Very Best of Sergeant Schultz*, YouTube (Mar. 20, 2017), https://www.youtube.com/watch?v=OsXrpxo4uC0 [https://perma.cc/JQ3L-QPCM].

[85] *See The Chief Justice of the United States: Responsibilities of the Office and Process*, EveryCRSReport (Sept. 23, 2005), https://www.everycrsreport.com/reports/RL32821.html [https://perma.cc/NZP8-BE3U]. This report, prepared at the time Chief Justice Roberts was nominated by President Bush and confirmed by the Senate, described specific duties of the chief justice, but noticeably absent is a suggestion that the chief justice is responsible for ensuring that other justices comply with standards of judicial ethics.

recuse themselves from a case. Perhaps the chief justice is doing more about Supreme Court ethics behind the scenes, but we do not know because what the justices say to each other is not disclosed.

Chief Justice Roberts joined all the justices in signing a statement about ethics attached to his 2023 letter to Senator Durbin. The statement was written before public disclosure of Justice Alito's fishing trip with Paul Singer and said nothing about it. Presumably, Roberts would have found out about Alito's fishing trip if he had asked his colleagues about any free travel they had accepted. Indeed, that was an obvious question Roberts could have asked his colleagues after the news stories about Justice Thomas and Harlan Crow. But Roberts apparently did not ask; he and his colleagues just signed the statement saying they were complying with ethics rules. Attached to that memo is Roberts's own letter to Senator Durbin declining the invitation to testify. What Roberts knew about these ethics lapses on the court before they became public is one more thing the public will probably never know.

Impeachment Isn't Happening

This problem is explored in more detail in Chapter 8 of this book. Suffice it to say here that threat of impeachment of a justice for corruption won't work. It may have worked in persuading Justice Fortas to resign in 1969, but in today's political climate, Congress is almost certain not to even begin the process of removing a justice.

After one Clinton impeachment[86] and two Trump impeachments[87] ended in acquittal in the Senate, we see how difficult it is to impeach, much less convict, a holder of high office. If a president cannot be convicted for trying to overturn an election to stay in power and for encouraging a lawless mob to go to the Capitol,[88] it is hard to imagine any offense that would lead to the conviction of a Supreme Court justice.

[86] *See* Articles of Impeachment Against William Jefferson Clinton, H.R. Res. 611, 105th Cong. (1998); 144 Cong. Rec. 28110-28111 (1998) (House resolutions to impeach President Clinton for obstruction of justice and false testimony under oath). The Senate acquitted Clinton. *See* 145 Cong. Rec. 274 (1999) (1999 trial of Clinton in the Senate).

[87] *See* H.R. Res. 755, 116th Cong. (2019) (enacted) (impeaching Donald John Trump, president of the United States, for high crimes and misdemeanors, namely abuse of power and obstruction of Congress, Dec. 18, 2019). On February 5, 2020, the Senate adjudged that Trump was not guilty as charged in the articles of impeachment. 166 Cong. Rec. S871 (2020). H.R. Res. 24, 117th Cong. (2021) (enacted) (impeaching Donald John Trump, president of the United States for high crimes and misdemeanors, namely incitement of insurrection); *see generally* 167 Cong. Rec. S589-S717 (2021) (trial and acquittal in the Senate, Feb. 9 to Feb. 13, 2021).

[88] *See* H.R. Rep. No. 117-663 (2022).

Only one justice, Samuel Chase, was impeached by the House, in 1804, on allegations he allowed partisanship to affect his decisions on the court, and he was acquitted by the Senate.[89] Today, with all the partisanship in the Senate surrounding confirmations to the Supreme Court, it is highly unlikely that the removal of a justice—which requires two-thirds of the Senate—would be any different. If thirty-four or more senators belong to the political party of the president who nominated a justice to the court, acquittal is all but certain.

Justice Fortas, who resigned to protect the reputation of the court, resumed the practice of law in Washington and died in 1982.[90] He did not live to see the day when a justice in an ethical quandary worse than his own would have the full support of the political party of the president who appointed him. Perhaps Justice Fortas, if he had known what the future held for the court, would have pushed back on the accusations against him and insisted that without the votes of sixty-seven senators against him he was not going anywhere.

[89] *See* Richard B. Lillich, *The Chase Impeachment*, 4 Am.J. of Legal Hist. 49 (1960); William H. Rehnquist, *Grand Inquests: The Historic Impeachments Of Justice Samuel Chase And President Andrew Johnson* (1992); *see generally Trial Of Samuel Chase, An Associate Justice Of The Supreme Court Of The United States* (1805).

[90] Linda Greenhouse, *Ex-Justice Abe Fortas Dies at 71. Shaped Historic Rulings on Rights*, N.Y. Times (Apr. 7, 1982), https://www.nytimes.com/1982/04/07/obituaries/ex-justice-abe-fortas-dies-at-71-shaped-historic-rulings-on-rights.html.

5
Are the Justices Absolutely Immune and Other Separation of Powers Questions

The Supreme Court vigorously defends its independence from the other two branches of government. This was highlighted in Chief Justice Roberts's 2023 letter to Senator Richard Durbin (D-IL) declining Durbin's invitation to testify before the Senate Judiciary Committee about alleged Supreme Court ethics breaches, explaining that "[t]estimony before the Senate Judiciary Committee by the Chief Justice of the United States is exceedingly rare, as one might expect in light of separation of powers concerns and the importance of preserving judicial independence."[1]

A broader problem is that some of the justices may think Congress can't impose ethics rules on the court. As Chief Justice Roberts noted in his 2011 year-end report, "As in the case of financial reporting and gift requirements, the limits of Congress's power to require recusal have never been tested."[2]

The question addressed in this chapter is whether Congress has the power to regulate the ethics of the court.

Federal judges and justices are not entirely beyond the control of the other two branches of government. They are not immune from criminal prosecution by the Department of Justice, and federal judges have been criminally charged while in office. US Court of Appeals Judge Otto Kerner, former governor of Illinois, did not resign from his judicial office until July 22, 1974—after he had lost his final appeal of his criminal conviction for corruption, and seven days before he went to prison.[3] Congress also can impeach and remove judges and justices.

Congress regulates the court by establishing the number of justices, which was set at six in the Judiciary Act of 1789 and most recently at nine in the

[1] Letter dated April 25, 2023, from Chief Justice Roberts to Senator Durbin.
[2] Chief Justice Roberts, 2011 Year-End Report at 7.
[3] Seth S. King, *Otto Kerner Goes to Jail Today His Once Shining Career at End*, N.Y. Times (July 29, 1974).

Conduct Unbecoming. Richard W. Painter, Oxford University Press. © Oxford University Press (2026).
DOI: 10.1093/9780197832301.003.0006

Judiciary Act of 1869.[4] Congress could increase the number of justices by passing a law providing for a larger court,[5] and Congress also could decrease the size of the court by attrition with a statute providing that retiring justices would not be replaced until the court reached a reduced size. Congress has the power to determine the court's appellate jurisdiction but not its original jurisdiction, or power to hear a case for the first time, which is established in the Constitution and cannot be changed.[6] Congress also sets the justices pay and allocates a budget for the court. In 1929, Congress voted to allocate funds to build the building for the Supreme Court. Before that, the court heard cases in the Old Senate Chamber inside the US Capitol building from 1860 until 1935. The court was a separate branch of government but was then located in the same building as Congress.

As explained further in this chapter, the argument for congressional power to regulate the ethics of the court is strongest in areas that regulate personal conduct of the justices, such as financial disclosure rules, gift rules, and restrictions on outside income. The extent of congressional power is more complicated in areas that impact procedural aspects of adjudication by the court, such as statutory requirements for recusal of a justice. Overly broad recusal rules enacted by Congress would be problematic, but as discussed below, the existing statutory recusal requirement is consistent with common law principles of impartiality and should be applied to the court.

Whether a statute passed by Congress is constitutional is a matter ultimately for the court to decide. In this instance, though, the justices would

[4] The Judiciary Act of 1789, ch. 20, § 1, 1 Stat. 73 (1789) set the number of justices at six, with four being a quorum. The Judiciary Act of 1801, ch. 4, § 3, 2 Stat. 89 (1801), reduced the number of justices to five, a provision the lame duck Federalist controlled Congress passed to keep President Jefferson from appointing a justice, a statute repealed the next year. The Judiciary Act of 1802, 31, § 1, 2 Stat. 156 (1802), confirmed that the total number of justices was six. The number of justices was raised to seven in the Seventh Circuit Act of 1807, ch. 16, § 5, 2 Stat. 420 (1807) (creating the Seventh Circuit in new western states and requiring that the new justice reside in the new circuit, a provision later repealed). The number was again raised by two additional justices in the Eighth and Ninth Circuits Act of 1837 is ch. 34, 5 Stat. 176 (1837). With the creation of the Tenth Circuit the number of justices was increased to ten in 1863 in the Tenth Circuit Act, ch. 100, § 1, 12 Stat. 794 (1863). The Judicial Circuits Act of 1866, ch. 210, 14 Stat. 209 (1866), reduced the number of justices from ten to seven, a statute Congress passed to prevent President Andrew Johnson from appointing new justices. When President Ulysses S. Grant took office, the Judiciary Act of 1869, ch. 22, 16 Stat. 44 (1869) set the number at nine justices, where it remains today.

[5] If Congress were to return to its pre-1869 approach there would be one justice for each court of appeals. Counting only the eleven regional circuits this would mean eleven justices, and counting also the District of Colombia Circuit and the Federal Circuit, this would mean a Supreme Court of thirteen.

[6] In *Marbury v. Madison*, 5 U.S. (1 Cranch) 137 (1803), the court held that Section 13 of the Judiciary Act of 1789, granting the court the power to issue writs of mandamus to government officials, was unconstitutional in cases the court heard for the first time, because Article III, Section 2 of the Constitution enumerates the types of cases where the court has original jurisdiction, and Congress cannot add additional cases to its original jurisdiction. By contrast, the Constitution specifically provides that "...the supreme Court shall have appellate Jurisdiction, both as to Law and Fact, with such Exceptions, and under such Regulations as the Congress shall make." U.S. Const., Art. III, Sec. 2, Cl. 2.

have a conflict of interest were they to strike down a statute imposing ethics rules on the court. As discussed later in this chapter, the court doing so could precipitate a constitutional crisis in which other branches of the federal government, and perhaps the states, ignore the court's rulings in other cases. The court, to preserve its position in the constitutional checks and balances of our government, should agree to follow the reasonable ethics rules enacted by Congress as well as the rules that other federal judges impose on themselves in the Code of Conduct for United States Judges.

Gifts, Financial Disclosure, Outside Income and other Personal Conduct

Congress has the power to impose, within reason, rules for personal conduct of justices, as it does for the officers of the executive branch. The Ethics in Government Act of 1978 requires the financial disclosure forms filed annually by the justices as well as by senior executive branch officials and members of Congress.[7] Congress also has the power to restrict gifts to federal officials, including judges, and as explained in Chapter 2, Congress had done so. A gift given in connection with a justice's vote in a case, of course, would violate the criminal statute on bribes and gratuities.[8] No Supreme Court justice would openly assert the power to take bribes, so the suggestion that Congress cannot regulate the personal conduct of justices is simply not correct. As Professor Amanda Frost told the US Senate Judiciary Committee in 2023, "The Justices' claim to be above the laws that govern all federal judges, as well as officials in the other two branches of the federal government, has no basis in constitutional text or history."[9]

Congress could conceivably go too far in regulating the personal conduct of justices—for example, a statute banning justices from participating in programs sponsored by the American Bar Association, the American Law Institute, law schools, or other organizations. It also would probably be excessive for Congress to ban justices from participating in programs of more ideologically oriented organizations such as the American Constitution Society, the American Civil Liberties Union, and the Federalist Society. At some

[7] The Ethics in Government Act of 1978 requires filing of financial disclosure reports. See 5 U.S.C. § 13103, formerly 5a U.S.C. § 101.

[8] 18 U.S.C. § 201 (prohibiting bribery).

[9] *See* Testimony of Amanda Frost Before S. Comm. On Judiciary, titled Supreme Court Ethics Reform (May 2, 2023); Amanda Frost, *Judicial Ethics and Supreme Court Exceptionalism*, 26 Geo. J. Legal Ethics 443 (2013) (concluding that Congress has broad constitutional authority to regulate the Justices' ethical conduct, although Congress's power to regulate justices' ethics is constrained by separation of powers principles, and the need to preserve judicial independence).

point, statutory prohibitions could violate the justices' freedom of association. Even matters such as membership in discriminatory social clubs and other organizations are best dealt with by judges and justices setting their own rules, as they have done,[10] rather than with a mandate from Congress.

This does not mean that justices should associate frequently with outside organizations, only that Congress probably cannot regulate this area of judicial conduct without getting into a conflict with the court over freedom of association. Repeated interaction with more ideologically oriented organizations, such as the Federalist Society and American Constitution Society, can create the appearance of bias, particularly if justices form close relationships with members of the Supreme Court bar, are exposed to thinly veiled *ex parte* communications about legal issues before the court, or are lured into making their own public statements about issues before the court. Restrictions on *ex parte* communications with justices by lawyers and parties about cases presently before the court are, of course, reasonable, and are presently imposed by the Code of Conduct for United States Judges.[11] Congress can insist that Supreme Court justices comply with those rules. Furthermore, risks of appearance of *ex parte* influence would be minimized if the justices limit their exposure to such organizations, particularly repeated interactions with the same ones.

Statutory restrictions on partisan political activity of justices, such as political fundraising or serving as a manager of a political campaign or an officer in a political party, are within reason. As discussed in Chapter 3, such restrictions are presently embodied in the Code of Conduct for United States Judges. If these rules were not complied with in the judiciary, Congress could impose similar restrictions on judges and justices, as Congress has already done in the Hatch Act,[12] restricting political activity of all employees of the executive branch except the president and the vice president. If Congress can tell executive branch officials that certain political activity is impermissible, Congress presumably can do the same for the federal judiciary.

For Congress to restrict the public statements of judges or justices, except statements about candidates in partisan elections, would in most instances probably be unconstitutional. A Supreme Court justice has a right to speak out on an issue of public concern. In 2002, the court on First Amendment

[10] Code of Conduct for United States Judges, Canon 2C ("A judge should not hold membership in any organization that practices invidious discrimination on the basis of race, sex, religion, or national origin.")

[11] *Ibid.*, Canon 3(A)(4) ("a judge should not initiate, permit, or consider ex parte communications or consider other communications concerning a pending or impending matter that are made outside the presence of the parties or their lawyers.")

[12] *See* 5 U.S. Code § 7323—Political activity authorized; prohibitions (applicable to employees of the executive branch).

grounds struck down a state law prohibiting candidates for elected judicial office from announcing their views on disputed legal and political issues,[13] and presumably the justices would claim a similar free speech right for themselves. However, a justice's public statements in some instances might create serious doubts about impartiality, requiring the justice to recuse from a case, an issue discussed below. The point here is that Congress regulating what justices say, like regulating the persons they associate with, would probably lead to a constitutional conflict with the court.

Recusal

Recusal is a difficult topic for several reasons, including the subjective tests that are often applied to assess whether a judge or justice can be impartial in a case. Bright-line rules—for example, requiring recusal from a case in which the judge or justice has a financial interest—are easier to apply. The merits of recusal rules are discussed in other chapters of this book. The issue here is whether Congress can constitutionally impose them.

Whether the recusal statute, 28 U.S.C. § 455, is constitutional as applied to the Supreme Court is a legitimate subject for debate. Congress, in this instance, is telling justices which cases they may and may not participate in, a statutory mandate that could go too far, although as explained below the present statute does not go too far.

One view is that Congress can never tell Supreme Court justices when they can vote on a case because of a conflict of interest. This view holds that Congress cannot by statute, including a conflict-of-interest statute, reduce the constitutional powers of federal officers heading any branch of government by prohibiting their participation in certain matters. This view would parallel the opinion of the Department of Justice Office of Legal Counsel that the federal financial conflict of interest statute for executive branch employees, 18 U.S.C. § 208, cannot constitutionally be applied to the president and vice president because it would interfere with enumerated powers.[14] Congress has exempted the president and vice president from that statute, and while most presidents

[13] *Republican Party of Minnesota v. White*, 536 U.S. 765 (2002).

[14] *See* Memorandum for Richard T. Burress, Office of the President, from Laurence H. Silberman, deputy attorney general, Conflict of Interest Problems Arising Out of the President's Nomination of Nelson A. Rockefeller to the Vice President Under the Twenty-Fifth Amendment to the Constitution (Aug. 28, 1974) (opining that the federal financial conflict of interest statute could not constitutionally be applied to the president and vice president).

voluntarily avoided financial conflicts of interest, President Trump has not.[15] Financial conflicts of interest that under the statute would be criminal for a cabinet officer, or for any other federal officer or employee, are legally permissible for the president. By similar reasoning, 28 U.S.C. § 455,[16] which requires recusal in the judicial branch from cases on account of a financial interest, would be unconstitutional if applied to a justice of the Supreme Court, even though the statute specifically states that it applies to any "federal judge or justice."

This reasoning with respect to both the president and the Supreme Court is probably wrong. This author has already argued that the federal financial conflict of interest statute for executive branch employees should be applied to the president and vice president.[17] The statute would not constrict performance of presidential duties because in almost all instances the financial asset creating a conflict of interest can be sold. For example, this author has suggested that Congress should prohibit the president from making substantial personal investments in cryptocurrency while at the same time overseeing federal regulation of cryptocurrency.[18] Congress has not enacted such a law prohibiting presidential conflicts of interest, but it probably would be within the power of Congress to do so.[19]

Similarly, 28 U.S.C. § 455, which prohibits judges and justices from participating in a case in which they have a financial interest, is likely constitutional. The judge or justice can dispose of the asset that creates the conflict to participate in the case. Or the judge or justice can recuse. The justices already acknowledge that they are supposed to do that to comply with the statute. As discussed in Chapter 2, in some instances justices have failed to recuse when they should, but thus far the justices have not claimed that this part of the recusal statute does not apply to them. Another bright-line area is the statutory requirement that a judge or justice recuse when a close relative is a party or a lawyer in a case. Here also Congress can constitutionally impose a requirement to recuse.

[15] See Richard W. Painter, *Trump's Business "Separation" Plan Does Nothing of the Kind*, N.Y. Times (Jan. 12, 2017).

[16] 28 U.S.C § 455—Disqualification of justice, judge, or magistrate judge.

[17] See Painter, *Getting the Government American Deserves: How Ethics Reform Can Make a Difference* (2009), Chapter 2.

[18] See Testimony of Richard W. Painter before the United States Senate Committee on Banking Hearing on July 9, 2025, titled "From Wall Street to Web3: Building Tomorrow's Digital Asset Markets" (discussing cryptocurrency conflicts of interest of President Trump and some members of Congress), https://www.banking.senate.gov/imo/media/doc/painter_testimony_7-9-25.pdf.

[19] But see Judge Silberman's 1974 OLC memo expressing the view that Congress cannot do so.

Apart from these bright lines in the recusal statute, the more subjective criteria in the statute could raise constitutional questions if interpreted and applied too broadly to the Supreme Court. The justices address this problem by allowing each justice to decide when to recuse from a case, a system that, as discussed in Chapters 2 and 3, has not worked well. An alternative approach would be for the entire court to determine application of the recusal statute to a justice, although that approach also has its complications. Finally, as suggested in the Chapter 6 of this book, a Supreme Court inspector general could report to Congress instances in which a justice did not recuse but in the view of the inspector general should have recused. 28 U.S.C. § 455 is not a criminal statute, and there has not been a case in which its application to a Supreme Court justice has been an issue before the court.

And at some point, a statute like this one could be unconstitutional if it were amended to impose unreasonable recusal requirements on the Supreme Court. For example, Congress probably could not constitutionally require justices to recuse from all cases involving the president who appointed them. The statute also probably could not constitutionally provide that a justice must recuse from any case argued by a member of the Supreme Court bar who supported the justice's nomination or confirmation. However, requiring a justice to recuse from cases involving individuals and organizations that spent large sums of money on the nomination and confirmation process would be within reason. Indeed, the Supreme Court has ruled that under the Due Process Clause of the Fourteenth Amendment, elected state supreme court justices must recuse from cases in which a party contributed substantially to their campaign.[20] It would be ironic if Supreme Court justices were to say that the same due process concern does not apply in cases before the court.

The better view on applying the recusal statute to the Supreme Court is that it is constitutional provided it is aligned with recusal criteria widely adopted by other judges. The American Bar Association Model Code of Judicial Ethics is remarkably similar to the scope of recusal requirements in the statute for federal judges and justices. There is nothing out of the ordinary that Congress is imposing on federal judges and justices. Congress probably does not have the constitutional right to expand the recusal statute into the extraordinary, inventing new conflicts of interest to impose on Supreme Court justices, but a statute requiring them to conduct themselves like other judges should pass constitutional muster.

[20] *Caperton v. A. T. Massey Coal Co.*, 556 U.S. 868 (2009).

Substantive Intrusion on the Powers of the Court

Very different from regulation of the justices' personal conduct and conflicts of interest would be Congress regulating the adjudication process or the substantive decisions of the court. The court's cases interpreting federal statutes can be overridden by Congress passing new statutes, but Congress trying to overturn the court's decisions on constitutional questions would precipitate a constitutional crisis. Such extreme action has been suggested on both the left and the right,[21] but as discussed in Chapter 3, empowering the political branches of the government to overrule the courts or to ignore court orders would remove an important check on authoritarian rule. Congress has not seriously considered doing this, although it has considered expanding the number of justices on the court.[22] Changing the number of justices is an unusual, but nonetheless constitutional, way of changing the direction of the court if a statute can be passed doing that. (The Constitution says nothing about fixing the number at nine, the number of justices specified in the Judiciary Act of 1869.)

But again, as pointed out in Chapter 3, the court needs to protect its own credibility, including its ethical credibility, if it is to repel intrusion on its authority by the political branches of government. If the court loses credibility, we face the risk that an authoritarian Congress, or an authoritarian president, at some point could seek to override the court's authority to interpret the law.

This means that preserving judicial independence requires a change in the culture at the Supreme Court. Taking great care to follow ethical rules should be the norm, not quarrelling with Congress about whether it has the constitutional power to legislate ethics rules for the court.

Instead of embracing the most permissive interpretations of ethics rules (e.g., Justice Alito's "empty seat theory" of permissible private plane travel discussed in Chapter 2), the justices should err on the side of over-compliance—for example, never accepting free luxury travel from anyone, including close personal friends. The justices do not help their cause by invoking separation of powers arguments to counter legitimate concerns in Congress about Supreme Court ethics, an approach that likely will only encourage the elected branches of government to more aggressively intrude upon the role of the courts.

[21] *See* the discussion in Chapter 3 of suggestions from the political left and right that Congress and the President should override judicial review.

[22] S. 1392, 75th Cong., 1st Sess. (1937), 81 Cong. Rec. 877, 880 (bill encapsulating President Roosevelt's court-packing plan).

The Immunity Problem

The argument that Congress cannot regulate the ethics of the court without compromising its independent Article III powers relies on the dubious theory that independence requires immunity from statutory law. Taken to its extreme, this theory would posit that justices should not only be immune from externally imposed ethics rules but also from criminal prosecution for performance of official duties. This issue has never come before the court, but a similar theory, conflating independent constitutional powers of a branch of government with immunity from prosecution, was embraced by the court in *Trump v. United States* in 2024. There the court held that broad immunity from prosecution was required to preserve the president's Article II powers.

Presidential malfeasance is not the subject of this book, but the implications of presidential immunity are profound. The court was asked by the Justice Department and amici in that case whether such immunity would extend to the hypothetical raised in oral argument of the same case in the court of appeals: the president ordering Seal Team Six to eliminate a political rival. Justice Sotomayor's dissent in *Trump v. United States* repeated that same question and her concern about how far immunity might go.[23] The six justices in the majority ignored these worst-case scenarios.[24]

Do the justices think of themselves as similarly immune from criminal law in the performance of their official duties? None of the justices had said or even implied that, but some of the court's own ethics lapses, such as allegedly willful disclosure violations, arguably violate criminal law.[25] At the beginning of July 2024, the month *Trump v. United States* was decided and sweeping immunity for the president was incorporated into separation of powers jurisprudence, two US senators wrote Attorney General Garland a letter requesting "that you appoint a Special Counsel to investigate possible violations of federal ethics and tax laws by Associate Justice of the Supreme Court Clarence Thomas."[26] The Supreme Court's ethics crisis and its embrace

[23] "The President of the United States is the most powerful person in the country, and possibly the world. When he uses his official powers in any way, under the majority's reasoning, he now will be insulated from criminal prosecution. Orders the Navy's Seal Team 6 to assassinate a political rival? Immune. Organizes a military coup to hold onto power? Immune. Takes a bribe in exchange for a pardon? Immune. Immune, immune, immune." *Trump v. United States*, 603 U.S. 593 (2024) (Sotomayor, J., dissenting).

[24] The author of this book has addressed the court's presidential immunity decision in *Trump v. United States* more extensively in another recent book. See E. Thomas Sullivan and Richard W. Painter, *The U.S. Presidency: Power, Responsibility and Accountability* (Cambridge U. Press 2025), 254-264.

[25] Potential applicability of criminal statutes, including the false statements statute at 18 U.S.C. § 1001, to the Supreme Court's recent ethics scandals is discussed in Chapter 2 of this book.

[26] Letter, dated July 3, 2024, from Senator Sheldon Whitehouse (D-RI and chairman of the Senate Committee on the Judiciary), and Ron Wyden (D-OR and chairman of the Senate Committee on Finance) to Attorney General Merrick Garland requesting a special counsel investigation of Justice Thomas.

of immunity theory for the president may be a coincidence, or it could be more. The court, vulnerable to its own scandals, is aware that immunity is one safeguard from criminal prosecution. Another and better safeguard, for presidents and justices, is complying with the law so that prosecution is not a possibility.

Extreme Separation of Powers and Where It Might Lead

The immunity doctrine is linked to another concerning development, which is the court's gravitation toward a theory of separation of powers whereby the three branches of government act with autonomy in exercising core powers. The court has struck down as unconstitutional acts of Congress that constrain the president's Article II powers—for example, statutes prohibiting the president from firing heads of independent federal agencies.[27] The court has held that a subpoena directed at the president's personal financial records cannot be enforced unless it is closely related to a specific legislative purpose of Congress, because of the separation of powers principles at stake, including the unique position of the president.[28] The court likely would be no more receptive to an attempt by Congress, or perhaps even a federal prosecutor, to subpoena personal financial records of a justice.

The court has not yet ruled on the question of whether Congress has the power to pass laws that regulate the internal affairs of the court. For over 200 years, the justices appear to have accepted the statutory limitations mentioned at the beginning of this chapter, with the exception of the Judiciary Act provision bestowing original jurisdiction on the court that the court rejected in *Marbury v. Madison*.[29] But the court could be hardening its position on separation of powers to such an extent that the justices believe themselves immune from laws made by anyone but themselves.

So, the question is this: If the court believes itself beyond the reach of Congress, that Congress cannot check the court's power, even with statutes imposing ethics requirements on the justices, why should Congress and the president allow the court to check their power? The president and Congress, unlike the justices, are elected by the people, and if they can't tell the justices what to do, why should the justices tell them what to do?

[27] *Seila Law LLC v. Consumer Financial Protection Bureau*, 591 U.S. ___ (2020); *Collins v. Yellen*, 594 U.S. ___ (2021).

[28] *Trump v. Mazars USA, LLP*, 591 U.S. ___ (2020).

[29] *Marbury v. Madison*, 5 U.S. (1 Cranch) 137 (1803).

This question was asked and answered already in Chapter 3, which posited the necessity of judicial review for the rule of law but also posited that judicial review could be put at risk if justices involve themselves in partisan politics. More broadly, judicial review is a separation of powers question. Complete separation of powers means each branch of government can do whatever it wants to do. Complete separation of powers would allow the court to make its own ethics rules but would also mean that in more monumental matters the court could not compel the other branches of government to act or refrain from acting.

In that world of complete separation of powers and no checks and balances, the president ultimately will prevail. The president is commander in chief and has an army. Congress and the court have none.

Is this really what the Supreme Court wants? Presumably not. But the court's insisting that it is entirely beyond the reach of checks and balances from the other two branches of government, even in matters as basic as judicial ethics, will undermine its credibility, its authority, and its meaningful role in our constitutional system.

6
An Inspector General for the Judiciary

As discussed later in this chapter, an inspector general (IG) is an independent official in a government agency charged with investigating ethics violations, waste, fraud, and abuse. This author served as the chief White House ethics lawyer for two and a half years for President George W. Bush. The White House has no IG to investigate allegations of wrongdoing. A year after leaving the White House, the author of this text recommended, in a separate book, that the White House should have an IG.[1] Perhaps now the White House needs an IG more than ever, but it doesn't have one.

The topic of this book, however, is ethics and the Supreme Court. Should the Supreme Court have an IG?

This chapter explores a proposal in legislation introduced in 2015 by Senator Charles Grassley (R-IA) that would install an IG for the entire judicial branch, including the Supreme Court.[2] That bill never advanced out of committee, but perhaps there should be one or more IGs in the judicial branch, with particular attention to investigating alleged violations at the Supreme Court.

The Supreme Court, and also each court of appeals and federal district court, also should have a designated ethics lawyer. The ethics lawyer would be the first line of defense against violations of ethics rules and standards, counseling judges and justices, working to ensure as much as possible a consistent interpretation of ethics law across the federal judiciary. The ethics lawyer would advise, hopefully to prevent violations, and would have a confidential attorney-client relationship with the court. The IG would investigate alleged violations when they occur and, if a violation is found, report it to Congress.

Chapter 5 discussed separation of powers issues and concluded that Congress can and should impose reasonable ethics rules and enforcement

[1] *See* Richard W. Painter, *Getting the Government America Deserves*, ch. 3 (2009) (discussing the need for an IG in the White House).

[2] Judicial Transparency and Ethics Enhancement Act, S. 1418, 114th Cong. (2015). See Richard W. Painter, "SCOTUS House: Can A Supreme Court Ethics Lawyer and Inspector General Help Get This Fraternity Under Control?," *Georgetown Journal of Legal Ethics* 37, no. 1 (2024): 347, discussing Senator Grassley's proposal and how it could be improved upon by also requiring a dedicated ethics lawyer at the court.

Conduct Unbecoming. Richard W. Painter, Oxford University Press. © Oxford University Press (2026).
DOI: 10.1093/9780197832301.003.0007

provisions on the Supreme Court. Provided the legislation were drafted carefully to respect the independence of the substantive work of the court, a statutory requirement that there be an IG and an ethics lawyer at the Supreme Court would align with other reasonable regulations Congress has passed with respect to the federal judiciary.

Senator Grassley's Proposal

In 2015, Senator Charles Grassley said in a speech on the floor of the Senate, "The fact remains that the current practice of self-regulation of judges with respect to ethics and the judicial code of conduct has time and time again proven inadequate."[3] Grassley was right, although ironically we have not heard much from him after the recent Supreme Court ethics scandals discussed in Chapters 2 and 3 of this book. His silence and the even more aggressive stance of some Senate Republicans in defending the ethics of the Supreme Court show how political this subject has become (recall Senator Kennedy's (R-LA) 2023 questioning of the author of this book about which justices are "bought"[4]). The Supreme Court today, with three new justices appointed by President Trump, is perhaps more to the liking of conservatives than the court in 2015,[5] but the ethics problems are the same. Senator Grassley was right to expose the problems then, and he would be right if he were to reintroduce his reform bill today.

Grassley called his bill the Judicial Transparency and Ethics Enhancement Act, S. 1418. This bill contained several proposals to improve ethics and disclosure in the judiciary. The focus here is its "Chapter 60—Inspector General for the Judicial Branch," which provided for an IG for the federal judiciary, including the Supreme Court.[6] The IG's responsibilities under the bill would include

> investigations of possible judicial misconduct, investigating waste fraud and abuse, and recommending changes in laws and regulations governing the federal judiciary. The bill would require the IG to provide the Chief Justice and Congress with an annual report on its activities, as well as refer matters that may constitute a

[3] 114 Cong. Rec. S3240 (daily ed. May 21, 2015) (floor speech by Sen. Grassley).

[4] See Introduction of this book (discussing Senator Kennedy bringing up this and other irrelevant topics at a 2023 Senate hearing on fossil fuel money in politics and climate change).

[5] In 2015, before President Trump appointed three justices, the court was more liberal than it is today. Among other things, the court that year struck down state laws restricting same sex marriage. *Obergefell v. Hodges*, 576 U.S. 644 (2015).

[6] Floor speech by Sen. Grassley, *supra*, note 3.

> criminal violation to the Department of Justice. In addition, the bill establishes whistleblower protections for judicial branch employees.[7]

This IG would "conduct investigations of alleged misconduct in the United States Supreme Court that may require oversight or other action within the judicial branch or by Congress."[8]

Senator Grassley suggested that the IG for the judiciary would conduct investigations and make reports; obtain information from government agencies, including the federal judiciary; subpoena witnesses and documents, administer oaths, and take affidavits; employ officers and outside experts, contract for audits, studies, analyses, and pay for the same out of a budget appropriated by Congress.[9]

Senator Grassley's bill was read twice and referred to the Committee on the Judiciary, where it died.

The Supreme Court Needs an Ethics Lawyer

An IG's job would be much easier if ethics violations were prevented. Federal judges and justices should get sound legal advice to begin with. An ethics lawyer in the Supreme Court would be the first line of defense against violations of rules and standards. Only if the ethics lawyer fails to prevent an alleged violation would an IG be needed to investigate. A federal court should have an ethics lawyer—each circuit court of appeals and each district court—but the focus of discussion in this chapter is the work an ethics lawyer would perform at the Supreme Court.

The role of ethics lawyers in the executive branch is a helpful model to examine. Executive branch agencies each have a designated agency ethics official (DAEO)[10] who coordinates the agency's ethics program. The DAEO is familiar with statutes and regulations promulgated for executive branch employees by the US Office of Government Ethics (OGE)[11] and works with OGE and agency employees to ensure compliance with those rules.

[7] *Ibid.*

[8] Judicial Transparency and Ethics Enhancement Act, S. 1418, 114th Cong. § 1023 (2015). *See generally* 161 Cong. Rec. 3240–41 (2015).

[9] *Ibid.* at § 1024.

[10] 5 C.F.R. § 2638.104(a) (2024) ("Each agency head must appoint a Designated Agency Ethics Official (DAEO). The DAEO is the employee with primary responsibility for directing the daily activities of the agency's ethics program and coordinating with the Office of Government Ethics.").

[11] 5 C.F.R. § 2638.104(b)(2) (2024) ("The DAEO must be an employee who has demonstrated the knowledge, skills, and abilities necessary to manage a significant agency program, to understand and apply complex legal requirements, and to generate support for building and sustaining an ethical culture in the organization.").

The responsibilities of the DAEO include maintaining agency ethics program records; overseeing an ethics education program and advising employees on ethics laws and regulations; taking appropriate action to resolve conflicts of interest through recusals, divestitures, waivers, and reassignments; notifying the agency IG of significant violations of ethics rules or other law; notifying the Department of Justice if there is evidence of a criminal law violation; providing the IG, upon request, with assistance in interpretating ethics laws and regulations; requiring timely compliance with senior officials' ethics agreements; conducting ethics briefings for senior officials;[12] and evaluating the agency's ethics program and making recommendations to the agency for improvement.[13] Federal regulations provide a detailed description of these functions in an agency ethics program.[14]

Ethics lawyers in the executive branch spend a lot of time ensuring compliance with financial disclosure requirements, which is one area where Supreme Court justices have faced difficulty. The DAEO in a federal agency oversees the filing and review of financial disclosure reports and takes appropriate action in the event of noncompliance, imposes late fees for untimely filing, and makes referrals to the IG or the Department of Justice in cases involving knowing and willful falsification of financial disclosure reports. The DAEO also certifies financial disclosure reports as being accurate and complete, meaning the filer alone is not the only person making disclosure decisions. This is a system very different from that followed by the Supreme Court, where each justice alone, perhaps working with a personal lawyer or accountant, makes financial disclosure decisions. An executive branch DAEO also uses information disclosed in financial disclosure reports to address conflicts of interest, once again not leaving it up to agency officials to be the lone decision makers about their own conflicts of interest.[15]

This author ran the White House ethics program from 2005 to 2007 and described some of how the White House ethics program worked in a book published in early 2009.[16] Although the White House does not have an IG (this author has suggested it should), its ethics office functions much like the

[12] 5 C.F.R. § 2638.305 requires that senior officials receive special ethics briefings.

[13] 5 C.F.R. § 2638.104(c) (2024) (describing responsibilities of the DAEO).

[14] Specific regulations address an agency ethics program's mission and responsibilities (Subpart A), procedures (Subpart B), government ethics education (Subpart C), correction of executive branch agency ethics programs (Subpart D), and corrective action involving individual employees (Subpart E). *See generally* 5 C.F.R. §§ 2638.101–2638.604 (2024).

[15] *See* 5 C.F.R. §§ 2638.101–2638.108 (2024).

[16] *See generally* Richard W. Painter, *Implementation and Enforcement of Ethics Rules in the Executive Branch: How Big Are the Gaps in the System?, Chapter 3 in* Getting the Government America Deserves: How Ethics Reform Can Make a Difference (2009).

federal agencies the president oversees. The standards for ethics programs outlined in OGE regulations apply across the executive branch. The White House ethics office also oversees the quality of ethics compliance in the agencies, assisting agency ethics lawyers in making sure that the president's senior appointees are complying with ethics statutes and regulations. Cabinet officers and other senior officials who resist the advice of agency ethics lawyers should get a call from the White House. The director of OGE, a presidential appointee, is also often involved in high-level discussions about ethics compliance in the agencies.

Such is the system of checks and balances built into the executive branch ethics program, where multiple ethics lawyers at different levels are involved in advice and compliance, a system lacking for the Supreme Court.

This executive branch ethics program, of course, only works as well as the people who implement it. In 2025, President Trump fired the head of OGE, as well as the head of the Office of Special Counsel, the agency responsible for enforcing civil service laws and the Hatch Act, which prohibits use of official government position to influence partisan elections. The president also fired over a dozen IGs in multiple agencies. These abuses of presidential power are addressed in another recent book by this author,[17] and illustrate that the judiciary is not the only branch of government where ethics rules and standards are put to the test. But at least the executive branch has a system for implanting an ethics regime if the president and his appointees want to use it.

Another model worth expanding upon is that used for the federal judiciary itself. The other federal courts have a system where ethics rules are administered by the Judicial Conference and judges adjudicate ethics matters concerning other judges. This system was described in the introduction and in Chapters 2 and 4 of this book.

Ethics compliance in lower federal courts would be even more robust, and probably fewer cases would need to be reported to the Judicial Conference, if judges had the benefit of expert advice of an ethics lawyer. An ethics lawyer on site for each court might help federal judges respond more appropriately to the appearance of impropriety that arises from travel to free seminars at luxury resorts paid for by corporate donors, a problem discussed in Chapter 1 of this book, conflicts of interest that arise when law clerks accept employment at law firms, and reports of sexual harassment of law clerks, a problem involving at least two Ninth Circuit judges that was discussed in Chapter 4.

[17] E. Thomas Sullivan & Richard W. Painter, *The U.S. Presidency: Power, Responsibility and Accountability* (2025).

But at least the other federal courts have the reporting and investigation apparatus of the Judicial Conference. There is a system to hold judges accountable. The Supreme Court has nothing.

So, for starters, the Supreme Court needs an ethics lawyer.

The court has a senior lawyer who serves as its legal counsel,[18] who provides legal services to the court and may have some responsibilities related to ethics, but this is not the same as an ethics lawyer. Much of the legal counsel's job is advising the justices and their clerks on complex procedural and jurisdictional aspects of litigation in cases before the court.[19] Ethics compliance is an entirely different job and needs a designated lawyer. The legal counsel on numerous occasions, at the direction of the chief justice, responds to inquiries by members of Congress about Supreme Court ethics, invariably reassuring Congress that ethics rules are being complied with,[20] but providing no information about a Supreme Court ethics program. That's because there isn't one.

The appointment of a Supreme Court ethics lawyer should be made by the chief justice with the concurrence of all the justices. A Supreme Court ethics lawyer who loses the support of a substantial minority of the justices (perhaps three) probably should be removed by the chief justice. Because the ethics lawyer's role is advisory, not enforcement, an ethics lawyer without the support of most of the justices, like any other lawyer without the support of a client, would likely be ineffective in gathering information and rendering advice. Justices requesting the removal of the ethics lawyer, however, should be required to explain why, and this information should be provided to both the ethics lawyer and the court's IG.

[18] The court says that the "[t]he Court's Legal Office, established in 1973, provides support to the Justices on a variety of case-related issues and legal services for the Court as an institution." Press Release, Supreme Court of the United States (November 20, 2013), https://www.supremecourt.gov/publicinfo/press/pressreleases/pr_11-20-13 [https://perma.cc/2VSW-TULR] (announcing appointment of Ethan V. Torrey as legal counsel to the court). Torrey replaced Scott S. Harris, who became clerk of the court in September 2013.

[19] *See* John W. Winkle III & Martha B. Swann, *When Justices Need Lawyers: The U.S. Supreme Court's Legal Office*, 76 Judicature 244 (1993) (discussing the operations of the Supreme Court Legal Counsel's office).

[20] *See, e.g.*, Letter from Ethan Torrey, Legal Counsel, the Supreme Court, to Senator Sheldon Whitehouse (D-RI) and Representative Henry Johnson (D-GA) (Nov. 7, 2022), https://www.whitehouse.senate.gov/imo/media/doc/2022.11.7%20-%20Letter%20to%20Chairman%20Whitehouse%20and%20Chairman%20Johnson.pdf [https://perma.cc/2D59-QJMZ] (referencing Torrey's prior letter of July 12, 2021, explaining that the justices rely on the Code of Conduct for United States Judges in evaluating ethics issues and "follow the same financial disclosure rules that are applicable to other federal judge."). *See also* Letter from Ethan Torrey, Legal Counsel, Supreme Court, to Senator Sheldon Whitehouse and Representative Henry Johnson (Nov. 28, 2022), https://www.documentcloud.org/documents/23320580-letter-from-scotus-counsel [https://perma.cc/8X7P-BZH7] (explaining that Justice Alito had no role in improperly leaking the court's decision in *Burwell v. Hobby Lobby Stores*, 573 U.S. 682 (2014)).

The ethics lawyer would not be an investigator. That would be the role of a Supreme Court IG. Rather, the ethics lawyer would have an attorney-client relationship with the court.[21]

The attorney-client privilege—and the obligation of confidentiality—for communications with the court's ethics lawyer probably should be waivable only by a majority of the justices. Absent a waiver—or some other exception to the attorney-client privilege[22]—communications between the ethics lawyer and the justices, clerks, or other court employees would be confidential and not be discoverable by persons outside the court (the relationship the ethics lawyer would have with the court's IG is discussed further below). The objective of this attorney-client relationship is to have an ethics lawyer the justices, clerks, and employees of the court can consult, knowing that the conversation will not be disclosed outside the court unless the court decides it should be disclosed.

The court's ethics lawyer would assist the justices in filing financial disclosure forms, review the gift rules, and make recommendations about speaking engagements, spousal income, offers of free travel, and any other situation that might give rise to ethics issues. A small staff of paralegals and other professionals could assist the ethics lawyer in these tasks. Instead of coordinating with OGE, which only has jurisdiction over ethics in the executive branch, the Supreme Court ethics lawyer would be a liaison between the court and ethics experts at the Judicial Conference of the United States.

The ethics lawyer would have no power to compel action on any matter, but when the resolution of a matter is arguable, the ethics lawyer could recommend that the chief justice seek an advisory opinion from the Judicial Conference ethics staff or from one or more court of appeals judges on recusal, financial disclosure, gifts, and other ethics issues. Circuit judges themselves face many of the same issues, are bound by many of the same laws, and could provide valuable advice to justices on how best to comply. The ethics lawyer could facilitate this advisory process, sometimes asking court of appeals judges more general questions without naming justices or other parties (e.g. "should a justice be required to recuse in such and such circumstances") and sometimes being more specific about which justice is considering recusal or some other action, such as divestment of financial assets or termination of a social relationship creating a conflict of interest.

[21] The Supreme Court ethics lawyer would represent the Supreme Court as an institution, not the individual justices. *See* American Bar Association Model Rules of Professional Conduct R. 1.13 (2018) (clarifying that the lawyer for an organization represents the organization, not its individual constituents).

[22] The attorney-client privilege is waived if the communications are in furtherance of a crime or fraud (e.g., if the ethics lawyer were asked to falsify a financial disclosure report).

These advisory communications between the ethics lawyer and court of appeals judges, and similar communications between justices and court of appeals judges, should also be kept confidential in most circumstances.

The ethics lawyer would represent the entire court as an institution, not any one justice. The ethics lawyer would consult with justices individually but would not conceal from other justices the information they should know. The lawyer also would be required to report to the chief justice, or to all the justices, and to the IG, evidence of a material violation of law by any justice, clerk, or employee of the court.[23]

One function of the ethics lawyer, like that of ethics lawyers in the executive branch, would be to prepare ethics agreements for new judges and justices and to update them regularly whenever circumstances change—new spousal employment, an inheritance, a speaking engagement or book contract, and so on. Suggestions for pre-confirmation and post-confirmation ethics agreements are discussed more in Chapter 7.

An Inspector General for the Supreme Court

But what if a justice, law clerk, or other employee of the court fails to consult with the ethics lawyer or doesn't disclose to the ethics lawyer important information? Ethics lawyers can't prevent ethics violations they don't even know about. Also, what if a justice or someone else refuses to take the ethics lawyer's advice or that advice is wrong? Potential and actual violations discussed in Chapters 2, 3, and 4 of this book involve areas as far reaching as impermissible gifts to justices, failure to disclose gifts and financial conflicts of interest, inappropriate political activity, failure to recuse from cases when required to do so, ex parte communications about cases, misuse of confidential information of the court, sexual harassment of clerks or staff, and other violations of statutes and regulations.

The court needs an IG who can initiate the enforcement process. The rest of the federal judiciary could also use an IG, although the Judicial Conference performs some analogous functions by investigating violations in lower courts. There could be one IG for the entire judiciary, including the Supreme Court, or separate IGs for each court.

For lower court judges, an IG would assist the Judicial Conference in enforcing its Code of Conduct for United States Judges and investigating

[23] American Bar Association *Model Rules of Professional Conduct*, Rule 1.13 requires a lawyer representing an organization to report unresolved law violations up the ladder to the highest governing authority in the organization, and that should be the obligation of the Supreme Court ethics lawyer as well.

wrongdoing by clerks, other staff, parties and lawyers appearing before the courts, and amici. Because the Judicial Conference already has a procedure for investigating misconduct, even without an IG, the role of the IG might be more limited. This chapter focuses on how an IG would interact with the Supreme Court.

The IG's application of rules and standards would need to be consistent with that of the Judicial Conference. There should not be two different compliance standards, one stricter and the other more permissive. In almost all circumstances, the same rules should apply to all federal judges, including Supreme Court justices. As discussed in Chapter 2, recusal from cases is the one area that is more difficult for Supreme Court justices, so there might be more emphasis on preventing conflicts of interest than on recusal. Selling stock, refusing gifts and free travel, and avoiding problematic social interactions are far preferable to a justice having to recuse from a case when no replacement justice is available.

But whatever the rules are, it is essential that they be enforced.

IGs in the executive branch are a useful role model for the court—assuming executive IGs do what they are supposed to do. This brings up an important caveat that should be mentioned before delving into the specifics of how executive branch IGs work: The executive branch ethics and compliance model is only as effective as the president and Congress want it to be. If the president fires IGs, or otherwise obstructs enforcement, and Congress lets him do that without threatening impeachment, the system won't work. Executive branch noncompliance also is encouraged when the Supreme Court interprets the "unitary executive theory" to allow the president for any reason to fire the heads of ethics watchdog agencies and agency IGs. In 2024, the court made matters worse by holding that the president is presumptively immune from criminal prosecution for official-capacity crimes in office.[24] Chapter 5 of this book explores the possibility that both the Supreme Court and the presidency could be headed toward complete autonomy, an extreme version of separation of powers in which each branch of government does whatever it wants with no checks and balances. In the case of a potentially lawless presidency, this author also addressed this problem in another recent book.[25]

Still, for purposes of modeling an IG regime for the Supreme Court, it is important to examine how the executive branch IG regime is supposed

[24] *See Trump v. United States*, 603 U.S. 593 (2024) (holding that the president has broad immunity from criminal prosecution for official acts) (citing and discussing *Seila Law v. CFPB*, 591 U.S. 197 (2020) (holding that under Article II of the constitution the president has broad power to remove heads of federal agencies)).

[25] *See* E. Thomas Sullivan & Richard W. Painter, *The U.S. Presidency: Power, Responsibility, and Accountability* (2025).

to work when the president does not act as if he and his subordinates are above the law. A Supreme Court IG will interact with the court differently than an executive branch IG interacts with agencies, but in some respects, the functions will be similar.

Under the Inspector General Act of 1978,[26] as amended by the Inspector General Reform Act of 2008,[27] there are over seventy statutory IGs in federal agencies throughout the executive branch. They are "appointed by the President, by and with the advice and consent of the Senate, without regard to political affiliation and solely on the basis of integrity and demonstrated ability in accounting, auditing, financial analysis, law, management analysis, public administration, or investigations."[28] IGs report to the head of their agency, but "[n]either the head of the establishment nor the officer next in rank below such head shall prevent or prohibit the Inspector General from initiating, carrying out, or completing any audit or investigation, or from issuing any subpoena during the course of any audit or investigation."[29]

Note that this statutory requirement that IGs be appointed "without regard to political affiliation and solely on the basis of integrity and demonstrated ability" is only effective to the extent that it is enforced by the Senate in the confirmation process. If the Senate allows a president to appoint a highly political IG, or one who lacks integrity, the system won't work. The same is true for any IG in the Supreme Court.

IGs can be removed by the president, but Congress must be given thirty days advance notice of removal and told the reason for removal.[30] Except for the Trump administration, where there were multiple firings of IGs in both the first and second terms,[31] IG removals have been rare, in part because of the appearance of scandal when an IG is removed. Once again, if a president does fire IGs for political or retaliatory reasons, and Congress lets the president get away with it by not conducting its own investigation, the system won't work.

[26] Inspector General Act of 1978, 92 Stat. 1101 (1978) (codified as amended at 5a U.S.C. § 3).
[27] Inspector General Reform Act of 2008, 122 Stat. 4302 (2008).
[28] 5a U.S.C. § 3.
[29] *Ibid.*
[30] *Ibid.*
[31] *See, e.g.*, Alexandra Marquez, *Sen. Adam Schiff Says Trump "Broke the Law" by Firing 18 Inspectors General*, NBC News (Jan. 26, 2025), https://www.nbcnews.com/politics/donald-trump/adam-schiff-trump-broke-law-firing-inspectors-general-rcna189327 (discussing firings of IGs in multiple agencies, including the Department of Defense, the State Department, Health and Human Services, and the Department of Labor). There were also notable firings of IGs during President Trump's first term. *See also* Melissa Quinn, *The Internal Watchdogs Trump Has Fired or Replaced*, CBS News (May 19, 2020), https://www.cbsnews.com/news/trump-inspectors-general-internal-watchdogs-fired-list [https://perma.cc/M6ZB-NF9W]; Charlie Savage, *Endorsing Trump's Firing of Inspector General, Barr Paints Distorted Picture*, N.Y. Times (Apr. 10, 2020), https://www.nytimes.com/2020/04/10/us/politics/barr-inspector-general-firing.html [https://perma.cc/Z7F3-K2S5] (discussing President Trump's firing of Michael K. Anderson, the intelligence community IG, over his handling of a whistleblower complaint that led to Trump's 2019 impeachment).

An IG thus is supposed to be inside the agency, yet independent from it. An executive branch IG has the authority and responsibility to investigate alleged waste, fraud, and abuse involving the agency, make recommendations to the agency head and to the White House, send criminal referrals to the Department of Justice, and send reports to Congress.[32]

IGs, in turn, appoint an assistant IG and other staff, including a whistle-blower protection coordinator, to prevent retaliation against agency employees for protected disclosures to the IG. Retaliation is a separate violation of federal law.[33] IGs in the executive branch are supposed to coordinate with each other through the Council of Inspectors General on Integrity and Efficiency.[34]

The Supreme Court, of course, is different from the executive branch. No single person is head of the judicial branch. Although the chief justice has special administrative duties, the other justices are not his subordinates; he cannot suspend them or remove them. Each justice has one vote on the court. The court collectively heads up an entire judicial branch of government.

For these reasons, an IG for the court ideally should be appointed with the consent of all nine justices (however, whether that is possible given some of the justices' resistance to outside supervision is an open question). An IG could be appointed with the consent of fewer justices, perhaps a majority, but this could result in accusations of bias if one of the other justices were the subject of an IG investigation. If one or more justices refuse to consent to the appointment of an IG for the court, an IG could be appointed by a majority of the justices, by the chief justice, or, if the court declines to nominate an IG, by the president or by the attorney general of the United States. An IG nominated without the consent of the entire court, or at least a substantial majority of the court, probably should serve a shorter term in office (e.g., two years), allowing the justices an opportunity later to agree on nomination of an IG. An IG nominated by the entire court should probably be allotted a longer term, perhaps eight to ten years. This would provide a measure of job protection sufficient to ensure independence but not the unaccountability too often associated with lifetime tenure.

IGs in the executive branch are confirmed by the Senate, and the same should probably be required for the Supreme Court IG. The Senate

[32] 5a U.S.C. § 4.

[33] 5a U.S.C. § 3.

[34] *See* The Council of the Inspectors General on Integrity and Efficiency (CIGIE), https://www.ignet.gov [https://perma.cc/X74A-AAMK] (last visited January 22, 2026) ("[CIGIE] is an independent entity established within the executive branch to address integrity, economy and effectiveness issues that transcend individual Government agencies and aid in the establishment of a professional, well-trained and highly skilled workforce in the Offices of Inspectors General.").

confirmation process would involve, among other things, a discussion of the nominee's understanding of the IG's responsibilities to report to Congress. Advice and consent to the nomination of the IG from the Senate as well as from the justices is the best way to instill public confidence in the performance of the IG's duties. An IG nominated by all the justices and confirmed by the Senate would be ideal.

Requiring the IG to be nominated by the justices and confirmed by the Senate reduces the likelihood of an IG being politically aligned with one party or faction in Congress that might try to use the IG to subject the court to intimidation or interference. An IG should not be nominated or confirmed if the IG does not understand the proper balance between the independence of the judicial branch and the need for accountability.

At the Supreme Court, the IG would initiate an investigation when there is probable cause to believe there was a violation of an ethics rule or other law by a justice, a clerk, or other employee of the court or by a party, an amicus party, or a lawyer in connection with a case before the court. Examples of investigations undertaken by the IG would include the alleged failure of justices to recuse themselves from a case when required to do so, improper attempts to influence justices, financial reporting lapses, leaks of draft opinions or other confidential information, sexual harassment, substance abuse, failure of parties or amici to make required disclosures to the court, and other matters.

The IG should report to Congress on any investigation that finds clear and convincing evidence of a breach—whether of federal statutes, the Code of Conduct for United States Judges, or other ethical standards—by a justice, an employee of the court, or any lawyer, party, or amici appearing before the court. For investigations with no finding of a violation, the IG should either not report to Congress or should inform Congress of the finding and the reasons for it.

A statute establishing the office of the IG could also give one or more parties in cases pending before the court standing, upon receipt of an unfavorable IG report, to petition the entire court for a rehearing of a matter or even an injunction against a particular justice or justices committing a future violation. For example, if the IG were to find that a justice received an undisclosed substantial gift from billionaire X, this finding could be the grounds for a party in a case in which billionaire X had a financial interest to move for a rehearing of a certiorari petition, a rehearing on the merits, and/or recusal of the justice. Making Supreme Court ethics itself an occasional case before the court would force the justices to own up to their collective responsibility to ensure that ethics rules are complied with and to acknowledge when they have failed or to explain in an opinion why they believe they have complied with the law.

If criminal conduct is involved, the IG should refer a matter to the Department of Justice, which would be expected to open an investigation and, if appropriate, obtain an indictment. Although the complexities involved with the criminal prosecution of a Supreme Court justice are beyond the scope of this book, and a special prosecutor would probably be required, sitting federal judges have been indicted while in office,[35] and there is no legal authority for the proposition that a sitting Supreme Court justice cannot be indicted.

The Justice Department has specific regulations for investigation of high-ranking officers in the executive branch, including the president, by a special counsel.[36] In fact, independent counsels have been appointed to investigate the president in the past two administrations.[37] If warranted, after a report from a Supreme Court IG, the Justice Department could appoint a special counsel to investigate a justice or other employee of the Supreme Court.

It also is important to have remedial measures short of indictment or impeachment of a justice. Censure of a justice by one or both houses of Congress after a report by the IG is an option.

The IG should also protect whistleblowers against retaliation. The IG's staff, like executive branch IGs, should have a whistleblower protection coordinator to prevent retaliation against court employees for protected disclosures, and it should be clear that retaliation is a separate violation of federal law.[38]

An IG who unduly threatens the independence of the court should be removed from office. Congress could stipulate that the IG could only be removed by unanimous decision of the justices or by a supermajority (six, seven, or eight justices). If the IG is removed by the court, the reasons for removal should be outlined in a written opinion of the court or a letter from the chief justice to Congress.[39] The IG should also be subject to impeachment by the House and removal by the Senate. An IG who fails to address wrongdoing on the court should be rigorously examined by Congress and perhaps impeached and removed.

[35] As discussed in Chapter 5, US Court of Appeals for the Seventh Circuit Judge Otto Kerner, former governor of Illinois, was indicted by a federal grand jury on charges of bribery, perjury, and tax evasion.

[36] *See* 28 C.F.R. § 600 (1999).

[37] *See* Office of the Deputy Attorney General, Order No. 3915-2017, Appointment of Special Counsel to Investigate Russian Interference with the 2016 Presidential Election and Related Matters (May 17, 2017), https://www.justice.gov/opa/press-release/file/967231/download [https://perma.cc/QN6T-JHQ8]; Office of the Attorney General, Appointment of Special Counsel (Jan. 23, 2023), https://www.justice.gov/opa/pr/appointment-special-counsel-1 [https://perma.cc/9C4D-SSG6] (appointing Robert K. Hur as special counsel to investigate the possible unauthorized removal and retention of classified documents discovered at the Penn Biden Center and the private residence of President Biden).

[38] Whistleblowers in the executive branch are protected by federal law prohibiting retaliation and by a whistleblower protection coordinator in the IG's office.

[39] IGs in the executive branch are removable by the president, but the president is required to give Congress thirty days advance notice. (*See* 5a U.S.C. § 3.) A similar rule could apply to an IG removed by the justices of the Supreme Court, although they could state their reasons in an opinion or memorandum instead of in a report to Congress.

Supervision Without Intrusion

The Supreme Court needs supervision of its internal affairs, but direct supervision of the court by Congress or by the executive branch could be abused and violate separation of powers principles. A Supreme Court IG would provide independent supervision without interference from the other two branches of government.

Having a Supreme Court IG, for example, is preferable to Congress calling the chief justice to testify whenever an ethics violation is alleged. This is what happened in 2023 when Senator Durbin (D-IL) requested that Chief Justice Roberts appear before the Judiciary Committee. Roberts refused, and Senator Durbin did not seek a subpoena, which would have resulted in a showdown with the court. Congressional testimony by a justice, and even a subpoena, might be appropriate after an IG finds serious violations of law, but not beforehand. The IG, not Congress, should conduct the initial investigation. The Justice Department should also, in most cases, decline to investigate a justice without a prior finding of wrongdoing by the IG.

Legislation installing an IG at the Supreme Court should not allow the IG to intrude into the substance of the court's work, and the IG should not be allowed to interfere unduly with court procedures. Achieving this goal will involve balancing the importance of investigatory objectives of the IG with the autonomy of the court. But it should be obvious that either extreme—an out-of-control IG investigation or having no investigation at all—is unacceptable.

In creating the office of the IG, Congress could also impose limits on the duration of an IG investigation—for example, in most cases, requiring the IG to close an investigation and issue a report within ninety days of a matter being referred to the IG.

Supervision Without Collusion

A Supreme Court IG would need to be independent of the parties, lawyers, and amici before the court. One way of accomplishing this is for the IG to be bound by the ethics rules that bind IGs and all other employees in the executive branch. These include statutes prohibiting financial conflicts of interest for government employees,[40] rules requiring recusal from matters in which

[40] 18 U.S.C. § 208 (prohibiting certain financial conflicts of interest for federal employees).

an employee's impartiality might reasonably be questioned because of personal or business relationships,[41] and the Ethics in Government Act annual disclosure requirements that bind executive branch employees as well as the justices.[42] All these requirements should apply to the Supreme Court IG and the ethics lawyer.

The IG, and the ethics lawyer, should also be as apolitical as possible and should not take sides in political or jurisprudential disputes. Restrictions on political activity of federal judges and justices, discussed in Chapter 3, should apply to the IG and ethics lawyer as well. The IG and ethics lawyer should also probably be prohibited from making public statements on the merits of cases before the court, before or after those cases are decided.

The IG also should not be under pressure to collude with the justices or their clerks.

The IG is not a colleague of the justices. Neither is the ethics lawyer. The IG should not dine or regularly socialize with the justices and certainly would not sit in on deliberations with the justices. The IG's office probably should be outside the Supreme Court, with the IG entering the building only as needed in specified circumstances. The ethics lawyer would be closer in proximity to the justices and their clerks, and like law clerks, the ethics lawyer should have an office in the Supreme Court building. But the ethics lawyer also should have as much independence as possible and avoid close ties with any one justice or group of justices or their law clerks.

Both the IG and the ethics lawyer, if they are independent, can be a useful check on the groupthink problem discussed in Chapter 4. Psychologist Irving Janis, when writing about groupthink, proposed a "devil's advocate" approach in which someone in a decision-making group argues a contrary position to challenge the others.[43] In their deliberations, the justices of the Supreme Court are adept at playing this "devil's advocate" role, arguing different sides of a case. In matters of ethics and personal conduct, however, they apparently do not do that—they just give each other a pass. The IG and ethics

[41] 5 C.F.R. § 2535.502 (OGE impartiality rule for executive branch officials).

[42] *See* discussion in Chapter 2 of the Ethics in Government Act annual financial disclosure requirements.

[43] *See* Janis, *supra*, at 2. In 2020, Muqtafi Akhmad, Shuang Chang, and Hiroshi Deguchi of the Tokyo Institute of Technology published a paper using an agent-based model of groupthink and simulations to assess the effectiveness of "devil's advocacy" techniques to overcome groupthink in different situations. *See generally* Muqtafi Akhmad et al., *Closed-Mindedness and Insulation in Groupthink: Their Effects and the Devil's Advocacy as a Preventive Measure*, J. Comput. Soc. Sci. (2020) (describing the agent-based model and various simulations) (citing a wide range of literature on groupthink, including Robert S. Baron, *So Right It's Wrong: Groupthink and the Ubiquitous Nature of Polarized Group Decision Making*, 37 Advances in Experimental Soc. Psych., 219–253 (2005); Marco Brambilla et al., *Morality and Intergroup Relations: Threats to Safety and Group Image Predict the Desire to Interact with Outgroup and Ingroup Members*, 49 J. Experimental Soc. Psych., 811–821 (2013)).

lawyer hopefully would not be ensnared in the "groupthink" about ethics that appears to have overtaken some of the justices. This groupthink appears to have spread as well to clerks, former clerks, and members of the Supreme Court bar who fail to recognize when ethics rules are violated or who minimize the seriousness of a violation. The IG and ethics lawyer can push back with a different view: that rules must be followed, and that there is no excuse premised on the "no harm, no foul" argument that violations might not affect case outcomes.

The IG and the ethics lawyer are also not as likely to be subjected to external influence. A billionaire probably won't invite the Supreme Court ethics lawyer or IG to join him with a justice on his yacht or invite them to an all-expense-paid fishing expedition with a justice. If that did happen, the ethics lawyer and IG would have to refuse the invitation or disclose the gift on their annual disclosure form, which would surely get the attention of the media.

Furthermore, neither the ethics lawyer nor the IG are unduly interested in defending the judiciary from the rule of law. Their professional reputation instead turns on the ethics of the judiciary. They should not be as headstrong as the justices in protecting the court's power as an institution. Executive branch IGs, if allowed to do their jobs, can counter the unchecked accumulation of presidential power, at least at the margins; similarly, a Supreme Court IG could check some abuses of power by the Supreme Court.

Supervision with Transparency

As discussed earlier in this book, transparency at the Supreme Court is a difficult and controversial matter, and considerations are different than for transparency in the executive branch. The IG report to Congress would provide important information about ethics compliance at the Supreme Court without disclosing the court's legitimate confidences.

When there is a serious violation of ethics rules or even criminal law, the IG's report to Congress would be essential to opening an impeachment investigation. Having a preliminary investigation by the IG, if there were a finding of wrongdoing, should make it easier for Congress to obtain testimony, including from the justices themselves. The court could refuse to comply with congressional subpoenas of the justices' records, triggering a constitutional crisis. But after release of a sufficiently compelling IG report, the justices might recognize that it is better to comply. This would be very different from a more politicized situation where a congressional committee, with no IG report, demands information from the court because the chair of the committee, or some of its members, think there has been a violation. In that instance, the court is almost certain to refuse.

An entirely separate issue, not the subject of this book, is the debate over greater transparency in the substantive deliberations of the court—for example, proposals to have television cameras in the courtroom, disclosure of draft opinions, and the like. Such issues do not involve the IG. Transparency about ethics compliance, however, does involve the IG and is critical to public confidence in the court. Findings of violations supported by sufficient evidence should be reported by the IG to Congress and become public. The IG should also testify about matters in the IG report if asked to do so by either house of Congress.

Supervision with Confidentiality

Confidentiality has always been vitally important to the court, and the justices will insist on strict limits on disclosure outside the court of internal deliberations. The office of the IG, who has a reporting obligation, not the ethics lawyer, who is sworn to confidence, will raise confidentiality concerns for the court. The IG would need to take special care to protect the confidentiality of the court while disclosing to Congress and the public what needs to be disclosed when a violation of ethics rules or other law occurs.

A lot more information is confidential in the court than in an executive branch agency. The court's deliberations, draft opinions, email, and other communications are not subject to Freedom of Information Act[44] requests the way similar communications often are in the executive branch. This means that the IG should examine only documents that are necessary to examine to conduct a thorough investigation of an alleged ethics breach and not delve into matters unrelated to the breach.

For example, in a recusal scenario, the federal recusal statute[45] requires recusal regardless of how a judge might decide a case. Recusal is a strict liability rule (it does not matter what the justice's position is in the case; he either must recuse or does not have to recuse). There is little need for an IG to go through records of a justice's thought process in deciding a case if the IG is investigating whether the justice should have been recused from the case. The *facts* of the case might be relevant to recusal, because the facts involve who has a financial or other interest in the case, but the facts can be discerned from the pleadings or other public records. Facts about a justice's relationship with

[44] 5 U.S.C. § 552.
[45] 28 U.S.C § 455.

parties or amici would be relevant to recusal, but these are distinguishable from the justice's thoughts about the merits of legal arguments in the case. The Supreme Court IG should only investigate facts that need to be investigated to decide the recusal question and leave the rest alone. If the IG does see communications about the justices' deliberations, these should never be disclosed by the IG unless they are directly linked to a demonstrated act of serious wrongdoing by a justice.

The IG thus should be required to protect the court's confidences as much as possible. The IG's report to Congress should only disclose confidential information of the court to the extent *necessary* to support a finding of wrongdoing. In most cases, the IG shouldn't have information about the justices' case deliberations, and such information—including draft opinions—should seldom be disclosed. An exception would be rare instances where the IG concludes that a justice changed a vote in a case due to a bribe, an impermissible ex parte contact by a party or amicus group, or other improper influence.

Indeed, absent probable cause concerning both a violation and its impact on a case, the IG should not be allowed to examine deliberative materials to begin with. The wrongdoing would be established by other means. For example, a justice who accepted a free vacation from an amicus in a pending case would violate ethics rules regardless of the impact on the justice's vote in the case, and the IG should report that to Congress. The IG could examine deliberative materials only upon obtaining evidence showing that a gift (e.g., a free vacation) influenced a justice's decision. Furthermore, that information would be reported to Congress only if clear and convincing evidence established that the free vacation influenced the justice's vote in the case.

The IG should be required to agree to a confidentiality pledge specifying what type information may or may not be disclosed in a report to Congress depending on the type of investigation. The statute creating the office of Supreme Court IG could impose specific penalties, including immediate dismissal, on an IG who makes unauthorized disclosures of the court's confidential information.

Supervision with Consultation

Most ethics violations can be avoided through prior consultation, ensuring that justices, law clerks, and others know what is permitted and what is not. The first line of defense is the ethics lawyer. The ethics lawyer can help by resolving an ethics issue so that it never gets to the IG. Because the ethics lawyer does not report to Congress and has an attorney-client confidential relationship with the court, the ethics lawyer is in the best position to find out about potential ethics problems and resolve them. The Supreme Court's code of conduct should require justices and their clerks to consult with the ethics lawyer whenever there is an arguable question of judicial ethics. In addition, the court might authorize the ethics lawyer, on a confidential basis, to seek advice from appellate judges or ethics lawyers working for the court of appeals about the best approach to specific situations.

If a matter does get to the IG, the IG should also have the power to request advisory opinions on recusals, financial disclosure, and other matters from one or more federal appellate judges. Unlike the Supreme Court ethics lawyer, who should probably only be permitted to seek such advisory opinions with the permission of the justices, the IG should be permitted to initiate a more formal review. For example, if justices refuse to recuse themselves from a case even though it appears that recusal is required, the IG could refer the matter to one or more appellate judges. Likewise, if a justice were to insist that a certain gift did not need to be disclosed on the annual disclosure form, the IG could consult appellate judges. The advisory opinion of the appellate judges would not be binding, but the IG would report to Congress a justice's decision to act contrary to that opinion. Alternatively, if the IG disagrees with the determination of the appellate judges, the IG could explain that in the report.

Appellate judges might be deferential to Supreme Court justices on matters of ethics because they, in some ways, are colleagues of the justices and can be overruled by the justices in the cases they decide. This is a reason for a Supreme Court ethics regime not to rely too much on consultation with appellate judges. Nonetheless, their input, coupled with an independent IG investigation, could help prevent the worse lapses of professional judgment on the Supreme Court.

Supervision Without Compulsion

The IG can investigate and release a report, but the IG can't make a justice do anything. If a justice still refuses to recuse themselves from a case despite a clear finding by the IG that the justice should recuse, or a justice refuses to disclose certain required information on a financial report, the other justices have the option of weighing in. But they might not be able to make the justice recuse or disclose either. Nonetheless, the IG's independent position, and duty to report to Congress, would be a powerful deterrent for a justice determined to violate the recusal statute, the disclosure statute, or any other ethics rule.

If the law is unclear, a justice's interpretation is likely to prevail over that of the IG. The IG's job is to apply the law to the facts and issue a report. If there is evidence of wrongdoing, the court and Congress both can decide what to do next.

Both the IG and the ethics lawyer know that Congress passes laws and the justices interpret the law. And only if a justice's interpretation of an ethics law is unreasonable, and a violation ensues, does the IG have the responsibility to report the matter to Congress. The IG probably would be subjected to severe criticism in Congress if the IG were to use poor judgment either in condemning a justice for conduct that was proper or allowing improper conduct. There is a risk of having an abusive or overzealous IG, and the nomination and confirmation process should be designed to ensure that doesn't happen. If it does, the IG can and should be removed by a vote of the justices and that decision explained by the court to Congress.

Why Can't the Justices Do It Themselves?

An argument against any proposal to involve an IG or other independent federal officer in the affairs of the Supreme Court is that the justices can do it themselves. Perhaps they could abandon the tradition of allowing individual justices to monitor their own compliance and instead take a more proactive and formal role in addressing each other's ethics issues. The court could decide ethics questions for the court by majority vote, for example. They could rely on their institutional memory and seek consistency.

There are several problems with this approach.

First, allowing the justices to decide which ethics laws apply to them violates that ancient rule "*aliquis non debet esse Judex in propria causa*"—no man ought to be a judge of his own cause—articulated by Sir Edward Coke in 1610.[46] Indeed, this principle is quoted by Supreme Court justices when they apply it to parties other than themselves.[47] Having the full court decide ethics questions that involve individual justices does not avoid this problem, as all justices are affected by these decisions.

Second, it could further divide the court to have justices ruling on whether each other behaved unethically or telling each other when they may and may not participate in a case. Deciding recusal motions based on alleged conflicts

[46] *Dr. Bonham's Case*, (1610) 77 Eng. Rep. 638, 646, 652; 18 Co. 107a, 114a, 118a (C. P.) (holding that the College of Physicians, although given power under the Physicians Act of 1523 to punish unlicensed practice of medicine, may not be "judges, ministers, and parties" in a case).

[47] *See Tellabs, Inc. v. Makor Issues & Rights Ltd.*, 551 U.S. 308, 329 (2007) (Scalia, J., concurring in the judgment) (citing and quoting *Dr. Bonham's Case, supra*, for this same Latin phrase).

of interest would itself involve conflicted justices, as a justice who disagrees with a colleague's position on a case would be deciding whether to require the colleague's recusal from that same case.

Third, to the extent justices have tried it, consulting with other justices hasn't worked. We don't know how much the justices discuss ethics issues among themselves. Justice Thomas said he consulted his colleagues about his financial disclosure issues,[48] but we don't know who he consulted. Justice Alito also appears to have had a poor understanding of the disclosure rules on gifts of free travel.[49] If justices do consult with each other, their strive for consistency could become a one-way ratchet toward a looser application of ethics rules. Once a justice has decided not to recuse or not to disclose in a certain situation, other similarly situated justices may decide to do the same, in order not to embarrass a colleague. Choosing the "less ethical" option may be the path of least resistance. In any event, the court's present difficulty with ethics issues suggests that if the justices are acting as ethics lawyers for each other, it is not working.

Why Can't the Law Clerks Do It?

One objection to having a Supreme Court ethics lawyer is that justices already get advice from law clerks. Judicial ethics rules are relatively straightforward, and clerks, even if recent law school graduates, are presumably intelligent enough to figure it out.

One problem with this approach is that clerks are not experts in judicial ethics, and some judicial ethics rules are not as straightforward as they might appear. Additionally, advice from law clerks may be inconsistent. For example, one justice might recuse from a case based on their clerks' counsel, whereas another justice, receiving different advice, does not. Some justices might want law clerks to be overly cautious on matters of ethics, and some might prefer a more permissive stance. Clerks also leave every year or two, so there may be weak institutional memory of how particular ethics matters were resolved in the past. Finally, law clerks expect to take away from their experience a lifelong close relationship with the justice and other clerks. Expecting a clerk to tell a justice they are doing something unethical is an unreasonable expectation. That likely won't happen.

[48] Mark Sherman, *Justice Thomas Says He Didn't Have to Disclose Luxury Trips*, The Associated Press (Apr. 7, 2023), https://apnews.com/article/supreme-court-justice-clarence-thomas-ethics-trips-2c0f59fd1b0d5d3617c1537a767c5325 [https://perma.cc/ET2D-JYYM].

[49] *See* discussion in Chapter 2.

It is here that the Supreme Court ethics lawyer will be invaluable. That lawyer would have expertise in judicial ethics and government ethics in general and would likely serve for longer than the one- or two-year span of a typical Supreme Court clerkship. The ethics lawyer would work for the entire court and not have an allegiance to a particular justice. To the extent law clerks are influenced by ideological divides, the ethics lawyer would be expected to stand apart from those battles. And the ethics lawyer would be expected to give consistent advice to all the justices, not advice tailored to the substance and style that justices most likely want to hear.

Concluding Thoughts

Having an ethics lawyer and an IG at the Supreme Court will not solve all the court's ethics problems, but it could help. There needs to be some independent oversight of ethics at the court, as the justices are not able to effectively do it themselves. However, allowing Congress or the executive branch to investigate the court would likely become political, violate separation of powers principles, and undermine the independence of the judiciary. An ethics lawyer and IG who are independent, yet part of the judicial branch, is the best approach, particularly if combined with other solutions discussed in the chapter that follows.

7
Other Ethics Reforms for the Supreme Court

Besides giving the Supreme Court and an ethics lawyer and an inspector general, Congress could enact other reforms to strengthen ethics compliance on the court. This chapter discusses some of the possibilities.

Three of the reforms discussed in this chapter focus on the front end of the court's ethics problem—the process by which new justices are selected. As discussed in Chapter 1, this is when special interest groups vie for influence in selecting and confirming a new justice. At this stage, special interest groups and individuals behind them establish close personal, and in some cases financial, ties with new justices. As also explained in Chapter 1, some of these groups and individuals may also employ or have other financial dealings with the spouses of justices they supported in the confirmation process.

Other reforms include improving transparency around the role of amici in briefing the court and enlisting appellate judges in advising the court on interpretation of ethics rules and standards.

The Elusive Goal of Transparent Judicial Confirmation Spending

The origin of the court's politicization and influence problem is discussed in Chapter 1. Hundreds of millions of dollars are spent on confirmation battles by organizations and people having interests before the court. Limiting expenditures on confirmation battles is impossible given the First Amendment considerations whenever political speech is involved. The Supreme Court in several cases, including *Citizens United v. FEC*,[1] has ruled that spending on communications to influence elections to Congress and the presidency is protected speech. The court is unlikely to view spending on judicial confirmation battles differently.

[1] *Citizens United v. FEC*, 558 U.S. 310 (2010).

Conduct Unbecoming. Richard W. Painter, Oxford University Press. © Oxford University Press (2026).
DOI: 10.1093/9780197832301.003.0008

Requiring more disclosure of funding sources for confirmation battles is a possibility. Some groups spending large amounts on confirmation battles already disclose information about their spending. They and their financial backers could be required to disclose more. Money flows through many different channels before it funds advertising campaigns for or against a Supreme Court nominee. Where the money originates should be public information.

The problem is that disclosure will not be complete unless the many trade associations, nonprofits, and other organizations that fund advertising in Supreme Court confirmation battles disclose who their donors are. And if these donors are yet other organizations, then those organizations should disclose their donors, and so forth. It is uncertain if Congress would enact a law requiring disclosure of donors through the entire nonprofit sector, not to mention the for-profit entities that funnel money through multiple entities before it arrives at its intended destination.

The court might also strike down such a broad disclosure law. In 2021, the court imposed an exacting scrutiny standard to strike down a California rule requiring charities to disclose their larger donors to the state attorney general. The court held the rule to be an unconstitutional infringement on freedom of association, holding that donors are presumptively entitled to privacy absent an important state interest in disclosure.[2] The court's exacting scrutiny standard was similar to that also used by the court to strike down campaign finance and electioneering communications regulations,[3] adhering to the court's longstanding view that not only people's speech, but also their money, enjoys First Amendment rights.

In sum, federal law probably should require a lot more disclosure of the sources of dark money spending on Supreme Court confirmation battles. This information would allow the public, as well as parties before the court, to know more about persons and organizations that might have earned the favor of one or more justices on the court. Yet disclosure of confirmation battle spending will never be complete. Disclosure mandates that are too expansive would probably be struck down by the court. Disclosure mandates that try to expose the original sources of confirmation battle spending would be difficult to enforce, as a practical matter, as money often flows through

[2] *Americans for Prosperity v. Bonta*, 594 U.S. __ (2021) (holding the California attorney general's office rule requiring charities to provide to it, on a confidential basis, information about their major donors, was an impermissible burden on the First Amendment rights of donors because the policy was not narrowly tailored to an important government interest), Slip Opinion at 7-11 (applying an exacting scrutiny standard in reviewing California's rule under the First Amendment).

[3] *Citizens United v. FEC*, *supra*, and *Buckley* v. *Valeo*, 424 U.S. 1, 64 (1976), cited in *Bonta*, *supra*, Slip Op. at 8-9 ("While exacting scrutiny does not require that disclosure regimes be the least restrictive means of achieving their ends, it does require that they be narrowly tailored to the government's asserted interest.").

multiple channels before reaching an organization that reports it. Finally, Congress would need to enact disclosure laws, and Congress is also influenced by these same organizations that spend massively on electioneering communications for Congress and the White House. Donors who don't want to be disclosed will not support politicians who vote for legislation requiring donor names to be disclosed.

In his 2010 State of the Union address, President Obama strongly criticized the court's holding in *Citizens United* and called on Congress to support a bill called the Democracy Is Strengthened by Casting Light on Spending in Elections Act (the DISCLOSE Act),[4] which would have required disclosure of where dark money political spending comes from. Justice Alito, sitting in a front row with the other justices, reacted to the president's criticism of the court's ruling by shaking his head and mouthing the words "not true."[5] The DISCLOSE Act has been introduced during multiple sessions in Congress but has never passed both houses to become law. A bill requiring disclosure of spending on judicial nominations and confirmations would likely meet a similar fate.

Disclosure of original sources of spending on Supreme Court confirmation battles, even if complete, would also only reveal that part of the judicial influence story that starts at the beginning of a justice's term. The continued story of influence will not be revealed unless the justices comply with requirements that they disclose free travel, gifts, other financial arrangements, sources of spousal income, and the like for each year they are on the court. Strengthening disclosure requirements for the justices and ensuring compliance are issues already discussed in Chapter 2 of this book, as well as in Chapter 6, which suggests that the court have an ethics lawyer and an inspector general (IG).

Pre-Confirmation Ethics Agreements for New Justices

If there is any point when a meaningful ethics pledge can be obtained from a Supreme Court justice, it's when the justice is first nominated to the court. They want the job, and this is the time for the president and the Senate to get specific commitments on ethics in return.

[4] See H.R.5175—DISCLOSE Act111th Congress (2009–2010) (passed the House but not the Senate); S.512—DISCLOSE Act of 2023 (introduced by Senator Whitehouse (D-RI), referred to the Committee on Rules and Administration, but no further action).

[5] Adam Liptak, *Supreme Court Gets a Rare Rebuke, in Front of a Nation*, N.Y. Times (Jan. 28, 2010). Justice Alito did not speak out loud during the State of the Union but did shake his head and mouth the words "not true" when President Obama was discussing *Citizens United*.

Supreme Court nominees do not enter into pre-confirmation ethics agreements tailored to their specific circumstances, although nominees are usually asked very general questions about recusal and other ethics issues in their confirmation hearing. In response, nominees almost always make very general promises to comply with rules applicable to other judges.[6] Now that the Supreme Court has an ethics code, nominees will probably be asked to promise to abide by the court's ethics code. And that's about it.

Most of the focus of confirmation hearings is on what the nominee did in the past. Senators opposing the nomination and their respective interest groups engage in a game of "gotcha," attacking the nominee's ethics while the nominee's supporters play defense, arguing that whatever the nominee did in the past was ethical. Rarely is there a meaningful discussion of the nominee's approach to judicial ethics, and the nominee almost never makes specific commitments about the future.

As the chief White House ethics lawyer from 2005 to 2007, this author screened candidates for nomination to the Supreme Court for past compliance with ethics rules when they were court of appeals judges. This ethics screening of Supreme Court nominees was retrospective, cross-checking a judge's financial holdings, including subsidiaries of companies in which the judge owned stock, with every case in which the judge participated on the court of appeals to detect arguable violations of the federal recusal statute.[7] Opposition groups and Democratic staff of the Senate Judiciary Committee likely were conducting similar searches for conflicts of interest in past cases and anything else they could find to challenge the integrity of the nominee. Some otherwise very qualified Supreme Court candidates, because of relatively minor missed recusals on the court of appeals, would not make the "ethics cut" because the White House would not be willing to risk opponents' attacking the nominee during confirmation.[8]

Judge Samuel Alito of the Third Circuit and Judge John Roberts of the District of Columbia Circuit passed this ethics review. This author helped prepare both for their Supreme Court confirmation hearings, posing questions likely to be put to nominees by the Senate Judiciary Committee. Pre-confirmation briefing sessions covered past recusal from cases, gifts, and

[6] Occasionally, but not often, a nominee makes a more specific commitment prospectively. *See, e.g., Supreme Court Nominee Jackson Says She Would Recuse Herself from Harvard Affirmative Action Case*, Wash. Post (Mar. 23, 2022), https://www.washingtonpost.com/politics/2022/03/23/ketanji-brown-jackson-supreme-court-hearing-live-updates/ [https://perma.cc/S8TG-YDUH].

[7] 28 U.S.C. § 455.

[8] This process of vetting Supreme Court nominees for ethics is discussed in Chapter 1.

financial conflicts of interest. Both confirmation hearings were almost entirely free of controversy over judicial ethics.[9]

But little attention was paid to the specifics of what these justices would do about ethics *after* they got on the Supreme Court. For example, John Roberts owned a significant number of individual stocks when nominated for the court, and he properly recused himself on the court of appeals in cases affecting these stocks, but neither the White House nor the Senate extracted from him a promise to sell these stocks before joining the court. As discussed in Chapter 2, these stocks would later require him to recuse in several cases on the court. A few times, justices who hold individual stocks have, probably inadvertently, missed recusals in cases where they should have recused. In retrospect, new justices should have been required to sell individual stocks before joining the court and promise not to buy new stocks afterward. Diversified mutual funds, where most Americans have their retirement accounts invested, do not pose similar conflicts of interest and should be the preferred investment vehicle for Supreme Court justices as well.

The process for nomination and Senate confirmation of cabinet officers and other executive branch nominees is different. The process, which this author also coordinated for the Bush White House, is more precise and exacting and involves written ethics agreements. US Office of Government Ethics (OGE) guidance enumerates issues that should be considered in drafting these ethics agreements.[10] The agreement is usually a letter from the nominee to the agency ethics lawyer and is tailored to the nominee's specific financial situation and employment history. A copy of the ethics agreement is sent to OGE and to the Senate committee conducting the confirmation hearing.[11]

These agreements may not be legally enforceable contracts, but some of the federal conflict of interest rules cited in these agreements are criminal statutes.[12] In signing such agreements, nominees acknowledge that they are aware of specific conflicts of interest and promise to avoid them. Violation of an ethics agreement could lead to a congressional investigation, firing by

[9] *See* Richard W. Painter, *I Did Alito's Ethics Prep for His Confirmation Hearing. His New Excuses Are Nonsense. Nearly 20 Years Later, I Must Ask: What Happened?*, MSNBC (June 25, 2023), https://www.msnbc.com/opinion/msnbc-opinion/alito-supreme-court-ethics-scandal-vacation-rcna90819 [https://perma.cc/8VGM-CS8Y].

[10] *See* Program Advisory from David J. Apol, General Counsel, to Designated Agency Ethics Off., U.S. Off. of Gov't. Ethics (July 31, 2020), https://www.oge.gov/Web/OGE.nsf/News+Releases/FE34D4F80EB2A056852585C20056BD26/$FILE/PA-20-05%20Revised%20Guide%20to%20Drafting%20Nominee%20Ethics%20Agreements.pdf [https://perma.cc/2TFQ-XZBU].

[11] *See, e.g.*, Letter from Janet L. Yellen, nominee of President Elect Joe Biden for Sec'y of the Treasury, to Brian J. Sonfield, designated agency ethics off., United States Department of the Treasury (Dec. 29, 2020), https://extapps2.oge.gov/201/Presiden.nsf/PAS+Index/18A4D129DD5675888525864F0081071C/$FILE/Yellen,%20Janet%20L.%20final%20EA.pdf [https://perma.cc/SG7U-D76D].

[12] *See, e.g.*, 18 U.S.C. § 208.

the president, or, in particularly egregious cases, even criminal prosecution or impeachment.

Nominees for the Supreme Court also should have an ethics agreement tailored to their own specific circumstances. The ethics agreement could address, among other things 1) divestment of stocks and other investments, 2) recusal from cases related to prior employment, nonprofit board memberships (including relationships with organizations that file amicus briefs), and organizations that assisted the nominee in the confirmation process, 3) limitations on income from book contracts, speaking engagements and other outside activities, 4) recusal on account of conflicts of interest from the employment of a nominee's spouse, and 5) known conflicts of interest involving grown children, siblings and other close relatives of the nominee. The ethics agreement could also provide that the nominee agrees to consult with the Supreme Court ethics lawyer, and follow the ethics lawyer's advice, when complying with existing law such as recusal requirements, restrictions on gifts and free travel, and completing annual disclosure filings required by the Ethics in Government Act of 1978. Finally, there should be a provision whereby the nominee promises to update the ethics agreement when circumstances change: an inheritance, change in marital status, a change in spousal employment, a new book contract, and so on. The Supreme Court ethics lawyer would work with each nominee for the court on drafting the ethics agreement, which would be presented to the Senate before confirmation.

Enforcement of ethics agreements once a justice is on the court would be more complicated than in the executive branch. A Supreme Court justice cannot be fired by the president. A congressional investigation could ensue if there were an alleged violation of a justice's ethics agreement, although as discussed in the Chapter 6, it would be preferable for a Supreme Court IG to investigate the matter first. If there were a finding of wrongdoing, an IG's report would be submitted to Congress.

Supermajority Vote for Confirmation of Judges and Justices

Would Supreme Court justices adhere more closely to ethics rules if confirmation required a supermajority of the Senate? Perhaps so, for two reasons. First, increasing the number of votes required for confirmation might allow the Senate to impose more exacting ethics standards on a nominee, retrospectively looking at past conduct and prospectively, looking at the nominee's commitments in an ethics agreement. Second, even if senators did not change their votes on a nominee because of ethics concerns, nominees who have broader support in the Senate might be more moderate in their judicial philosophy and less likely to have ties to the partisan special interest groups that spend massively on confirmation battles for nominees having the support of Senators in only one political party.

Federal judges and justices are confirmed by a bare majority vote in the Senate. Until the early 2000s, appellate court judges could be blocked by a senate filibuster, which could only be ended by a sixty-vote cloture vote.[13] The Senate's approach to Supreme Court justices was more nuanced; the Senate rarely used filibusters for Supreme Court nominations, but some senators refused to support a nominee who lacked some support in the other political party.

Filibusters of nominations for the appellate courts were abandoned in a 2013 Senate rule change during the Obama administration,[14] a politically palatable move given the history of the filibuster which had been used to try to block civil rights legislation in the 1960s. Republicans were furious at the rule change, but looked forward to a time when they could control the White House and get their own nominees through by a bare majority. In 2017, the Senate also formally ended filibusters of Supreme Court nominees when Republicans sought to overcome opposition to the nomination of Justice Gorsuch.[15]

When the Democrats regained the White House in 2021, liberal interest groups could also help the White House ram through judicial nominees with a bare majority of the Senate.

The point relevant to the subject of this book—judicial ethics—is that the Senate's abandonment of a supermajority requirement strengthens the hand of partisan special interest groups and the people and organizations that fund them. The polarized confirmation battles discussed in Chapter 1 are that much more intense, and as discussed in Chapter 1, the nomination and confirmation processes are where many personal and financial relationships that underlie future ethics problems of Supreme Court justices begin. Not worried about appealing to the minority party in the Senate, presidents are more likely to select nominees with close ties to the interest groups from their

[13] *See* Michael Gerhardt & Richard W. Painter, *Majority Rule and the Future of Judicial Selection*, 2017 Wis. L. Rev. 263 (2017); Michael Gerhardt & Richard W. Painter, *"Extraordinary Circumstances": The Legacy of the Gang of 14 and a Proposal for Judicial Nominations Reform*, 46 U. Rich. L. Rev. 969 (2012).

[14] Jeremy W. Peters, *In Landmark Vote, Senate Limits Use of the Filibuster*, N.Y. Times (Nov. 21, 2013) ("Under the change, the Senate will be able to cut off debate on executive and judicial branch nominees with a simple majority rather than rounding up a supermajority of 60 votes. The new precedent established by the Senate on Thursday does not apply to Supreme Court nominations or legislation itself.").

[15] Matt Flegenheimer, *Senate Republicans Deploy "Nuclear Option" to Clear Path for Gorsuch*, N.Y. Times (Apr. 6, 2017).

political "base" and rely on massive spending by those groups to ram through nominees with a bare majority of senators.

Nominees affiliated with the Federalist Society and other conservative groups in Republican administrations and with the American Constitution Society and other liberal groups in Democratic administrations gain the upper hand in the selection process. The other side is predictably furious and spends millions fighting the nomination. This massive spending, and the bitterness of confirmation battles, cements relationships between nominees and the special interest groups that push them through the Senate. Most will make it. Ever since Robert Bork's failed nomination in 1988, every Senate confirmation floor vote has been successful.[16]

The Senate imposing a supermajority requirement, by reinstating the filibuster or by senators simply refusing to vote for a nominee without bipartisan support, would change this dynamic. Special interest groups powerful in one political party but disliked in the other party would have less influence; candidates they are close to, and likely would remain close to after confirmation, would be less likely to be nominated and confirmed. This would not eliminate all special interests from the nomination and confirmation process but would mitigate the impact of the most polarizing interest groups. Some of the pre-confirmation relationships that become after-confirmation relationships with justices might be avoided.

Arguably, the Senate imposing a supermajority requirement for confirmation is antimajoritarian and undemocratic. But the Senate was never designed to be a democratic institution. Senators serve six-year terms, so shifts in power in the Senate can lag considerably behind shifts in public opinion. Until 1913, senators were chosen by state legislatures, not directly by the people, as now provided for under the Seventeenth Amendment, and there still are two senators for each state, large and small.[17] As discussed in Chapter 1, all three of President Trump's nominees to the court—Justices Gorsuch, Kavanaugh, and Barrett—were confirmed by a vote of a bare majority in the Senate representing less than half the American population, and they were appointed by a president who, in 2016, won the Electoral College but lost the popular vote. If the Senate is evenly split on a nomination, the vice president casts a tie-breaking vote, almost certainly on the side of the president's nominee. Taking all these factors into consideration, the "majority rule" principle of representative democracy does not dictate that the Senate must confirm judges and justices with a bare majority. Perhaps judges and justices should be confirmed

[16] President Bush's 2006 nomination of Harriet Miers was withdrawn before a vote in the Senate.

[17] See Lawrence Lessig, *They Don't Represent Us: Reclaiming Our Democracy* (2019) (discussing and proposing reform of a wide range of antidemocratic characteristic of our political system including the composition and governance of the Senate).

on the premise that a successful nominee needs sufficiently broad support—for example, sixty senators or even two-thirds or sixty-seven senators—and not just barely squeak by with the support of fifty.

The practical problem, however, is that a supermajority requirement imposed by Senate rules would be all too easy to reverse when one party or the other controls both the White House and a slim majority of the Senate. Senate rules can be changed by majority vote, which is exactly what happened when the threshold for confirmation was reduced to fifty senators in 2013 for nominees to lower federal courts, and in 2017 for the Supreme Court. The most recent four nominees to the court were only confirmed by a handful of votes: Gorsuch (54–45), Kavanaugh (50–48), Barrett (52–48), and Jackson (53–47). It's hard to imagine a president and the president's party giving up another such opportunity because the Senate agreed to return to a supermajority requirement for confirmation. The Senate, by fifty votes, would simply change the rule back to where it is now.

One way around this would be for a handful of Senators concerned about political polarization on the Supreme Court, and the corrupting influence of polarized special interest groups, to pledge to each other and to voters in their states that they will not vote for a Supreme Court nominee lacking support of a supermajority, whether fifty-five senators, sixty senators, or even sixty-seven (two-thirds). This pledge might remain intact while those senators are in office, although senators often break promises, and a senator agreeing to a supermajority requirement could come under immense political pressure from a president of their own political party. Many special interest groups supporting a nominee also likely would not agree with it, as a supermajority requirement could force the president to choose someone more moderate. These groups' political spending could then be turned against a senator who stood in their way.

This takes us back to the issue raised in Chapter 1. The ethics problems of the Supreme Court will be difficult to solve without curtailing special interest groups' role in nomination and confirmation of justices, and that problem relates to the broader problem of unregulated and undisclosed electioneering communications influencing the other two branches of government. The Supreme Court itself has contributed to this corruption problem with its holdings equating dark money electioneering spending with "free speech."[18] People and organizations having this power to influence all three branches of government with their money will turn with a vengeance on anyone who tries to take it away from them.

[18] *E.g., Citizens United v. FEC, supra.*

Amici Reform

Over a thousand amicus briefs are filed with the court each term,[19] a dramatic increase from decades earlier when amici were relatively rare.[20] Their value to the court is contested among legal scholars, some saying amicus briefs are written by expert lawyers in the Supreme Court bar who help the justices select which cases to decide and how by connecting specific cases with broad legal principles.[21] Critics claim authors of amicus briefs are really sophisticated lobbyists, usually hired to advance pro-business interests before the court.[22]

Both observations are probably true. Many, not all, Supreme Court amicus briefs are very well written and help the justices connect specific cases with important legal principles the justices want lower court judges to apply in future cases. Amicus briefs also aren't cheap and are paid for by financial backers having interests before the court, in other similar cases if not the specific case at hand.

The names of amici and their counsel are disclosed in the brief, and the "interest of amici" is vaguely described. Who's funding the organizations paying the lawyers to write the amicus brief is not disclosed. Until recently, amici sought permission from opposing counsel before filing a brief. Consent was routinely given so that the justices would not be burdened with a contested motion to file the brief without consent, as neither side wants to annoy the court. The consent process at least provided some advance notice of a brief and perhaps an opportunity to research who might be behind it before it was filed. But the court's rules, effective January 1, 2023, no longer require consent to file an amicus brief.[23]

Sometimes justices and their clerks can guess who's funding a brief; they also may know if their friends or acquaintances are supporting a brief. But other justices may not know. Parties to the case may know who's paying for

[19] Kelsey Reichmann, *Supreme Court "Friends" Leave Justices More Questions Than Answers: Interactions with the Justices Are Few and Far Between but Just About Anyone Can Inject Their Opinion into the latest Supreme Court Legal Battle Set to Shape Decades of American Life*, Courthouse News Service (Oct. 23, 2024).

[20] Joseph D. Kearney & Thomas W. Merrill, *The Influence of Amicus Curiae Briefs on the Supreme Court*, 148 U. Pa. L. Rev. 743, 749 (2000) (noting that while the court decides roughly the same number of cases on the merits as it did in the 1950s, by 2000 the number of amicus filings had increased by more than 800 percent).

[21] Allison Orr Larsen & Neal Devins, *The Amicus Machine*, 102 Va. L. Rev 1901–1968 (2016).

[22] Paul M. Collins Jr., *Friends of the Supreme Court: Interest Groups and Judicial Decision Making* 46 (2008); *Id.*, at 27 (discussing how amici function in the court like lobbyists in the legislature, helping justices maximize policy preferences in terms of effective law).

[23] The requirements for amicus briefs are set forth in Supreme Court Rules 33.1, 34, and 37. See Memorandum to Those Intending to File an *Amicus Curiae* Brief in the Supreme Court of the United States, from Scott S. Harris, clerk of the court, January 2023.

amicus briefs on their side (lawyers for parties and amici often talk to each other although parties are not supposed to assist amici with brief writing). Lawyers on the opposing side often do not know about who's paying for amicus briefs filed against them.

As discussed in Chapter 2, Senator Sheldon Whitehouse described this phenomenon in his 2021 article *A Flood of Judicial Lobbying: Amicus Influence and Funding Transparency*, published in the *Yale Law Journal Forum*. His example of the "flotilla" of amici phenomenon was ironically a case before the court involving the very issue these organizations may care about most—nonprofit organizations' "right" not to disclose their donors: *Americans for Prosperity Foundation v. Bonta*,[24] in which the Americans for Prosperity Foundation, the 501(c)(3) arm of the Koch network's 501(c)(4) group Americans for Prosperity, objected to a California state regulation that required nonprofits to confidentially disclose to the state attorney general their largest donors.[25]

The *Bonta* case was discussed earlier in this chapter because of its broader impact on the problem of how organizations funding Supreme Court confirmation battles do not want to disclose their donors. These groups benefited from the court articulating a broad privacy principle in *Bonta* arising in a very different context. (The California attorney general was trying to compel disclosure of donors to protect the public from charity fraud.) As discussed above, the *Bonta* decision could be an obstacle to a federal law requiring more disclosure of who funds nonprofit organizations, including those that bankroll Supreme Court confirmation battles.

The story told by Senator Whitehouse, is how an "armada of amici" helped make this decision happen. Supreme Court deliberations are confidential, and we usually do not know what impact the amici had on the court's ruling, but in *Bonta* the court was explicit in acknowledging their influence. The opinion of the court observed:

> The gravity of the privacy concerns in this context is further underscored by the filings of hundreds of organizations as amici curiae in support of the petitioners. Far from representing uniquely sensitive causes, these organizations span the ideological spectrum, and indeed the full range of human endeavors: from the American Civil Liberties Union to the Proposition 8 Legal Defense Fund; from the Council on American-Islamic Relations to the Zionist Organization of America; from Feeding

[24] *Americans for Prosperity Foundation v. Bonta*, 141 S.Ct. 2373 (2021).

[25] Sheldon Whitehouse, *A Flood of Judicial Lobbying: Amicus Influence and Funding Transparency*, Yale L.J. F. (Oct. 24, 2021), https://www.yalelawjournal.org/forum/a-flood-of-judicial-lobbying-amicus-influence-and-funding-transparency [https://perma.cc/8J6C-9NDQ].

> America—Eastern Wisconsin to PBS Reno. The deterrent effect feared by these organizations is real and pervasive, even if their concerns are not shared by every single charity operating or raising funds in California.[26]

It is true, as the court states, that this was not entirely a "right-wing" armada of amici, as Senator Whitehouse suggests. But still, Whitehouse rightly points out that many of the amici had ties to a single organization on the political right—the Koch family organization. As discussed in Chapter 1, organizations on the left play the same game of influencing elections, legislation, and Supreme Court nomination battles, and they also do not want their donors disclosed. Donor secrecy is a principle that unites special interests across the political spectrum, and in *Bonta*, they were able to convince the majority of the justices to make it into a constitutional principle. The court itself acknowledged that the amici influenced its decision.

The influence of amici however is not absolute. The three liberal justices—Sotomayor, Breyer, and Kagan—dissented in *Bonta* even though at least some liberal organizations had filed briefs trying to persuade them to join the majority.

Dark money funding of amicus briefs is an even bigger conflict of interest problem for the court if the same monied interests deploy other means of influencing justices (e.g., gifts of luxurious travel). As discussed in Chapter 2, some of the gift donors omitted from justices' financial disclosure forms—including Harlan Crow and Paul Singer—are involved with organizations filing amicus briefs.

This is in addition to whatever "amicus curiae" (friend of the court) briefing on broad legal issues, even if not specific cases, could take place in private conversations during a justice's free travel on yachts or private planes. The two problems are interrelated, and the common theme is that the "dark money" paying for the justices' free travel, and perhaps other benefits, and paying for amicus briefs is not adequately disclosed, and, in some instances, the source of that money may be the same.

Opaque funding of amicus briefs was one of several issues addressed in the Supreme Court Ethics, Recusal and Transparency (SCERT) Act of 2023, which was sponsored by Senator Sheldon Whitehouse and Representative Hank Johnson (D-GA).[27] The bill would have required amici curiae

[26] *Bonta* at ___, slip op. at 17–18.

[27] The bill was cosponsored by, among others, Jeff Merkley (D-OR), Cory Booker (D-NJ), Kirsten Gillibrand (D-NY), Jack Reed (D-RI), Richard Durbin (D-IL), Dianne Feinstein (D-CA), Mark Warner (D-VA), Bernie Sanders (I-VT), and Mazie Hirono (D-HI). S. 359, 118th Cong. (2023).

to disclose more about their sources of funding, recent gifts, travel, or reimbursements they have given to a justice; and lobbying or money they recently spent promoting a justice's confirmation to the court.[28]

Additional disclosure when amicus briefs are filed would increase transparency. Justices should know where the money is coming from when they read these briefs. Counsel of record on amicus briefs, in each case a member of the Supreme Court bar, should be required to disclose that. More disclosure by amici would help inform the court about who is behind the arguments presented and whether there is overlap with other potential conflicts of interest justices might have.

Nonetheless, there is only so far disclosure can go. Counsel of record for a brief can inquire of the amicus party who its funders are but has little ability to ascertain where its funders are getting their money, and so forth. It would be naïve to think a federal statute, or a rule of the Supreme Court, on amicus briefs can ever make disclosure complete.

Ethics Opinions from Appellate Judges

SCERT would also require the court to have a process for parties, counsel, and the public to submit ethics complaints against the justices; and for a review panel of appellate court judges[29] to investigate and make recommendations on those complaints.[30] This also is probably a good idea, but this approach also has its limitations.

First, opening the door to complaints from the public, rather than only from parties and their counsel, means that there will be a lot of unmeritorious complaints against the justices. Someone will need to screen through perhaps thousands of complaints to ferret out the few that raise genuine issues of law and fact suggesting that there could be an ethics violation on the court.

Second, appellate judges would play a more useful role before unethical conduct occurs on the Supreme Court. Chapter 6 discussed how a Supreme Court ethics lawyer and IG could consult with appellate judges when there is disagreement with a justice about disclosure, acceptable gifts, recusal, and other matters. The next best solution would be for appellate judges to be

[28] *See* S. 359, at Section 3 (disclosure by justices), Section 6 (disclosure by parties and amici).

[29] *See* S. 359, 118th Cong. § 367(b) (2023) (the 2023 Senate version of SCERT) (providing for a "judicial investigation panel, which shall be composed of a panel of 5 judges selected randomly from among the chief judge of each circuit of the United States").

[30] *See* S. 359, at Section 2 (Code of conduct for Supreme Court justices) including an amendment to 28 U.S.C. adding a new section 367 governing complaints against justices and a judicial investigation panel of appellate judges.

enlisted to resolve an ethics violation that has already occurred but before it reaches a point where a public complaint is made. When possible, appellate judges should be enlisted in preventing or mitigating ethics violations at the Supreme Court rather than adjudicating them.

Third, it may be a bridge too far to expect appellate court judges to investigate complaints against justices of the Supreme Court. That is function better performed by a Supreme Court IG, as discussed in Chapter 6. Appellate judges are adjudicators not investigators, and likely will not welcome an investigatory role. Indeed, it could be a conflict of interest for them to investigate justices who have the power to overrule them. It would be far better for an IG to ascertain the facts in a matter while appellate court judges stick to the role of the judicial branch, which is to say what the law is. Appellate judges' conclusions on ethics statutes and rules, particularly in close cases where the law could be interpreted either way, would carry more weight with Congress and with the public than the conclusions of the IG alone, and it is in this capacity where appellate judges could be most useful.

Finally, there is the question of whether appellate court judges' determinations in matters of ethics should be binding on the Supreme Court. Although the Supreme Court usually has the last word in interpreting the Constitution and the laws, there is also the ancient principle "*aliquis non debet esse Judex in propria causa*" (no man ought to be a judge of his own cause).[31] An ethics matter involving a justice of the Supreme Court should be decided by judges who are not on the Supreme Court. Ethics panels of federal appellate judges should perhaps perform this function, and Congress could provide that in cases where the Supreme Court justices are conflicted because a case involves themselves or their colleagues, the adjudications of designated ethics panels of appellate judges are final. For example, if an appellate panel ordered a Supreme Court justice to amend previous years' financial filings to disclose all free travel paid for by a particular billionaire, the justice would have to do that. These ethics orders would be binding on the Supreme Court justices, who, if they did not comply, would lose all credibility when they insist that their own orders in all other cases be obeyed by everyone else.

[31] See the discussion of this principle in Chapter 6, citing *Dr. Bonham's Case*, 8 Co. 107a, 114a, 118a, 77 Eng. Rep. 638, 646, 652 (C. P. 1610).

8

Impeachment and Other Things Congress Can Do About the Court

The separation of powers framework in the US Constitution reflects the political theory of checks and balances between different branches of government. This theory was most famously articulated by Baron De Montesquieu in 1748 in *The Spirit of Laws*:

> When the legislative and executive powers are united in the same person, or in the same body of magistracy, there can be no liberty; because apprehensions may arise, lest the same monarch or senate should enact tyrannical laws, to execute them in a tyrannical manner. Again, there is no liberty, if the power of judging be not separated from the legislative and executive powers.[1]

The framers expected Congress to be a check on abuse of power by the president.[2] Since *Marbury v. Madison* was decided in 1803, the judiciary, has been a check on both the president and Congress.[3] But who is a check on federal judges and justices? The founders surely did not intend for judges and justices to be accountable to nobody.

The Impeachment Clause of the Constitution provides that "[t]he President, Vice President and all civil Officers of the United States, shall be removed from Office on Impeachment for, and Conviction of, Treason, Bribery, or other high Crimes and Misdemeanors."[4] This includes federal judges. Article III, Section 1 of the Constitution provides that federal judges

[1] Charles de Secondat, Baron De Montesquieu, *The Spirit of Laws* 216 (1823; repr. of 1748 ed).

[2] *See The Federalist No. 48* (James Madison) (arguing that the branches of government must have sufficient power to impose some restraints over each other to operate effectively). *See* Maurice J. C. Vile, *Constitutionalism and the Separation of Powers* (1967) (tracing the history of constitutional governance and examining criticisms of the doctrine), and William B. Gwyn, *The Meaning of the Separation of Powers: An Analysis of the Doctrine from Its Origin to the Adoption of the United States Constitution* (1965) (analyzing the doctrine of the separation of powers from its origin to its adoption in the US Constitution).

[3] *Marbury v. Madison*, 5 U.S. 137 (1803) is the most famous case in which the Supreme Court asserted the power of the judiciary to check the power of the executive as well as Congress.

[4] U.S. Const., Article II, Section 4. The House of Representatives has sole power to impeach, and the Senate sole power to conduct impeachment trials. See Article I, Section 2, Clause 5; Article I, Section 3, Clause 6. An impeached and convicted federal officer is removed from office and can be barred by the Senate from holding future office. Article I, Section 3, Clause 7.

Conduct Unbecoming. Richard W. Painter, Oxford University Press. © Oxford University Press (2026).
DOI: 10.1093/9780197832301.003.0009

shall hold their seats during "good behavior,"[5] clearly implying that they are among federal officers who can be impeached by the House and removed by the Senate.

Impeachment in Theory

Federal officers can be impeached by the House for "high crimes and misdemeanors." This language in the Impeachment Clause appears open ended, yet the requirement of a two-thirds vote in the Senate to convict assures that in a successful impeachment this language will be construed quite narrowly. In the case of federal judges, however, there is also the "good behavior" language in Article III, Section 1, which suggests a somewhat lower threshold for impeachment and removal. This makes sense because judges, unlike presidents and cabinet officers, have lifetime tenure, and a higher standard of behavior is expected of judges than, for example, politicians.

At the same time, the entire purpose of lifetime tenure would be undermined if federal judges were subjected to politically motivated impeachment and removal. The only impeachment of a Supreme Court justice in US history illustrates that point. Justice Samuel Chase was impeached by the House in 1804 on allegations he allowed partisanship to affect his oversight of trials in the lower federal courts, which was a routine duty of Supreme Court justices in the early years of the Republic. The impeachment of Justice Chase was instigated by President Thomas Jefferson and had clear political overtones, as the Democratic-Republicans were trying to remove Federalist appointees from the bench. Chase himself engaged in conduct that appeared partisan, but the Senate acquitted him.[6] Of the votes taken on eight separate charges against Chase, the highest number was eighteen Senators in favor of conviction, with sixteen for acquittal.

Chief Justice William Rehnquist later wrote a book about the impeachment of Chase.[7] He and other observers saw in the verdict of acquittal validation of the independence of the judiciary. Although judges should not conduct themselves in a partisan manner, impeachment of a judge for partisanship is an even greater threat to the independence of the judiciary and has not been tried since the Chase trial over two centuries ago. With respect to the political partisanship today of Justices Thomas and Alito, and of the late Justice Ginsburg,

[5] U.S. Const., Article III, Section 1.

[6] *See* Richard B. Lillich, *The Chase Impeachment*, 4 Am.J. of Legal Hist. 49 (1960); *see generally Trial of Samuel Chase, An Associate Justice of the Supreme Court of the United States* (1805).

[7] William H. Rehnquist, *Grand Inquests: The Historic Impeachments of Justice Samuel Chase and President Andrew Johnson* (1992).

discussed in Chapter 3 of this book, their conduct may have been improper, but the precedent set in the Chase impeachment is that partisanship alone would not be grounds for impeachment and removal.

Corruption, however, is a different matter. There are different categories of corruption, ranging from financial conflicts of interest of judges to bribes and judges receiving secret gifts from persons with interests before them. At some point, a judge is sufficiently corrupt that removal from the bench is the appropriate remedy.

Two crimes are specifically mentioned in the Impeachment Clause of the Constitution. One is treason. (As mentioned later in this chapter, lower court federal judges were impeached and removed for the crime of rebellion during the Civil War.) The other crime is bribery.

Bribery for purposes of impeachment does not necessarily mean what modern criminal bribery statutes say it means.

The Constitution does not define bribery. If one adheres to the originalist interpretation of the Constitution embraced by today's Supreme Court, the common law meaning of the word "bribery" when the Constitution was ratified should guide interpretation.[8] That common law definition of bribery is sufficiently broad that today's justices, in view of their own conduct, described in Chapter 2 of this book, might feel uncomfortable with it.

William Hawkins's *A Treatise of the Pleas of the Crown* (1716), said:

> But Bribery in a large sense is sometimes taken for the receiving or offering of any undue Reward, by or to any Person whatsoever, whose ordinary Profession of Business relates to the Administration of public [] Justice in order to incline him to do a Thing against the known Rules of Honesty and Integrity . . . [This corruption] deserves the severest of Punishments.[9]

Similar definitions appear in other publications, such as *Russell on Crimes* (1819).[10]

Dr. Samuel Johnson's 1773 dictionary defines a "bribe" as "[a] reward given to pervert the judgment or corrupt the conduct."[11] Johnson defined "bribery" as "[t]he crime of taking or giving rewards for bad practices."[12] Bribery thus does not require that a particular official act be exchanged for a reward, an

[8] At the time of the founding, bribery was a common law crime of "giving, and offering to give, [any] improper rewards" to a public official. Frank Bowman, *High Crimes and Misdemeanors: A History of Impeachment for the Age of Trump* 243 (2019).

[9] William Hawkins, *A Treatise of the Pleas of the Crown* (1716).

[10] William Oldnall Russell, *Treatise on Crimes and Misdemeanors*, (1853; repr. of 1819 ed.).

[11] Bribe, in 1 Samuel Johnson, *A Dictionary of the English Language* (1978; repr. of 1773 ed.).

[12] Bribery, in *Ibid.*

express quid pro quo, but rather the focus is on the purpose of the reward itself. Why was it given? It is a reward given to pervert judgment, corrupt conduct, or result in bad practices? If so, it is a bribe and should not be offered or accepted.

William Blackstone defined "bribery" as "the next species of offen[s]e against public justice; which is when a judge, or other person concerned in the administration of justice, takes any undue reward to influence his behave[or] in his office."[13] Under this definition, if a judge knows that someone is giving a gift to influence performance of judicial duties, it is a bribe. This is true even if the judge never intended to change the way he performs his judicial duties because of the gift and does not do so. If the gift giver intended to influence the judge and if the judge knows that is so, the judge has accepted a bribe.[14]

As Professor Zephyr Teachout explains in her book *Corruption in America*, the law defining bribery and corruption in Britain and colonial America existed for the primary purpose of removing public officials and preventing them from holding future office.[15] A wide range of corrupt practices could result in impeachment of a public official, and the outcome of impeachment trials turned on a mixture of factors both legal and political.[16]

In 1621, Lord Chancellor Francis Bacon was the first judge impeached for bribery, in a prosecution led by Sir Edward Coke. Bacon had received thousands of pounds in gifts, payments, and loans from litigants in cases before him but insisted that he did not change his rulings and, in fact, had entered decrees against some of the payors.[17] But even if a quid pro quo exchange could not be proven in these instances, "Bacon had made Chancery produce cash"[18]—a lot of it. He eventually confessed and was convicted by the Lords.

One hundred years later, Lord Chancellor Thomas Parker, 1st Earl of Macclesfield, was impeached in 1725 for bribery and corruption and was convicted by the Lords. Macclesfield not only had received undisclosed payments but had also in return awarded appointments to unqualified persons as chancery master (an administrative office roughly equivalent to a US magistrate judge today), misappropriated funds, and in several other ways allowed

[13] 4 William Blackstone, *Commentaries on the Laws of England* 139 (1765).

[14] *See* Richard W. Painter, *Bribery Law: Is Anything Left?*, 46 Cardozo L. Rev. 1775 (2025) (containing a similar comparison of common law definitions of bribery with modern criminal statutes).

[15] Zephyr Teachout, *Corruption in America: From Benjamin Franklin's Snuff Box to Citizens United* (2016).

[16] *See, e.g.*, H. of Lords, Gr. Brit. Parliament, Report from the Lords Committees Appointed to Examine Precedents Relative to the State of the Impeachment Against Warren Hastings Esquire, Brought Up from the Commons and Proceeded Upon in the Last Parliament (1791) (compiling English precedent during an investigation of the charges against Warren Hastings).

[17] John T. Noonan Jr, *Bribes: The Intellectual History of a Moral Idea* (1987) at 356.

[18] *Ibid.* at 358.

his own financial interest to influence performance of his duties as lord chancellor.[19]

Parallel to these impeachment proceedings against public officials, common law defined bribery as a tort, committed when a person corrupts another person's private fiduciary. The vice of secrecy is important, because the fiduciary's receipt of the secret payment is a breach of the duty of loyalty that the principal is entitled to expect, resulting in remedies at equity[20] and common law[21] including recission of a transaction approved by the corrupt fiduciary regardless of whether the payment altered the conduct of the fiduciary.

If a private transaction can be rescinded and other damages awarded because of the corruption of a fiduciary by gifts and other things of value, there surely must also be a remedy for similar corruption of a judge.

Following the impeachment and common law precedents in English law, the word "bribery" is expressly mentioned in the US Constitution's Impeachment Clause.[22] Removal from office is the purpose; the Constitution does not allow infliction of additional criminal punishments in the impeachment proceeding. The threshold of culpability for removal of a public official is understandably different than that required for imposing imprisonment or other criminal penalty.

In eighteenth-century England, common law bribery was a "high misdemeanor," meaning that guilty persons could be barred from public office.[23] The US Constitution refers to bribery and also refers to "high crimes and misdemeanors," and the Constitution furthermore provides that an impeached and removed public official can be tried separately in criminal court.[24] This means that impeachment and the criminal case for bribery are two different proceedings with different objectives. And different law applies.

[19] See Julia Rudolph, *Jurisdictional Controversy and the Credibility of Common Law, in* Questioning Credible Commitment: Perspectives on the Rise of Financial Capitalism 104–124 (2013) (discussing the Maccelesflied impeachment)

[20] Jordan English, *Bribery and Secret Commissions: A Common Law-Equity Divide?*, Lloyd's Mar. & Com. L.Q. (2025). "Starting with liability in equity, where a bribe or secret commission is paid to a fiduciary—that is, a person owing fiduciary obligations—the payment will amount to an unauthorised profit obtained by the recipient in breach of their obligation of loyalty. The bribe recipient will therefore be required to account for and disgorge the profits obtained in breach of fiduciary duty, which would include the value of the bribe." *Id* at 4.

[21] "At common law, the ground of rescission [of a transaction] is the bribery itself. For a transaction to be liable to be rescinded for bribery, all that need be shown is that the transaction the principal is seeking to have set aside was entered into while the agent was 'tainted by bribery' and that the counterparty to the contract was aware of the payment of the bribe. There is no need to prove that the bribe was a cause of the transaction being entered into or that the agent's mind was influenced in any way." *Id* at 6.

[22] U.S. Const. art. II, § 4.

[23] Teachout, *Corruption in America*, *supra* at 110–111.

[24] U.S. Const., art. I, § 3, cl. 6–7 ("Judgement in Cases of Impeachment shall not extend further than to removal from Office, and disqualification to hold and enjoy any Office of honor, Trust or Profit under the United States: but the Party convicted shall nevertheless be liable and subject to Indictment, Trial, Judgement and Punishment, according to Law.").

The definition of bribery, in impeachment trials or at common law, was not precise. But still, it is helpful to consider whether each of the following scenarios would have been considered a bribe at the time of the founding:

- A businessman in an industry impacted by frequent cases before the Supreme Court, even when his company is not a party to a case before the court, gives a justice of the court an interest-free loan to pay the entire purchase price of an extravagant coach, which costs more than an average house, and then forgives that loan.
- A businessman whose financial interests are impacted by cases before the Supreme Court frequently invites a justice of the court to be his companion on luxurious travel excursions, buys a house belonging to the justice's mother but allows her to continue living there, and pays a private school tuition bill for a minor nephew of the justice for whom the justice is a guardian.
- A businessman invites a justice on a free expenses-paid fishing trip, including luxury travel and lodging; the businessman's company later has a case before the court, and the justice does not recuse from the case.[25]

Assume also that in each of these instances the justice does not disclose the gift even though the justice is required to do so, and that the justice signs a writing incorrectly stating that the justice has disclosed everything he is required to disclose.

Absent an express quid pro quo exchange of the gift for an official act, none of these gifts would be a bribe under the modern US criminal statutes discussed separately later in this chapter. But what is not so clear is whether these gifts would be considered bribes under common law, and the understanding of corruption in the impeachment trials of Sir Francis Bacon (1621) and Thomas Parker (1725).

The first gift—the very large forgiven loan—is hard to explain with a motive other than the donor's hope to influence the court. Even the wealthiest people do not ordinarily give gifts of such magnitude to their friends, and if they do, they ordinarily do not characterize them as "loans" that are never repaid. It is possible that this donor is exceptional in his generosity, and that this gift has nothing to do with the recipient being a Supreme Court justice. But it's unlikely. Even if the justice never changed his vote in a case because of this

[25] These three hypotheticals track some of the alleged financial conflicts of interest of today's Supreme Court justices discussed in Chapter 2.

very large gift, the purpose of the gift is suspicious at best, and at common law it might be considered a bribe.

The second example involves multiple gifts from the same source that cumulatively are worth a lot. Separately, each gift might have a credible explanation other than an attempt to influence the court, and thus each gift if considered separately probably would not be a bribe. But this gift giver keeps on giving, and the cumulative pattern is as concerning as the first example. The frequency of the gift giving over many years might reflect a close friendship as a motive for the gifts, and hence not a bribe, but the pattern might be considered in its entirety to be a bribe at common law.

The third example, the fishing trip, probably falls short of a bribe at common law unless it is known at the time that the donor will have a case before the court. The one free trip is probably not enough to suggest that the donor could expect it to influence the court, particularly when there is no pending case. The fact that a case comes before the court later does not make it into a bribe retroactively. Still, the fact that the justice does not recuse from the donor's case demonstrates, at a minimum, insensitivity to public perception that the gift could have a corrupting influence.

In all three examples, the failure of the justice to disclose the gift(s) is troubling, and as discussed above, secrecy is a relevant factor in civil bribery cases at common law. The failure to disclose might have been because of forgetfulness, or a misunderstanding of disclosure rules, or alternatively could be an indication of a guilty conscience because the justice knew there was a corrupt reason for the gift, or perhaps some other reason that the justice did not want the gift to be disclosed.

Defining common law offenses is sometimes uncertain, which is why modern criminal cases turn instead on statutes such as the federal bribery statute discussed below. But these three examples of undisclosed gifts to justices, particularly the first two, come dangerously close to what the English courts and the framers of our Constitution might have thought of as bribes. If so, such conduct of a justice of the court, particularly if repeated might be grounds for impeachment in the House and conviction in the Senate. This conclusion, of course, assumes that both the House and Senate in impeachment proceedings apply common law concepts of bribery and corruption in defining "high crimes and misdemeanors."

Also, none of the three examples above is illustrative of "good behavior" in office, the constitutional definition of the terms for a federal judge's life tenure, and if repeated such conduct might be sufficient for impeachment and removal on those grounds. Again, however, the applicable standard in an impeachment proceeding, is for the House and Senate to decide.

The discussion in this chapter now turns to examining the current state of US criminal law defining bribery, not because it defines how a justice of the Supreme Court should behave, nor the definition of "good behavior" or "high crimes and misdemeanors" under the Constitution, but because this is the narrower definition of bribery the House and Senate in impeachment proceedings might prefer. If so, impeachment of a justice for any of the above examples of undisclosed gifts would be extremely unlikely without a proven quid pro quo. Conviction by the Senate would be even less likely.

One would think the justices would adhere to a higher standard of conduct than the narrow definitions in criminal law, paying closer attention to common law understandings of bribery, and avoiding the breach of trust involved with receipt of a secret gift, particularly when there is a legal duty to disclose it. But some of the examples of justices' behavior discussed in Chapter 2 suggest otherwise. If criminal definitions of bribery alone are the standard applied in impeachment proceedings, the House and Senate may let the justices get away with it.

The statutory definition of bribery in the United States has become narrower since the first version of the statute was enacted in 1853.[26] Today, the prosecution must prove intent to enter into a quid pro quo exchange of an official act for the bribe, which is described as a "thing of value."[27] The current federal criminal code, specifically 18 U.S.C. § 201(b), provides that the crime of bribery occurs if someone "directly or indirectly, corruptly gives, offers or promises anything of value to any public official . . . with intent . . . to influence any official act"[28] Section 201(c), as interpreted by the Supreme Court, prohibits "gratuities," which is the acceptance of a reward after an official act even if there was no corrupt intent before the official act.[29]

Think of a gratuity as a "tip," not for a waiter or taxi driver but for a public official as a reward for doing a "good job." It's a crime in the case of a federal official, if it can be proven that the gift to the public official was a reward for the official act. For example, a billionaire likes the way a justice has decided one or more cases in favor of big businesses, and to reward the justice for this

[26] Teachout, *supra.*

[27] *Ibid.*

[28] 18 U.S.C. § 201(b).

[29] *See* 18 U.S.C. § 201(c). While Section 201(c) does not explicitly use the phrase "gratuities," the Supreme Court recently explained the difference between a bribe and a gratuity under the statute in *Snyder v. United States.* 603 U.S. 1, 8 (2024) ("Importantly, because bribery can corrupt the official act, Congress treats bribery as a far more serious offense than gratuities. For example, if a federal official accepts a bribe, federal bribery law provides for a 15-year maximum prison sentence. By contrast, if a federal official accepts a prohibited gratuity, federal gratuities law sets a 2-year maximum prison sentence." [citations omitted] (citing 18 U.S.C. § 201(b), (c)). In *Snyder*, the court ruled that a separate federal criminal statute applicable to state and local officials, 18 U.S.C. § 666(a)(1)(B), only prohibits bribes and not gratuities, which are left to regulation under state laws. *Snyder*, 603 U.S. 1.

the billionaire buys the justice an expensive present or invites him on an all expenses paid luxury vacation. The present or free vacation is a gratuity and could be prosecuted as a violation of the federal criminal statute.

Unlike an impeachment proceeding, which focuses only on the public official, the criminal bribery statute covers *both* the public official and the giver or offeror of the bribe. But there must be an official act connected to the bribe. Without an official act being offered, solicited or agreed upon (the act does not have to be performed), there is no bribe for purposes of the criminal bribery statute.

Under the statute, an official act furthermore does not include just an opportunity to meet with a public official. The public official must *do something* in exchange for the bribe.

The statute does not specifically address this point, but that is how the Supreme Court has interpreted it. The Supreme Court's unanimously held in *McDonnell v. United States* that selling access to a public official for cash or other consideration is not a bribe.[30] The governor of Virginia, Robert McDonnell, was convicted of exchanging official meetings for gifts to himself and his wife, but the court, in 2016, reversed these convictions, holding that an "official act" is an action that "involve[s] a formal exercise of governmental power."[31] Agreeing to a meeting is not an "official act" under the bribery statute.[32] Buying access to a public official thus is permitted so long as the public official does not promise to do a specific official act in exchange for the bribe.

If *McDonnell* had been decided differently, or if the federal bribery statute were amended to specifically provide that agreeing to a meeting to discuss official business is itself an official act, many public officials might be in jeopardy. For example, campaign contributors often donate a specified amount to attend private gatherings with public officials where official government business is discussed. In addition to the usual campaign dinners and cocktail parties, this includes weekend retreats, golf outings, and other events with elected officials, sometimes with officers in the executive branch attending as well. In 2025, the president of the United States had a private dinner with purchasers of his meme coin,[33] although it is not clear how much official government business was discussed.

[30] *McDonnell v. United States*, 579 U.S. 550, 579–581 (2016).
[31] *Id.* at 555, 574.
[32] *Id.* at 574.
[33] Michelle Conlin et al., *Wealthy foreign crypto investors descend on President Trump's Golf Club for $148 Million Meme Coin Dinner*, Reuters (May 22, 2025), https://www.reuters.com/world/us/trump-draws-global-crypto-investors-with-148-million-meme-coin-dinner-2025-05-22/.

And, more to the point of this book, in view of the *McDonnell* case, none of the conduct described in Chapter 2 of this book could be prosecuted as bribery. Buying access to a Supreme Court justice with gifts of free travel, even if the pot is sweetened with a $250,000 recreational vehicle or buying the Justice's mother's house, is not a crime. Even if a justice expressly agreed to a private meeting in exchange for a gift (there is no evidence that any of the justices have done so), that would not violate the bribery statute.

Supreme Court justices' conversations with billionaire hosts on free vacations might just be about fishing, or yachting, or politics, but some conversation might be about legal issues, if not specific cases, before the court. Nobody knows. Judicial ethics rules prohibit *ex parte* communications with justices about specific cases by a party or lawyer in a case pending before the court. Still, the criminal bribery law apparently is not violated even if someone paid for the opportunity to have a conversation with the justice.

But as discussed above, *McDonnell* is the legal rule for criminal bribery prosecution, not necessarily the legal rule for impeachment. The common law definition of bribery is broader. If an originalist interpretation of the Impeachment Clause is at all important, as this court says it is when interpreting other parts of the Constitution, it is important to note that the founders probably thought it was a bribe for a public official to agree to a meeting to discuss official business in exchange for a thing of value.

There is no record of deliberation over the definition of bribery at the Constitutional Convention, but a famous scandal soon thereafter illustrated that the founders knew what a bribe was. American diplomats were hit up for cash payments by French officials while trying to negotiate peace with France in the 1790s.[34] The bribes were solicited by officials associated with Charles Maurice de Talleyrand, the French foreign minister.[35] American diplomats had traveled all the way to Paris only to be faced with demands for payment in exchange merely for getting "a public audience" with French officials.[36] The French officials requesting these payments—referred to as "X," "Y" and "Z" in correspondence rather than by their actual names—did not promise a particular official act for the payments, but access to high-ranking officials who in turn would provide an opportunity to influence France's governing

[34] For an account of the XYZ Affair, see Stanley Elkins & Eric McKitrick, *The Age of Federalism: The Early American Republic, 1788–1800*, at 549–79 (1993). *See also* Richard W. Painter, *Bribery Law: Is Anything Left?*, *supra* (contrasting the Supreme Court's holding in *McDonnell v. United States*, 579 U.S. 550 (2016) (holding that payment only for a meeting with the governor is not a bribe under federal law) with the "XYZ Affair," in which Thomas Jefferson and others expressed anger at French Foreign Minister Talleyrand demanding payment from American diplomats in exchange for a meeting).

[35] Elkins & McKitrick, *The Age of Federalism* at 550.

[36] *Id.* at 569.

Directory.[37] This extortion scheme, known as the XYZ Affair, angered the Americans.[38]

Thomas Jefferson, who hoped to avoid war with France, was appalled.[39] He wrote to his nephew Peter Carr in 1798:

> As the instructions to our envoys [and] their communications have excited a great deal of curiosity, I [e]nclose you a copy. [Y]ou wlll perc[ei]ve that they have been assailed by swindlers whether with or without the participation of Taleyrand is not very apparent. [T]he known corruption of his character renders it very possible he may have intended to share largely in the 50,000 £. demanded.[40]

The American delegation came home from Paris, diplomatic negotiations failed, and there soon followed the Quasi-War between the United States and France in which the two nations attacked each other's ships on the seas.[41]

Would the founders have intended that officers of the United States or of the states could do the same thing and request or accept payment in return for a meeting? Likely not. Unless the founders for some unexplained reason thought that which was corrupt for Talleyrand would not be corrupt for the governor of Virginia, they likely would have thought that an agreement to grant an official meeting in exchange for a thing of value was a bribe. The Supreme Court in *McDonnell* merely interpreted a modern criminal statute; the court did not redefine the concept of bribery.

At least some of the conduct described in Chapter 2 of this book treads dangerously close to the founders' understanding of bribery that, among other things, likely included payment of a thing of value for access to a public official. There is no proof that any justice has changed the way they vote on cases to enrich themselves, and there is no evidence that any of the justices demanded payment in exchange for a meeting. But lavish gifts from persons with interests before the court, gifts that might not be given but for the official position of a justice, presents a prima facie case that the purpose of the gift is to gain access to the justice at a minimum, and perhaps more. The meeting need not be in the justice's chambers, and it could be on a yacht, on a fishing expedition or at a lodge in the Adirondacks. The gift given to gain access is just the same. If the gift is not disclosed despite a legal requirement that it be

[37] *Id.* at 550, 571, 573.
[38] *Id.* at 550.
[39] Letter from Thomas Jefferson to Peter Carr (Apr. 12, 1798), https://founders.archives.gov/documents/Jefferson/01-30-02-0180 [perma.cc/JN35-9C9V].
[40] *Id.*
[41] Alexander DeConde, *The Quasi-War: The Politics and Diplomacy of the Undeclared War with France, 1797–1801* (1966).

disclosed, and if the justice subsequently participates in a case affecting the gift giver, the situation is so much worse. Impeachment might be justified.

But once again, the legal standard for impeachment is for the House and Senate to decide. If the House or Senate decides that a judge is only to be removed from office for receipt of a bribe within the meaning of the federal criminal statute, as it is interpreted by the Supreme Court, which in essence requires a quid pro quo for an official act, in almost all instances an impeachment will not succeed.

And meanwhile, it is the justices themselves who shape this criminal law when they narrowly interpret federal bribery statutes. In doing so, the justices may lure themselves into believing that this criminal law is the only definition of bribery that applies to them. If the House and Senate choose not to exercise their prerogative to apply a different definition in impeachment proceedings, the justices will have been allowed to define the law that applies in their own case, the legal standards by which they are to remain in office.

Impeachment in Practice

As discussed above, only one Supreme Court justice has ever been impeached. Associate Justice Samuel Chase was impeached for political partisanship on the bench and was acquitted. This is a clear indication that if precedent is a guide, the partisanship of some of today's justices discussed in Chapter 3, however troubling, would not be grounds for impeachment.

No justice has been impeached for corruption. As discussed in Chapter 4, Justice Abe Fortas was threatened with impeachment for receipt of large payment from a businessman with interests before the court, but he resigned before he could be impeached. His fate suggests that, at least fifty-seven years ago, indicia of corruption, even falling short of criminal bribery, were viewed as grounds for impeachment.

Over the nation's history, fourteen lower federal judges have been impeached by the House, some for corruption but others for offenses such as drunkenness and neglect of duty, and one for rebellion during the Civil War. Impeachments for abuse of power or other more ambiguous charges in connection with official duties were often less successful.

John Pickering, judge, US District Court, District of New Hampshire, was impeached on March 2, 1803, for intoxication on the bench and unlawful handling of property claims, found guilty by the Senate, and removed from office.

James H. Peck, judge, US District Court, Western District of Tennessee, was impeached April 24, 1830, for abuse of the contempt power, but acquitted in the Senate.

West H. Humphreys, judge, US District Court, Western District of Tennessee, was impeached May 6, 1862, on charges of refusing to hold court and waging war against the US government, convicted by the Senate, removed from office, and barred from future office.

Mark H. Delahay, judge, US District Court, Kansas, was impeached February 28, 1873, for intoxication on the bench and resigned prior to trial.

Charles Swayne, judge, US District Court, Northern District of Florida, was impeached December 13, 1904, on charges of abuse of contempt power and other misuses of office and acquitted by the Senate.

Robert W. Archbald, associate judge, US Commerce Court, was impeached July 11, 1912, for improper business relationship with litigants, found guilty by the Senate, removed from office, and disqualified from future office.

George W. English, judge, US District Court, Eastern District of Illinois, was impeached April 1, 1926, for abuse of power and resigned.

Harold Louderback, judge, US District Court, Northern District of California, was impeached February 24, 1933, for favoritism in the appointment of bankruptcy receivers and acquitted.

Halsted L. Ritter, judge, US District Court, Southern District of Florida, was impeached March 2, 1936, for favoritism in the appointment of bankruptcy receivers and practicing law as a sitting judge, found guilty, and removed from office.

Harry E. Claiborne, judge, US District Court of Nevada, was impeached July 22, 1986, for income tax evasion and for remaining on the bench following a criminal conviction, found guilty, and removed from office.

Alcee L. Hastings, judge, US District Court, Southern District of Florida, was impeached August 3, 1988, for perjury and conspiring to solicit a bribe, found guilty, and removed from office.

Walter L. Nixon, judge, US District Court, Southern District of Mississippi, was impeached May 10, 1989, for perjury before a federal grand jury, convicted, and removed from office.

Samuel B. Kent, judge, US District Court for the Southern District of Texas, was impeached June 19, 2009, for sexual assault, obstructing and impeding an official proceeding, and making false and misleading statements; he resigned.

G. Thomas Porteous Jr., judge, US District Court, Eastern District of Louisiana, was impeached March 11, 2010, for accepting bribes and making false statements under penalty of perjury, convicted, removed from office, and barred from holding future office.[42]

But what about Supreme Court justices? As discussed in Chapter 4, Justice Fortas came close to impeachment before he resigned from the court in 1969. There is no evidence that any of the current justices violated the criminal bribery statute, but the undisclosed gifts and business transactions described in this book in Chapter 2 are not "good behavior."[43] As discussed above, some of these gifts and transactions would approach the common law understanding of bribery if the intent of the donor was to influence a justice of the court. The answer to the question US Senator John Kennedy (R-LA) asked the author of this book in a June 2023 Senate Budget Committee hearing ("which justices do you think are bought?")[44] depends on what one means by "bought." The founders' understanding of corruption and bribery and the modern criminal bribery statute suggest different answers to that question.

Furthermore, as discussed in Chapter 2, many of these gifts and transactions were not disclosed despite a legal requirement that they be disclosed, and despite the justice's attestation and signature certifying that their disclosure was complete. Under 18 U.S.C. 1001, a knowing false statement on a disclosure form, like a knowing false statement on an income tax return, is a crime. As discussed in Chapter 2, the justices who failed to disclose claim this was inadvertent or due to a misunderstanding of the disclosure requirements.

Reasonable persons can differ as to whether this conduct rises to the level of "high crimes and misdemeanors" described in the Impeachment Clause, and whether the reference in Article III to judges holding office only during "good behavior" suggests a different threshold for impeachment and removal of a federal judge than an officer in the executive branch who does not have life tenure.

But no serious effort has been undertaken in Congress even to open an impeachment investigation of any of the justices, much less have a vote on impeachment. Even short of impeachment, the House has not subpoenaed a justice of the court to testify about any of these ethics breaches that might result in impeachment. The chairman of the Senate Judiciary Committee asked the chief justice to testify about Supreme Court ethics, but he refused. A subpoena did not follow.

Congress could do more to oversee the court and insist that ethics rules be complied with, but it doesn't. This chapter now turns to the reasons

[42] *See* US House of Representatives, Archives, List of Individuals Impeached by the House of Representatives, https://history.house.gov/Institution/Impeachment/Impeachment-List/.

[43] U.S. Const. Article III, Section 1.

[44] *See* Introduction of this book, describing this author's 2023 colloquy with Senator Kennedy.

why, at this time in our history, the remedies for judicial misconduct contemplated in the Constitution—congressional investigation and, in the worst cases, impeachment—are not working.

Congress's failure to be a meaningful check on the president and other officers of the executive branch is an equally serious matter that this author has addressed in another book.[45] Here the focus is on why Congress is not willing to do anything about the ethics crisis at the Supreme Court.

The Problem of Partisanship

A big part of the problem in Congress is the influence of political parties. Supreme Court justices appointed by Republican presidents are defended by Republicans at all costs, and vice versa for Democrats. All the partisanship in confirmation battles, described in Chapter 1, reemerges if a justice is accused of misconduct. Outside organizations that spend millions of dollars supporting and opposing nominations to the court also get involved, weighing in on matters of judicial ethics in the media, through a partisan lens. Cable news follows suit: A justice whom MS NOW (formerly MSNBC) says is unethical, and should be impeached, is the epitome of virtue on Fox News. And so on.

The founders' word for this partisanship was "faction." The founders feared faction for reasons not that different from what we are experiencing today.

Political parties grew quickly after the Constitution was ratified. Politicians who supported a strong central government, with a powerful executive, were called Federalists. Those who wanted more power for the states, and a weaker central government, were called Anti-Federalists. The Federalists formed a party by that name in 1789 under the leadership of Alexander Hamilton. Their opponents formed the Democratic-Republican Party in 1792, and later defeated the Federalists, electing Thomas Jefferson as president in 1800. Jefferson refused to deliver commissions to judges appointed at the last minute by his predecessor John Adams, including William Marbury, the plaintiff in *Marbury v. Madison*. Then, in 1804, Jefferson prodded partisans in Congress to impeach Justice Samuel Chase for his partisanship on the bench. The federal judiciary, and questions of judicial conduct, were already being politicized in Congress.

The framers had worried that factionalism would emerge with political parties. James Madison, in *Federalist*, no. 10, "The Utility of the Union as a Safeguard Against Domestic Faction and Insurrection," defined faction as

[45] E. Thomas Sullivan & Richard W. Painter, The *Presidency: Power, Responsibility and Accountability* (2025).

"a number of citizens, whether amounting to a minority or majority of the whole, who are united and actuated by some common impulse of passion, or of interest, adverse to the rights of other citizens, or to the permanent and aggregate interests of the community."[46] More specifically, Madison warned that

> [a] zeal for different opinions concerning religion, concerning government, and many other points, as well of speculation as of practice; an attachment to different leaders ambitiously contending for pre-eminence and power; or to persons of other descriptions whose fortunes have been interesting to the human passions, have, in turn, divided mankind into parties, inflamed them with mutual animosity, and rendered them much more disposed to vex and oppress each other than to co-operate for their common good.

Madison believed that factionalism could be mitigated if representatives in Congress were chosen by a larger number of people spanning different geographic regions, so factions would balance each other out.[47]

It hasn't worked out that way. Each member of the House of Representatives today represents approximately 761,000 Americans, many times the number each member represented at the time of the founding, yet the House is as bitterly divided as ever. Senators too, particularly from larger states, represent many more Americans than they used to, but in the Senate Supreme Court confirmation battles are highly partisan. So is any discussion of Supreme Court ethics.

James Madison lived a quarter millennium before cable news, social media, and other modern mediums for spreading partisanship across the country almost instantaneously. Many voters hear news, including the latest ethics scandal at the Supreme Court, through the tainted lens of partisanship within hours of the news breaking. Soon thereafter, many voters have made up their minds. Members of Congress cling to popular sentiment in their districts. They also listen to special interest groups that fund their campaigns. The message is clear: Conservative justices are good [or bad] and liberal justices vice versa; there is no such thing as an unethical conservative [or liberal] justice, and a member of Congress who goes against prevailing sentiment in

[46] James Madison, *Federalist No. 10*, "The Utility of the Union as a Safeguard Against Domestic Faction and Insurrection" (Nov. 23, 1787).

[47] "The influence of factious leaders may kindle a flame within their particular States, but will be unable to spread a general conflagration through the other States. A religious sect may degenerate into a political faction in a part of the Confederacy; but the variety of sects dispersed over the entire face of it must secure the national councils against any danger from that source. . . . In the extent and proper structure of the Union, therefore, we behold a republican remedy for the diseases most incident to republican government." *Ibid.*

their political party likely will face a well-funded primary challenger in the next election.

This partisan message similarly drives how members of Congress respond to alleged malfeasance of presidents, which is why oversight of the executive branch is also extremely partisan. Impeachment of a president has never in US history resulted in conviction in the Senate. As mentioned above, that is a topic this author discusses elsewhere.[48]

The Supreme Court justices have contributed to this atmosphere of extreme partisanship. First, some justices appear to be partisan themselves, the topic of Chapter 3 of this book. Second, in a series of decisions the court has ruled that the vast sums of money financing highly partisan electioneering communications is protected under the First Amendment, beyond the reach of regulation.[49]

Political allegiance and animosity—that which the founders referred to as "faction"—thus stands in the way of Congress performing its constitutional duty. This includes the duty to ensure that the justices who interpret and apply the law also obey the law.

If it were not for the partisan roadblock, there is much Congress could do short of impeaching a justice, a remedy appropriate only in the most extreme cases. Congress could investigate alleged ethics breaches at the court, calling witnesses, including justices themselves. Congress has not done so. Congress could pass legislation improving enforcement of ethics rules on the court, including Senator Grassley's (R-IA) 2015 bill that would install an inspector general in the court, and Congress could also install the Supreme Court ethics lawyer discussed in Chapter 6 of this book. Congress has not done so. Senator Grassley himself has been silent about Supreme Court ethics, and never reintroduced his inspector general bill in 2023, when ethics scandals involving Republican appointed justices made headlines.

Indeed, if Congress is only capable of approaching Supreme Court ethics from a highly partisan vantage point, the country is probably better off if Congress does nothing. Contrived investigations, and faux impeachments of justices, would be worse than Congress doing nothing at all. Despite its drawbacks, the two-thirds vote in the Senate required to convict a federal officer impeached by the House may be a good thing. Had a mere majority vote been required in the Senate, as discussed above, Justice Samuel Chase could have been convicted in 1805 in a trial that was essentially about his politics. Other similar cases would have followed, with Supreme Court justices and other

[48] *See* E. Thomas Sullivan & Richard W. Painter, *The U.S. Presidency, supra.*
[49] *See Citizens United v. Federal Election Commission*, 558 U.S. 310 (2010).

federal judges serving only at the pleasure of a majority in both houses of Congress.

The partisanship problem has gotten worse. In 1969, powerful members of Congress from both political parties exerted sufficient pressure on Justice Abraham Fortas that he resigned from the court after discovery of previously undisclosed payments from a wealthy businessman with cases in the federal courts. Five years later, a bipartisan group of senators persuaded President Nixon to resign in 1974 rather than face impeachment for the Watergate scandal. There have been times when, despite partisanship, Congress does its constitutional duty. But not now.

9
Will Term Limits Help?

This book mostly avoids discussing proposals for structural change to the composition or the jurisdiction of the Supreme Court, a topic that has been discussed often by other authors. For example, this book avoids the highly controversial suggestion that Congress should add additional seats to the court so that new justices can be appointed, an idea that hasn't been taken seriously in Congress since President Roosevelt unsuccessfully tried to pass a statute allowing him to appoint additional justices in the late 1930s.[1]

Most structural change proposals would require an amendment to federal statutes on the judiciary, and some would require a constitutional amendment. Some proposals seek to align the decisions of the court more closely with the political sentiment in the country. Others aim to bring more transparency to the court, to limit its use of a "shadow docket" where substantive decisions are made without adequate briefing or argument, or otherwise to change the court's procedures or jurisprudence.

This book, by contrast, is about improving the court's ethics. Better ethics may result in the court making better decisions, but this book has avoided speculating about the impact of ethics on the outcome of specific cases. Any reform that will improve the court's compliance with rules and expectations about ethics, however, should improve public confidence in the court and its decisions.

The structural change discussed in this chapter is limiting justices' active full-time service on the Supreme Court to a term of years—perhaps fifteen to twenty years. When this term is over, justices would retain their offices and their compensation with lifetime tenure, but perform other judicial duties, such as substituting for active justices on the court when they are required to recuse from a case, hearing cases on the court of appeals, or performing the duties of a district court judge. A statute reallocating judicial duties

[1] *See* Jeff Shesol, *Supreme Power: Franklin Roosevelt vs. the Supreme Court* (2010); James F. Simon, *F.D.R. and Chief Justice Hughes: The President, the Supreme Court, and the Epic Battle over the New Deal* (2012).

Conduct Unbecoming. Richard W. Painter, Oxford University Press. © Oxford University Press (2026).
DOI: 10.1093/9780197832301.003.0010

in this manner would probably be constitutional if applied to new justices appointed after such a statute is enacted by Congress. Shortening terms of service, or changing other conditions of employment, for the court's current justices would be more problematic without a constitutional amendment, but that possibility is discussed here as well.

The constitutional arguments for and against such a proposal are discussed below, as are the advantages and disadvantages from the vantage point of Supreme Court ethics.

The United States as Outlier

The United States is nearly alone among nations in allowing justices on its highest court to serve for a lifetime with no term limits and no mandatory retirement age.[2] One reason for this is that our written constitution is older than those of most representative democracies, and some, such as Great Britain, have no written constitution at all. Our Supreme Court, like other arguably antiquated portions of our constitution such as the Electoral College, was set in stone nearly two hundred and forty years ago.[3]

Life spans were much shorter when our constitution was ratified in 1789 than they are today, and once a judge reached an age where appointment to the court was likely, the probability of a twenty- or thirty-year tenure were not high. Some justices served for several decades—for example, Chief Justice Marshall served for over thirty years, from 1801 to 1835—but this was the exception. In 2006, Professors Steven Calabresi and James Lindgren observed that "the average tenure of a Supreme Court Justice from 1789 to 1970 was 14.9 years, for those Justices who have retired since 1970, the average tenure has jumped to 26.1 years."[4] The justices who retired or died while on the court after 2006, with one exception, served even longer: John Paul Stevens (thirty-five years), Antonin Scalia (thirty years), Anthony Kennedy (thirty years), David Souter (nineteen years), Ruth Bader Ginsburg (twenty-seven years) and Stephen Breyer (twenty-eight years).[5]

[2] *See* Lisa Hilbink, *Life Tenure for U.S. Supreme Court Justices Is a Global Oddity with Clear Costs*, Brennan Ctr. for Just. (Nov. 20, 2024), https://www.brennancenter.org/our-work/analysis-opinion/life-tenure-us-supreme-court-justices-global-oddity-clear-costs

[3] *See* Lawrence Lessig, *They Don't Represent Us: Reclaiming Our Democracy* (2019) (discussing needed reform of antidemocratic characteristics of our constitution, including the Electoral College and the undemocratic composition of the Senate).

[4] Steven G. Calabresi & James Lindgren, *Term Limits for the Supreme Court: Life Tenure Reconsidered*, 29 Harv. J.L. & Pub. Pol'y 769, 770–71 (2006).

[5] *See* Tyler Cooper et al., *Retiring Life Tenure: On Term Limits and Regular Appointments at the Supreme Court*, 42 Cardozo L. Rev. 2763 (2021), Table 1 (listing these justices and their dates of service, with the exception of Justice Breyer, who retired in 2022).

These terms are far longer than in other countries. Professor Lisa Hilbink, in 2024, researched high courts around the world and found no other country where judges of the highest court serve such lengthy terms. The highest after the United States was Norway, where the average was 15.2 years. In Canada, the average was 12.2 years, Brazil 13.8 years, Germany 12 years, France 9 years, and Japan 5.6 years. The United Kingdom created a new high court in 2009, and if the sitting judges depart at the mandatory retirement age of 75, the average term of service will be 7.6 years.[6] For whatever reason, countries that established their high courts after the United States chose different rules about term limits and mandatory retirement ages and have high court judges who serve less than half as long as our Supreme Court justices serve.

Are Supreme Court Term Limits Constitutional?

Article III, Section I of the US Constitution provides the following:

> The judicial power of the United States, shall be vested in one Supreme Court, and in such inferior courts as the Congress may from time to time ordain and establish. The judges, both of the supreme and inferior courts, shall hold their Offices during good behaviour, and shall, at stated times, receive for their services, a compensation, which shall not be diminished during their Continuance in Office.

The relevant question is whether these judicial "Offices" are necessarily attached to lifetime service on a particular court or whether a judge or justice can hold the same office while serving on different courts, or in the case of a fully retired judge or justice, serving on no court at all. *Booth v. United States*, 291 U.S. 339 (1934), an important case involving compensation of retired lower court federal judges, addressed the distinction between retirement pursuant to the terms set forth in an act of Congress and resignation from judicial office. A retired judge does not relinquish the office:

> By retiring pursuant to the statute a judge does not relinquish his office. The language is that he may retire from regular active service. The purpose is, however, that he shall continue, so far as his age and his health permit, to perform judicial service, and it is common knowledge that retired judges have in fact discharged a large measure of the duties which would be incumbent on them, if still in regular active service. It is scarcely necessary to say that a retired judge's judicial acts would

[6] *See* Hilbink, supra, note 2.

> be illegal unless he who performed them held the office of judge. It is a contradiction in terms to assert that one who has retired in accordance with the statute may continue to function as a federal judge and yet not hold the office of a judge. The Act does not, and indeed could not, endue him with a new office, different from but embracing the duties of the office of judge. He does not surrender his commission, but continues to act under it.[7]

Booth concerned the pay of federal judges who voluntarily retired but continued to perform the duties prescribed for retired judges by Congress. The holding was that these judges continued to hold the same office they did before and were entitled to the same compensation under the constitution, which specifically provides that compensation shall not be reduced during a judge's term in office. The judge holding judicial office is distinct from the duties the judge performs, which are specified by an act of Congress. As the court explained in *Booth*, "But Congress may lighten judicial duties, though it is without power to abolish the office or to diminish the compensation appertaining to it."[8]

Does the same logic apply to retirement of a judge or justice that is prescribed by statute, whether a mandatory retirement age or a limited term of service on a particular court? *Booth* suggests the answer to that question as well, at least in circumstances where a judge's duties are reduced because of mental or physical capacity:

> There is provision for appointment by the President of an additional judge for the circuit or district court where a sitting judge is found unable efficiently to discharge all his duties by reason of mental or physical infirmity of a permanent character. In that case, the sitting judge unquestionably retains his office, and it is significant that the act declares either a retired judge, or one whose mental or physical condition has caused the President to appoint an additional judge, shall be treated as junior to the remaining judges of the court.[9]

Retired US District Judge Nancy Gertner is among legal scholars who have made a persuasive argument, based in part on the court's holding in *Booth*, that term limits for a justice's service on the Supreme Court are constitutional provided the justice retains the office and salary of a justice of the Supreme Court and continues to perform judicial duties in the federal courts to the extent the justice is able to do so.[10] Diane P. Wood, retired US judge for the

[7] *Booth v. United States*, 291 U.S. 339 (1934).
[8] *Ibid.*
[9] *Ibid*, at 350.
[10] Nancy Gertner, *The Constitution Allows for Term Limited Supreme Court Justices*, Brennan Ctr. for Just. (Dec. 19, 2024).

Seventh Circuit Court of Appeals, and presently director of the American Law Institute, has also made a cogent argument for a statutorily mandated eighteen-year term of active service on the Supreme Court, also relying on the court's holding in *Booth.*[11]

A variation on this plan would allow a sitting justice to be nominated again by a new president and confirmed by the Senate for what would amount to a second term: a commission to serve on the court for a new period of years in place of the justice's old commission. Under this arrangement, a justice would not necessarily have to wait until the end of the first term to be nominated for a new commission to the court, as the politics of renomination and confirmation might be more suitable at another time.

Admittedly, the current justices of the court might strike down such as statute if term limits on active service were to be imposed on them. They might view Congress changing the duties of a sitting justice as an unacceptable diminution of the office and a workaround what they thought was their constitutional power to sit on the court for as long as they were willing and able. How the court might rule on this is uncertain, but it is not inconceivable that the justices would distinguish *Booth* as being a case about a judge's compensation and nothing else, or cast aside much of the above quoted language in *Booth* as dicta and insist that justices have the constitutional power to perform all of their duties on the court until they choose to retire, which Congress cannot take away from them. Whether this constitutional construction is correct, the court would have the final say. Congress, to avoid a confrontation with the court, might wisely limit a term limits law to justices who are appointed to the court after the law is enacted. New justices could also be asked in their Senate confirmation hearings whether they will abide by the statutory term limits.

Advantages of Term Limits

But will term limits for justices help fix the court's ethics problem?

In some ways, probably yes.

Bringing new justices more frequently onto the Supreme Court might mean an institution that is less ingrown and clubby. There would be more justices, even if only nine were actively serving on the court at any one time.

[11] *See* Diane P. Wood, *Why Term Limits for Supreme Court Justices Make Sense*, Brennan Ctr. for Just. (Aug. 19, 2024), https://www.brennancenter.org/our-work/analysis-opinion/why-term-limits-supreme-court-justices-make-sense; *See also* The Case for Supreme Court Term Limits, Am. Acad. of Arts & Scis. (2023) (report of a working group, which included Judge Wood, concluding that, relying on Booth, Supreme Court term limits may be imposed by statute).

This might mean less groupthink, a problem discussed in Chapter 4. Less groupthink might result in better judgment in matters of ethics and perhaps less willingness to accept the premise that because other justices did something in the past, it is the right thing to do.

Justices who will not serve a lifetime on the Supreme Court, but who someday will likely join or rejoin the court of appeals, might also be more deferential to the views of other judges on the court of appeals. This could help considerably if court of appeals judges are enlisted in guiding the Supreme Court on ethics, and providing ethics opinions to the court, as contemplated in Chapters 6 and 7 of this book.

Reputation should matter for a justice who is thinking about what comes after service on the court. This is particularly true if the statutory arrangement allowed for a sitting justice to be nominated again by a new president and confirmed by the Senate for what would amount to a second term. Recall from Chapter 1 that no matter how exacting the ethics scrutiny of Supreme Court nominees (this author can attest from experience in the White House that the scrutiny is exacting),[12] there is no second round, so justices' ethics standards may loosen considerably once they are confirmed. A statutory scheme that envisioned the possibility of a second round of confirmation hearings for a justice could help solve this problem.

Finally, if justices whose term of service on the court has expired could fill in for recused justices, that could help alleviate the court's recusal problem. Recusal on the Supreme Court has more serious consequences than on the court of appeals because there are no substitute judges, and retired justices are not permitted to replace justices who recuse from a case. As discussed in Chapters 2 and 3 of this book, there are too many instances in which justices should recuse as a matter of ethics, whether because of a gift, a personal friendship, an investment, or the appearance of political partisanship, but they don't recuse. A statutory scheme that contemplated there being more justices who have departed from active service and allowing them occasionally to sit in for recused justices could make it easier for a justice to recuse.

Disadvantages of Term Limits

But there are downsides to term limits as well.

Term limits for Supreme Court justices would mean more nominations and more confirmations. The contentious confirmation battles described in

[12] *See* Chapter 1, *supra* (discussing ethics screening of Supreme Court nominees).

Chapter 1 are highly political and attract enormous sums of outside spending. Term limits could make justices more dependent on outside interest groups, particularly if the statute allowed the possibility of a justice being nominated for a second term. Justices contemplating renomination would probably maintain even closer relationships with the people and organizations that helped them get on the court to begin with. This could mean more free fishing trips, yacht excursions, and hunting trips, not fewer. The justices might also keep much closer ties with the political branches of government, undermining not only their ethics but also their independence.

The other possibility is that some justices at the expiration of terms of active service on the court would leave the judiciary altogether and enter the private sector. With the present system of lifetime tenure with active service on the court, this has almost never happened. Only two Supreme Court justices have resigned to practice law. Justice Benjamin Robbins Curtis resigned from the court in 1857 in protest over Chief Justice Taney's notorious *Dred Scott*[13] decision, from which Curtis and one other justice, John McLean, bitterly dissented. Curtis returned to a lucrative Boston law practice and eventually represented President Andrew Johnson at his impeachment trial. Justice Abraham Fortas resigned in 1969 in the ethics scandal discussed in Chapter 4 of this book, and he resumed the practice of law in Washington, DC.[14]

But leaving the judiciary for the private sector might be a lot more attractive if justices' years of active service on the court were limited by statute. Justices considering private practice would have an incentive to maintain close relationships with wealthy businesspeople and lawyers. Ethics rules would require justices to recuse from cases involving parties and lawyers with whom they are negotiating for employment, but that is not enough. Even ethics rules prohibiting justices from negotiating for employment before they leave the court would not prevent them nurturing private sector relationships that precede negotiating for employment. The prospect of justices looking for other jobs while deciding cases of great importance to finance and industry could make the ethics problems on the court worse.

One way to reduce the lure of the private sector would be to change the generous retirement plan for federal judges and substantially reduce benefits for judges—or at least Supreme Court justices—who resign their office to enter private practice or other lucrative private sector employment. The present plan usually gives a judge or justice a pension equal to the full salary

[13] Dred Scott v. Sandford, 60 U.S. (19 How.) 393 (1857) (holding that the constitution did not confer citizenship on persons of African descent).

[14] Justice Arthur Goldberg resigned from the Supreme Court in 1965 to become US ambassador to the United Nations and later entered private law practice upon leaving that post in 1968.

upon retirement if the judge's years of service plus the judge's age equal eighty (e.g., a seventy-year-old judge with ten years of service, or a sixty-year-old judge with twenty years of service, gets a full pension).[15] These pensions are justified because the vast majority of federal judges do not retire to practice law. Those who do leave the judiciary for the private sector should arguably receive less.

But once again, changing the terms of employment, particularly pension plans, for current judges and justices would be both legally and politically impossible. Different retirement plans for new justices might be designed to reduce the incentive to enter the private practice of law upon leaving the court. Still, the lure of private practice for a term-limited justice might be hard to overcome, and the ethics problems likely to come with it might also be difficult to resolve.

In sum, there are disadvantages as well as advantages to term limits from an ethics perspective. They would help in some ways, bringing the court new people and new ideas, and perhaps create an incentive to be on "good behavior" that is more meaningful than the low bar the House and Senate are willing to accept before contemplating impeachment. However, justices considering their next career move, whether it be another term on the court, a political career, or making money in the private sector, may be even more conflicted than justices who serve for a lifetime.

[15] 28 U.S.C. § 371 (Retirement on salary; retirement in senior status).

10

Do We Need a Constitutional Amendment to Fix the Court?

Finally, we turn to the question of whether the Supreme Court is so intractable in refusing to confront its ethics problem and eager to strike down any attempt by Congress to regulate its affairs that a constitutional amendment is required. Such an amendment could be written in different ways, but generally would provide that the justices of the court must adhere to ethics rules binding on other federal judges and that Congress should establish a process for enforcement of ethics rules on the court.

Constitutional amendments pertaining to the court have been recommended before. One of these is an amendment imposing term limits, the idea discussed in Chapter 9 (as also discussed in that chapter, some term limit arrangements might not require a constitutional amendment). An amendment that limited terms of current justices of the court, however, would probably not be ratified in conservative states where the present court's decisions are popular. Indeed, with three-fourths of the states needed to ratify an amendment to the constitution, any amendment likely to change the substance of the jurisprudence of the court will almost certainly fail.

The court's ethics, however, are not so popular with voters anywhere on the political spectrum.[1] Outside the context of ethics attacks on specific conservative justices, for example, there will be no groundswell of support among conservatives for the proposition that Supreme Court justices should be allowed to accept free vacations, recreational vehicles, or other gifts of substantial value from billionaires. There will be no groundswell of support for permitting a justice to enter real estate transactions that are lopsided in the justice's favor, nor will there be popular support for the proposition that a justice should participate in a case argued by a law firm that recently made substantial payments to the justice's spouse. These topics only become heated and partisan when the conduct of a particular justice is at issue.

[1] The widespread lack of public confidence in the court is discussed in the introduction of this book and in Chapter 1.

Conduct Unbecoming. Richard W. Painter, Oxford University Press. © Oxford University Press (2026).
DOI: 10.1093/9780197832301.003.0011

Disclosure rules for justices are also likely to have broad public support as a matter of principle, even if the discussion takes a different turn when someone's favorite justice is accused of violating these rules. Finally, Senator Grassley's (R-IA) 2015 proposal for an inspector general (IG) in the court is neither partisan nor ideological. Grassley or another Republican in Congress would probably reintroduce the bill again today if the most recent Supreme Court scandals involved liberal justices instead of conservatives. A constitutional amendment strengthening ethics on the court likewise could attract broad popular support provided it was not perceived as being targeted at a particular justice.

A constitutional amendment would not need to be specific like the bills that have been introduced in Congress.[2] A one-sentence amendment could simply provide that Congress shall provide an enforceable code of ethics for the Supreme Court. The important point is that there is nothing partisan nor ideological about the proposition that the court should be bound by ethics rules that apply to the rest of the judicial branch and that these rules should be enforced.

Ratification of a constitutional amendment often takes time, but Congress could pass *both* such an amendment and a separate more specific statute imposing an enforceable ethics regime on the court. The constitutional amendment would require a vote of two-thirds of the House and of the Senate, but would not require the signature of the president, to be sent on for ratification by three-fourths of the states[3]; the statute by contrast would become law either with a majority vote in the House and Senate and the signature of the president, or in the case of a presidential veto a two-thirds vote to override a veto in the House and Senate.[4] If both the constitutional amendment and the ethics statute were to pass in Congress, and the court were to abide by the statute, the amendment would not be necessary, and states could decide not to ratify it or to delay ratification. If, however, the court were to embrace the more extreme separation of powers and immunity arguments discussed in Chapter 5, and strike down the statute, or refuse to comply with the statute, political momentum could build in state legislatures to ratify the amendment. Because there is no time limit for ratification of an amendment by the states unless the amendment's language imposes a time limit, states would have an opportunity to wait and see what the court does.[5]

[2] *See, e.g.*, Chapter 7, *supra* (discussing the SCERT Act).

[3] U.S. Constitution., Article V (setting forth procedures for amendment)

[4] U.S. Constitution., Article I, Section 7 (setting forth procedures for passing legislation)

[5] *See Dillon v. Gloss* , 256 U.S. 368 (1921) (holding that Congress has the power to fix a definite period for ratification of a constitutional amendment); and *Coleman v. Miller* , 307 U.S. 433 (1939) (holding that

What Would the Amendment Say?

There are different ways a constitutional amendment could be written, but simpler language is probably better. The objective of an amendment would be to allow, or require, Congress to regulate the ethics of Supreme Court justices without authorizing Congress to intrude into the deliberations of the court or the substance of its decisions.

For example, the text of an amendment could provide that "the justices of the Supreme Court shall comply with rules of ethics and procedures for enforcement of such rules that Congress shall enact into law, provided such rules are not substantially more burdensome that those applicable to other judges and do not interfere with the substantive deliberations of the Court." It is important to emphasize that this language is a fair characterization of the powers Congress already has under the constitution, the issue addressed in Chapter 5 of this book. The amendment would not be necessary unless the court would disagree and adopt an extreme separation of powers doctrine that places the justices beyond congressional oversight. The amendment would be there just in case.

Alternatively, an amendment could empower the federal judiciary, district court judges, and/or appellate court judges, by majority vote, to establish ethics rules binding on themselves and on the Supreme Court.

Inserting more specifics into a constitutional amendment—for example, requiring the court to have an IG—would probably be too much detail. Such decisions about enforcement are best made by Congress or by the federal courts themselves.

The amendment can, and probably should, be passed by Congress side by side with a law that specifies ethics rules and procedures for the Supreme Court. That law should go into considerably more detail than the amendment and could, for example, install an IG and ethics lawyer at the court, as discussed in Chapter 6, and perhaps implement other reforms discussed in Chapter 7. Alternatively, the law could delegate to the entire judiciary the power and duty to promulgate ethics rules binding on all federal judges, including the Supreme Court, and perhaps also the power to appoint an IG for the judiciary. As also discussed in Chapter 7, some Supreme Court ethics bills have already been introduced in Congress. In a less-heated political

Congress, not the judiciary, has authority to impose a time limit so an amendment will not lose its vitality due to the passage of time, and that if Congress does not specify a deadline the amendment remains pending indefinitely until Congress determines otherwise). For example, the 27th Amendment, which prohibits any law that changes the compensation for members of Congress from taking effect until after the next election of the House, was proposed in 1789 and not ratified until 1992, over 202 years later.

environment when the conduct of specific justices is not contested, one of these bills might pass. As discussed in Chapter 5, such a law would be consistent with the current constitution, or such is the better view, and only if the court strikes down the law would the constitutional amendment be necessary.

How Would Ratification Work?

The flexibility of the ratification process is that states can ratify a constitutional amendment whenever they want unless Congress has imposed a deadline for the states reaching the three-quarters ratification threshold.[6] In the case of a Supreme Court ethics amendment, a deadline would not be advisable because ratification could take time. Supreme Court ethics is still perceived to be a partisan issue, even though it shouldn't be, and for many states, there will be no rush to ratify the amendment. Also, it is not necessary if Congress already has the authority to regulate Supreme Court ethics. The political climate would likely change quickly if the Supreme Court were to strike down an ethics law as unconstitutional.

With no deadline imposed by Congress, states could ratify the amendment gradually, and as political winds shift, different states could consider ratifying for different reasons. If there is a scandal or alleged scandal involving a liberal justice, another Abe Fortas,[7] the political right will be up in arms and support Senator Grassley's idea of a Supreme Court IG. The retirement of Justice Thomas (age 77 at the time of this writing), who appears to be the worst offender in ethics scandals described in Chapters 2 and 3, would tone down the politics surrounding Supreme Court ethics as well.

Meanwhile, as discussed above, Congress should also pass a Supreme Court ethics statute, which can provide considerably more detail than a constitutional amendment. If the court were to strike down that statute as

[6] *See* cases cited in note 5 supra. See also U.S. Dep't of Just., Off. of Legal Couns., *Effect of 2020 OLC Opinion on Possible Congressional Action Regarding Ratification of the Equal Rights Amendment*, Memorandum for the Counsel to the President, Jan. 26, 2022 (affirming conclusions in Ratification of the *Equal Rights Amendment*, 44 Op. O.L.C. __ (Jan. 6, 2020)) ("Congress imposed a seven-year deadline when it initially proposed the ERA in 1972. Our opinion concluded that Congress had constitutional authority to impose that deadline and that, because 38 states had not ratified the proposed amendment before that deadline's expiration, the ERA is not a part of the United States Constitution.") The 2022 opinion acknowledged ambiguity on other questions such as whether a state can rescind its ratification of an amendment and whether Congress can modify its own deadline. *See* Memorandum from John M. Harmon, Assistant Att'y Gen., Off. of Legal Couns., on Constitutionality of Extending the Time Period for Ratification of the Proposed Equal Rights Amendment (Oct. 31, 1977). This OLC Memo was not formally published, but it is reprinted in a Congressional hearing. See Equal Rights Amendment Extension: Hearings on H.J. Res. 638 Before the Subcommittee on Civil & Constitutional Rights of the House Committee on the Judiciary, 95th Cong. 7–27 (1978) (testimony of Assistant Attorney General Harmon).

[7] *See also* Chapter 2, *supra* (discussing justices' book royalties, noting that Justice Sotomayor earned more in royalties than most of her colleagues on the court).

unconstitutional, or openly disobey its requirements, that would provide additional impetus toward ratification of the amendment.

The Dangers of Constitutional Amendments

The Supreme Court is not a popularly chosen branch of government, and right now the court is not a popular institution. The court has never been very popular, but today its popularity, in part because of its ethics scandals and in part because of its perceived partisanship, has reached another low.

But public anger at the court is nothing new and does not permanently reside in any one faction or political party. Over the past century, hostility toward the court has shifted from left to right and back again. Democrats were angry at an arch-conservative court that struck down President Roosevelt's New Deal legislation, and Congress even considered, but rejected, Roosevelt's court-packing scheme.[8] The political right was furious at the court's civil rights rulings in the 1960s and early 1970s, some calling for impeachment of Chief Justice Earl Warren.[9] Now, once again, the political left is angry at a court perceived to curtail civil liberties and issue pro-business rulings while some justices have ethically dubious relationships with billionaires.

None of these scenarios is a good political backdrop for Congress to consider a constitutional amendment affecting the court. The risk is that the move to amend could go well beyond Supreme Court ethics and turn toward weakening the power of the court to interpret the constitution and the laws. The risk of introducing any constitutional amendment about the court, even one limited to the ethics of the court, is that populists on the left or right in Congress could take it further and tack on provisos that change the composition of the court or abolish the principle of judicial review, abolish the jurisdiction of the court over certain cases, or alter the legal effect of its opinions. The idea of imposing term limits on the justices, discussed in Chapter 9, is popular,[10] even if, as also discussed in Chapter 9, it is not clear that term limits would improve ethics on the court. An even more extreme example of curbing the power of the court would be a constitutional amendment giving states, majorities in Congress, or perhaps even the president the power to override rulings of the court.

[8] *Aim to Pack Court, Declares Hoover. Roosevelt Move Transcends Any Partisanship Question, Ex-President Holds*, N.Y. Times (Feb. 6, 1937), page 1.

[9] *Birchers Chart Warren Attack. Welch Tells of Plan for New Drive for Impeachment*, N.Y. Times (Jan. 12, 1967), page 23.

[10] *See* Jessica Gresko & Emily Swanson, *AP-NORC poll: 2 in 3 in US Favor Term Limits for Justices*, AP News (July 25, 2022), https://apnorc.org/ap-norc-poll-2-in-3-in-us-favor-term-limits-for-justices/.

The court should not want its power of judicial review, accepted since *Marbury v. Madison*,[11] to be the subject of a constitutional amendment. The court should also want its orders to be obeyed. At different times, populist politicians have flouted court orders, including when President Andrew Jackson ignored the court's injunction against the State of Georgia's treatment of sovereign Indian tribes in *Worcester v. Georgia*,[12] and when Alabama Governor George Wallace tried to prevent court-ordered desegregation of public schools.[13] The court should want to use its power of judicial review sparingly, for important battles establishing constitutional principles, as it did in the civil rights era[14] or, perhaps today, in its growing number of cases rebuffing government intrusion on religious liberty.[15] The court should not want to engage in unnecessary and self-interested confrontation with popularly elected branches of government over the justices' ethics. A contrived separation of powers argument that justices have the constitutional power to take undisclosed excursions on yachts and private planes, receive expensive gifts, and earn unlimited book royalties is a strange hill for the constitutional powers of the court to die upon.

But that is a decision for the justices to make. If they choose to push this issue, to insist that in matters of ethics they are accountable to nobody but themselves, the popularly elected branches of government will at some point respond. A constitutional amendment is one way for the representatives of the people to respond. Given the alternatives, depending on what the amendment says, it might be an orderly way for the people to tell the justices they are not above the law. But once again, an amendment that goes further and weakens the power of judicial review could be even more dangerous than Congress doing nothing at all.

[11] *Marbury v. Madison*, 5 U.S. (1 Cranch) 137 (1803).

[12] *Worcester v. Georgia*, 31 U.S. (6 Pet.) 515 (1832).

[13] James T. Wooten, *Wallace Urges a Defiant South*, N.Y. Times (Feb. 9, 1970), page 1 ("George C. Wallace urged Southern governors today to defy Federal Court integration orders and promised to seek the Presidency again in 1972 'if Nixon doesn't do something about the mess our schools are in.'").

[14] *See, e.g., Brown v. Board of Education*, 347 U.S. 483 (1954).

[15] *See Mahmoud v. Taylor*, 606 U.S. __ (2025) (June 27, 2025) (ruling unconstitutional a school board policy that did not allow parents of schoolchildren to opt out of instruction on LGBTQ+ issues because the government cannot condition the benefit of free public education on parents' acceptance of instruction that violates their religious beliefs).

Conclusion

Without taking sides in the ideological battles over the composition of the Supreme Court or its judicial philosophy, this book has sought to explain an ethics crisis at the court that undermines public respect for the court and its authority. Furthermore, the court is not willing to recognize the seriousness of its ethics problems and address them on its own.

Remarkably, the court seems unaware that not only its moral authority but also its constitutional authority could be at stake. Judicial review of acts of the executive and the legislature is assumed. As Chief Justice John Marshall wrote in 1803: "It is emphatically the province and duty of the judicial department to say what the law is."[1] But today, we have a sitting president who has said he is not so sure, a vice president who has said the president can disregard Supreme Court orders,[2] and a handful of academics on the right[3] and left[4] who seem to agree.

With the authority of the judiciary on the line, now is the most inopportune time for the justices to squander their credibility defending bad personal conduct. Surely there are constitutional and legal principles more important to this court than the prerogative of justices to circumvent long-accepted norms of judicial ethics by accepting gifts from persons with interests before the court, going on luxurious excursions on the private planes and yachts of billionaires, violating financial disclosure rules, and engaging in unnecessary and overt political partisanship.

[1] *Marbury v. Madison*, 5 U.S. (1 Cranch) 137, 177 (1803).

[2] Charlie Savage and Minho Kim, *Vance Says "Judges Aren't Allowed to Control" Trump's "Legitimate Power,"*, N. Y. Times, Feb. 9, 2025. https://www.nytimes.com/2025/02/09/us/politics/vance-trump-federal-courts-executive-order.html. "Vance Denies Judges' Power Over President," appeared in the print edition of the New York Times on Monday, February 10, 2025, on Section A, Page 18.

[3] Asher Boiskin, *"Yale Law School Should Be Embarrassed": Vance LAW '13 Clashes with Legal Scholars over Judicial Power*, Yale Daily News, Feb. 19, 2025 (reporting that Yale law professor Jed Rubenfeld said Vance was "correct" and that "judges cannot constitutionally interfere" in areas where the executive branch has authority under the constitution). https://yaledailynews.com/articles/yale-law-school-should-be-embarrassed-vance-law-13-clashes-with-legal-scholars-over-judicial-power-and-trumps-agenda

[4] Samuel Moyn & Ryan Doefler, *We Are Already Defying the Supreme Court, The Risks of Calling on Politicians to Push Back Against the Court Must Be Weighed Against the Present Reality of a Malign Judicial Dictatorship*, Dissent, Vol. 71, No, 1 (Winter 2024), pages 108–116. https://dissentmagazine.org/article/we-are-already-defying-the-supreme-court/

Conduct Unbecoming. Richard W. Painter, Oxford University Press. © Oxford University Press (2026).
DOI: 10.1093/9780197832301.003.0012

Now may be the most important time in our nation's history for the court to double down instead on the basic principles that underlie what it means to be a judge: neutrality and personal distance from the parties before the bench, freedom from personal financial interests that could influence judgements, transparency about conflicts of interest, detachment from partisan politics, and independence from the executive and legislative branches of government. The justices also need to distance themselves from the financial behemoth that has taken over our presidential and congressional elections[5] and seeks to dictate nominations and confirmation to the federal judiciary.[6]

Congress could hold the court to account, but it won't. There, judicial ethics, like government ethics in general, is viewed through a principally partisan lens. Congress could more aggressively investigate alleged ethics breaches on the court, but representatives and senators of the same political party as the president who appointed a justice will dismiss ethics allegations as spurious. Congress could avoid such partisan feuds about alleged misconduct of justices by passing legislation that prospectively enacts stricter rules for the entire court on gifts, outside income, book deals, disclosure requirements, and conflicts of interest, and by providing the court an inspector general or another enforcement mechanism. That hasn't happened either. The constitutional checks and balances envisioned by the founders are not working to hold the Supreme Court accountable any more than they are working to hold the president accountable.[7]

Finally, the court's ethics problems are a sufficient threat to our representative democracy that the public should take a keen interest in pressuring Congress to confront the court with investigations of the justices' ethics and with ethics reform legislation. And if that does not work, public support should build for a constitutional amendment. Such an amendment, however, should be limited to addressing the ethics of the court and avoid the temptation to undermine the court's power of judicial review or allow the political branches to interfere with the work of the court.

Regardless of whether the court's ethics problems may relate to its political leanings, which are significantly to the right of the US general population as a whole and favor wealthy economic interests, focusing on ideology in public discourse about Supreme Court ethics could prove counterproductive. Politicizing ethics will make reform less likely, at least in the present highly

[5] *See Citizens United v. FEC*, 558 U.S. 310 (2010).

[6] *See* Chapter 1 discussing massive spending by special interest groups on judicial nominations and confirmations.

[7] *See* E. Thomas Sullivan & Richard W. Painter, *The U.S. Presidency: Power, Responsibility, and Accountability* (2025).

polarized climate. This book has sought to explain why Americans of all political viewpoints should be concerned about corruption at the Supreme Court and should embrace reform.

At different times, but within the past ten years, political leaders at both ends of the political spectrum have supported Supreme Court ethics reform. It is imperative for our republic that we get it done.

Index

For the benefit of digital users, indexed terms that span two pages (e.g., 52–53) may, on occasion, appear on only one of those pages.

Some entries in this Index are for names of Supreme Court justices and terms that appear repeatedly throughout this book. This Index lists page numbers containing the more significant discussion for those entries.